SUSTAINING THE ASIA PACIFIC MIRACLE

ANDRÉ DUA
DANIEL C. ESTY

SUSTAINING THE ASIA PACIFIC MIRACLE
Environmental Protection and Economic Integration

Institute for International Economics
Washington, DC
October 1997

André Dua is director of the Asia Pacific Trade and Environment Project, Yale University, and Research Scholar, Yale Law School. He is author or coauthor of a number of articles and studies on economic development and trade.

Daniel C. Esty, *Senior Fellow* in 1994, is Director of the Center for Environmental Law and Policy and Associate Professor in the Schools of Law and Forestry at Yale University. He served as the US Environmental Protection Agency's Deputy Assistant Administrator for Policy, Planning and Evaluation, as EPA's Deputy Chief of Staff, and as Special Assistant to EPA Administrator William Reilly. He was EPA's chief NAFTA negotiator. He is the author of a number of articles and studies on trade, competitiveness, environment, and development, including *Greening the GATT* (1994).

INSTITUTE FOR INTERNATIONAL ECONOMICS
11 Dupont Circle, NW
Washington, DC 20036-1207
(202) 328-9000 FAX: (202) 328-5432

C. Fred Bergsten, *Director*
Christine F. Lowry, *Director of Publications*

Printing and Typesetting by
Automated Graphic Systems
Cover design by Michelle M. Fleitz

For reprints/permission to photocopy please contact the APS customer service department at CCC Academic Permissions Service, 27 Congress Street, Salem, MA 01970.

Printed in the United States of America
99 98 97 5 4 3 2 1

Library of Congress Cataloging-in-Publication Data

Dua, André
    Sustaining the Asia Pacific miracle : environmental protection and economic integration / André Dua and Daniel Esty.
        p.   cm.
    Includes bibliographical references and index.

    1. Environmental development—Environmental aspects—Pacific Area.   2. Environmental policy—Pacific Area.   3. Pacific Area—Economic policy.   4. Pacific Area cooperation.   5. Asia Pacific Economic Cooperation (Organization)   I. Esty, Daniel C.   II. Title.
HC681.Z9E5355   1997
363.7'0099—DC21   97-30700
                                                CIP

ISBN 0-88132-250-4

To our parents
Jagdish and Sushma Dua
John and Katharine Esty
To whom we are deeply indebted

Contents

Preface

The linkages among growth, trade, and environmental protection have become a central concern of economic policy around the world. These concerns are nowhere greater than among the countries of the Asia Pacific Economic Cooperation (APEC) forum, which includes both the fastest growing and most heavily polluting nations on earth. Since APEC comprises half the world economy, it has both a responsibility and an opportunity to play a leading role in dealing with the growth-trade-environmental complex.

This volume develops the case for collective international action on environmental problems, suggests that a major regional grouping such as APEC has a clear role to play within that context, and proposes a series of specific measures that could be launched at APEC's next summit in Vancouver, Canada in November 1997. Daniel Esty, an internationally renowned trade and environment expert, has previously addressed the global dimension of these issues in *Greening the GATT: Trade, Environment and the Future,* published by the Institute in July 1994. His proposal in that volume for the creation of a new Global Environmental Organization (GEO) has recently been endorsed by a number of major governments including Brazil, Germany, Singapore, and South Africa. A summary version of *Sustaining the Asia Pacific Miracle,* entitled "APEC and Sustainable Development," is included in the Special Report *Whither APEC? The Progress to Date and Agenda for the Future* that I have edited and is being released simultaneously by the Institute.

The Institute for International Economics is a private nonprofit institution for the study and discussion of international economic policy. Its purpose is to analyze important issues in that area and to develop and communicate practical new approaches for dealing with them. The Institute is completely nonpartisan.

The Institute is funded largely by philanthropic foundations. Major institutional grants are now being received from The German Marshall Fund of the United States, which created the Institute with a generous commitment of funds in 1981, and from The Ford Foundation, The Andrew W. Mellon Foundation, and The Starr Foundation. A number of other foundations and private corporations also contribute to the highly diversified financial resources of the Institute. The AT&T Foundation and the GE Fund provide support for the Institute's work on Asia Pacific studies. About 12 percent of the Institute's resources in our latest fiscal year were provided by contributors outside the United States, including about 6 percent from Japan.

The Board of Directors bears overall responsibility for the Institute and gives general guidance and approval to its research program—including identification of topics that are likely to become important to international economic policymakers over the medium run (generally, one to three years), and which thus should be addressed by the Institute. The Director, working closely with the staff and outside Advisory Committee, is responsible for the development of particular projects and makes the final decision to publish an individual study.

The Institute hopes that its studies and other activities will contribute to building a stronger foundation for international economic policy around the world. We invite readers of these publications to let us know how they think we can best accomplish this objective.

C. FRED BERGSTEN
Director
September 1997

Acknowledgments

We are particularly indebted to C. Fred Bergsten for his support and encouragement of our efforts and his insightful comments as we prepared and refined the manuscript. Special thanks also go to our research assistant Michael Burstein whose unflagging efforts—researching, compiling data, synthesizing information, typing, proofreading, and assembling the manuscript—made an invaluable contribution to the final product and helped us meet an otherwise impossible deadline. Both the John D. and Catherine T. MacArthur Foundation and the Institute for International Economics provided funding for this study and we are very grateful for their support. Our environmental analysis of Asia builds on work funded by the Rockefeller Brothers Fund and the W. Alton Jones Foundation.

Many other people contributed to this project. We received detailed comments on early drafts from Steve Charnovitz, Jonathan Dawe, Jason Hunter, Patrick Low, Charles Pearson, David Runnals, John Whalley, and John Williamson. We also benefited from comments, suggestions and guidance from Kym Anderson, Jamie Art, Tim Beresford, Carter Brandon, Dan Ciuriak, John Curtis, Kim Elliott, Christopher Flavin, Ross Garnaut, Edward M. Graham, Dale Hathaway, Gary Hufbauer, John Jackson, Abraham Katz, Ambassador Tommy Koh, Lawrence Krause, Frank Loy, Sandeep Mangalmurti, Jerry Mashaw, Greg Mertz, Todd Millay, Molly O'Meara, Kristen Needham, Peter Petri, Jeffrey Schott, Miranda Sissons, Noordin Sopiee, Mathias Turck, Edie Wilson, and Ambassador John Wolf.

We were able to considerably sharpen our thinking by presenting versions of our work at a number of conferences and seminars. In this regard we would like to thank Stephen Parker and the Asia Foundation for convening a workshop on "APEC and Sustainable Development" in San Francisco, John Kirton for inviting us to Toronto to speak at a conference on "Canada and the Challenge of APEC," and Don Rothwell and John Armour for organizing seminars at the University of Sydney and University of Nottingham Law Schools, respectively. In addition we would like to express our gratitude to the participants of the study group organized by the Institute for International Economics.

We also appreciate the help given by Marge Camera and Ann Wallace in typing the manuscript and offering a range of administrative assistance. We also wanted to thank Nicole Itano who proofread, typed revisions, and laboriously compiled the figures for this study, as well as Rachel Hampton and Shalini Ramanathan who tracked down the data and materials that informed much of this study. At the Institute, we received extraordinary assistance from Christine Lowry, Brigitte Coulton, Alice Falk, David Kryzwda, Helen Kim, Michelle Madia, Erin Sullivan, and Tracy Temanson.

1

Introduction

APEC—the Asia Pacific Economic Cooperation forum—boasts the three largest economies in the world and nine of the world's ten fastest-growing economies, and it accounts for half of global output and trade. APEC members, however, are also home to seven of the world's ten most polluted cities and include four of the six countries with the highest greenhouse gas emissions, while the Asia Pacific region has the highest annual deforestation rate of any part of the world. Nowhere else on the planet are such large and growing economies juxtaposed with such serious and worsening environmental harms. The confluence of these trends raises the following question: *Is economic growth in the context of deepening regional economic integration compatible with a commitment to improved environmental quality?*

This study concludes that economic expansion and environmental protection can, in fact, be made mutually supportive—and APEC is well-positioned to be at the vanguard of such efforts. But without natural resource management and carefully constructed pollution prevention and control policies, the nations of APEC and the region as a whole face serious—and in some cases devastating—public health and ecological problems.

Why should APEC—an economic community (see box 1.1 for an overview of APEC)—concern itself with environmental issues? First, the environmental stresses accompanying the region's economic success cause productivity losses and require public health expenditures that together can cost countries between 3 and 8 percent of GDP, a significant offset against the social welfare gains of economic growth.

Box 1.1   APEC: An Overview

Membership

The Asia Pacific Economic Cooperation (APEC) forum was inaugurated at a ministerial meeting—at which 12 Asia Pacific economies were represented—in Canberra, Australia, in 1989.[1] APEC now includes 18 "member economies": Australia, Brunei, Canada, Chile, China, Chinese Taipei, Hong Kong, Indonesia, Japan, Malaysia, Mexico, New Zealand, Papua New Guinea, the Philippines, Singapore, South Korea, Thailand, and the United States.[2]

Goals

APEC began as an informal discussion group aimed at fostering regional economic cooperation among its participating nations in light of the growing economic interdependence around the Pacific Rim. It has now refined its mission to focus on three "pillars": (1) trade and investment liberalization, (2) facilitation, and (3) economic and technical cooperation ("ecotech"). APEC's most dramatic accomplishment has been to agree on the goal of "free and open trade and investment" in the region by 2010 for developed countries, and 2020 for developing members. In accomplishing this goal, APEC is committed to avoiding creation of a new preferential trading agreement—"open regionalism" is the guiding principle (APEC 1994b). Beyond their economic aspirations, the overarching aim of APEC's members is to create an Asia Pacific "community."

Structure

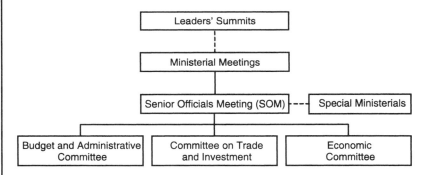

Working Groups

- Fisheries
- Human Resources Development
- Industrial Science and Technology
- Marine Resources Conservation
- Regional Energy Cooperation
- Telecommunications
- Transportation
- Tourism
- Trade and Investment Data Review
- Trade Promotion

Advisory Groups

- ABAC, 1996-
- PBF, 1994-1995
- EPG, 1993-1995

Miscellaneous

- Ad hoc Policy Level Group on Small and Medium Enterprises
- Agricultural Technical Cooperation

(continued)

Since its inception in 1989, the highest-level official meeting in APEC has been the annual meeting of ministers[3] from each APEC economy. However, since 1993, the leaders[4] of all the APEC nations have met informally immediately after each ministerial meeting in an APEC "Summit." Drawing on the work of the ministers and the recommendations of advisory groups,[5] the leaders have taken to fashioning a yearly declaration that sets out APEC's objectives and broader vision.

These Leaders' Summits have been held in Seattle, United States (1993); Bogor, Indonesia (1994); Osaka, Japan (1995); and Manila, Philippines (1996). Forthcoming summits are scheduled for Vancouver, Canada (1997); Malaysia (1998); New Zealand (1999); Brunei (2000); and China (2001).

Once the leaders make decisions on broad policy goals, designated senior officials carry out APEC's activities. These senior officials—who on average meet four times a year—are generally foreign or trade ministry bureaucrats at the assistant secretary or vice-ministerial level. The senior officials (1) coordinate and oversee the activities of APEC's working groups, (2) manage the efforts of APEC's Trade and Investment, and Economic Committees, and (3) act as a conduit between the general ministerial meeting and ad hoc meetings of ministers representing specific portfolios.

APEC's ten working groups meet frequently to advance issues important to APEC members in specific sectoral areas. APEC's committees have a broader mandate. The Committee on Trade and Investment, for example, is the key organ involved in helping countries implement the liberalization and facilitation components of the Osaka Action Agenda. The Economic Committee, in addition to analyzing economic trends and studying specific issues, manages APEC's ecotech program. Finally, the "special" ministerial conferences bring together ministers from each APEC country to focus on particular areas—such as energy, the environment, finance, industrial science and technology, human resource development, small and medium-sized enterprise, telecommunications, trade, and transportation—in ways that connect to the broader APEC program.

---

1. For a detailed discussion of APEC's history, see Funabashi (1995).

2. For the sake of simplicity and varied diction, we refer to the APEC "countries," even though APEC refers to them as "member economies." We also use the term "Taiwan" even though, in deference to Chinese sensitivities, this juridiction is called "Chinese Taipei" in the APEC forum.

3. Usually, members select a trade or economic minister to represent their economy.

4. "Leaders" refers to the presidents and prime ministers of APEC's members.

5. Currently, the APEC Business Advisory Group is the only active advisory group. Previously APEC's leaders have received input from the Pacific Business Forum (PBF) and the Eminent Persons Group (EPG).

Second, because many of the environmental harms that confront APEC's members are attributable to uninternalized externalities, poor management of common resources, and government policies that distort resource prices, allocative inefficiency is widespread and the integrity of the regional economic system cannot be assured. Thus, the imperative to pursue sound environmental policies derives from a desire not only to limit environmental degradation but also to improve allocative efficiency across APEC.

Third, environmental tensions may spill over into the economic realm, jeopardizing the prospects of continuing trade and investment liberalization and further economic integration. Any number of disputes could prove to be flash points that precipitate a retreat from a commitment to open markets. In particular, if developing countries feel that health and environmental standards in developed countries unreasonably threaten their market access, or that trade measures imposed unilaterally by the United States are being unfairly used to achieve extraterritorial environmental goals, they may slacken the pace of their liberalization.

Equally important, political leaders and the public in developed countries, especially the United States, fear that economic integration has placed domestic industries at a competitive disadvantage vis-à-vis competitors in low-environmental-standard countries. The debate over the North American Free Trade Agreement (NAFTA), in which the fear of unfair advantage accruing to industries operating in Mexico remained salient to the day of the final vote, showcases the seriousness of this concern. Low environmental standards in many Asian countries, including China, raise the specter of a magnified version of this debate in the APEC context. Perhaps the most important development, however, is the growing discomfort of Americans with the environmental choices of their trading partners and the accompanying calls to respond to such behavior. Each of these tensions places a strain on the commitment of APEC's members to openness, threatening the economic growth that accompanies freer trade.

The goal of APEC governments should be—and is, at least in rhetoric—"sustainable development," defined as economic growth that "meets the needs of the present without compromising the ability of future generations to meet their own needs."[1] Thus, APEC's members cannot simply maximize material gains but must attend to social welfare broadly, across both economic and environmental variables. Maximizing welfare more broadly and over time requires a dual policy approach. APEC must maintain its commitment to trade and investment liberalization, which supports economic growth, increases national incomes, and expands individ-

---

1. This definition of sustainable development comes from the World Commission on Environment and Development (1987), better known as the "Brundtland Commission."

ual material well-being. But the drive for economic integration and expansion must be matched by careful attention to environmental issues—locally, regionally, and globally—which are also important determinants of quality of life.

To be sure, one might accept the argument about the importance of good environmental policies that are integrated with economic goals without embracing the need for APEC to play a role in this process. Thus, the more specific question remains: *Why should APEC act rather than national governments or existing international organizations?*

APEC is the best institutional response to pollution and resource management problems on a regional scale. Since government intervention to respond to externalities should be at the scale of the harm to be addressed, to the extent that externalities exist at the regional scale the logic for an APEC environment program is unimpeachable.

Of course, the fact that spillovers—physical, economic, and psychological—occur at a variety of geographic scales argues strongly for a multi-tiered structure of environmental governance. Thus, problems that arise at the local level should be handled by national governments and their subjurisdictions, and issues with a global dimension should be addressed by international institutions. But in many cases, the efforts of national governments and international organizations are either substandard or nonexistent because of regulatory failures or political constraints. In these cases, APEC intervention may improve outcomes in practice, no matter that some other body is theoretically better positioned to respond to the harm or issue.

Moreover, as we explain in detail in the following chapters, deepening economic integration in APEC requires the evolution of a regional "community" in APEC. While all of APEC's members agree on the *de minimus* objective of creating an economic community, a narrow focus on strengthening economic interdependence cannot be sustained without attention to noneconomic issues. The beginnings of this process in the APEC context are best illustrated by the demands—at annual "People's Summits"[2]—that APEC address environmental, labor, and human rights issues. Continuing economic integration must be undergirded by the development of shared values and norms along environmental and other social dimensions. And the deeper the economic connections, the broader the set of common values that will be required to sustain the commitment to freer trade. APEC thus has an important role to play in Asia Pacific community building as a foundation for continued economic integration.

---

2. Since 1994, a parallel "civil society" conference has been convened immediately prior to (and, where possible, in the same city as) each Leaders' Summit. These "People's Summits" focus on the social and economic impacts of Asia Pacific integration and the commitment to further trade and investment liberalization.

Promoting environmental quality involves more than simply carving out the appropriate role for governments and intergovernmental bodies like APEC. Understanding the role that nongovernmental actors—the private sector and environmental nongovernmental organizations (NGOs)—can play in improving environmental performance across APEC is also critical.

Taking advantage of private-sector investment activity stands as a central challenge to environmental policymakers, particularly in APEC's developing countries, because the cost of environmental investments required in those countries far exceeds the available public funds. Environmental infrastructure needs across APEC top $40 billion per year today and could rise to $200 billion annually by 2020 (ADB 1997). Meanwhile, total official development assistance (ODA) given to APEC's developing countries by the World Bank, the Asian Development Bank, the Global Environment Facility, other international organizations, and bilateral foreign aid donors amounts to just a few billion dollars per year. Sustainable development in the Asia Pacific region therefore requires harnessing the $70 billion in private-sector foreign direct investment—together with the hundreds of billions in portfolio equity investment and debt finance—that is flooding into APEC's developing economies each year.

Environmental NGOs can also play an important role in improving APEC's environmental performance. Environmental groups can, in particular, sharpen the public's understanding of environmental issues, giving rise to public concern that will then motivate governments to strengthen their environmental programs. NGOs may also serve as the "connective tissue" that links individuals and local groups to the distant governmental bodies—such as APEC—that make environmental decisions and carry out policies on their behalf. In addition, environmental groups and other organizations often act as a source of "competition" to governments. They are able to generate alternative data, science, analysis, and policy options that force government officials to rethink their own approaches to environmental protection.

Chapter 2 lays the foundation for our argument about the need for an APEC environmental program with an analysis of the economic trends in the Asia Pacific region. The analysis shows impressive performance across the board: APEC's Asian members continue to experience extraordinary economic growth, its Latin American members are showing consistently strong growth, and its North American and Australasian members are proving to have the developed world's most vibrant economies. APEC's economic trajectory is also marked by deepening economic integration in the region in the form of expanded intraregional trade and investment.

Chapter 3, which surveys the environmental problems of APEC countries, shows that environmental degradation has become a significant offset against the quality-of-life gains brought to many Asia Pacific countries by economic growth. Each APEC country confronts a unique set of threats that derive from its stage and pace of development, income levels, and industrial structure. The major problems, which vary in severity from country to country, are land degradation, deforestation, water pollution, air pollution, hazardous and solid waste disposal, fisheries depletion, ozone layer thinning, climate change, and biodiversity loss. In examining these problems, we differentiate among local/national problems, regional issues, and global harms for two reasons: first, the optimal policy response and level of required government intervention varies depending on the geographic scope of the harm, and second, the scale of the problem often helps to determine how difficult the issue will be to address.

Chapter 4 analyzes the underlying reasons for the deterioration of the environment across so many APEC countries. Market failures, particularly externalities and problems of the commons, emerge as the primary source of environmental harms. Because polluters and resource users are able to spill the environmental costs of their activities onto others, overconsumption of resources and suboptimal levels of environmental protection result.

In some cases, market-failure-driven environmental problems can be overcome by properly allocating, defining, and enforcing property rights. Many harms, however, are not amenable to solutions based on property rights, making government intervention to protect the environment a necessity if the welfare losses of degradation are to be avoided. Even when the need for regulatory intervention is understood, the complexity of environmental policymaking and systemic regulatory incapacity frequently render the response to environmental problems suboptimal. In addition, governments often adopt policies in nonenvironmental areas—in particular, price-distorting subsidies for energy and agricultural activities and inputs—that have unintended negative effects on the environment. More broadly, a focus on economic development without attention to the effects on environmental welfare contributes significantly to environmental degradation. Additional environmental problems arise as a result of "public choice" problems, when governments fail to faithfully and accurately represent the views of their citizens.

Transboundary harms—"super externalities"—are especially difficult to address. In such cases, countries spill harms onto other countries or onto the commons largely without consequence as a result of a mismatch between the regulatory reach of national environmental authorities and the scale of the environmental harm in question. Empirical evidence shows that government responses to localized pollution harms improve as countries become wealthier. Better environmental performance can be attributed to improved government and private-sector capacity to make the necessary environmental investments and to demands by a richer public that governments improve local environmental quality. Regional and global trans-boundary harms, however, continue to worsen, even as incomes rise. When harms can be spilled onto other countries or the commons, there is little incentive to pay the costs of abatement since much of the benefit will accrue to citizens in other countries.

Chapter 5 examines the tensions at the economy-environment inter-face—environmental standards that obstruct market access, the use of trade measures to advance environmental goals, competitiveness con-cerns, and discomfort with trading partners' environmental choices—that endanger the continued commitment of APEC's members to trade and investment liberalization. An additional threat to openness comes from environmental NGOs in developed countries, which argue that expanded trade and the economic growth it generates are fundamentally at odds with environmental quality.

Chapter 6 explains why APEC must act in the environmental sphere—and addresses the specific question: What is APEC's environmental "value added?" Most directly, an APEC environmental regime would respond to the need for environmental governance to address regional super exter-nalities. From the perspective of economic theory, the reach of government should match the scope of the public goods that must be provided. Given that the geographic extent of environmental problems varies widely, gov-ernment response structures must concomitantly exist at various levels. Currently, no such structures exist at the overarching Asia Pacific level. APEC can fill the breach.

In addition to its potential to resolve regional-scale environmental issues, APEC could also make up for deficiencies at the national and global level—an important "second-best" institutional role. APEC could improve environmental policymaking at the national level by helping its less-developed members overcome their regulatory capacity constraints, facilitating collaboration among its members in response to common envi-ronmental problems, and enriching policy debates by sharing important environmental information with NGOs and the public as well as with governments.

APEC could similarly intervene at the worldwide level to make up for systemic problems in the global environmental regime. In this regard, it could act strategically in international negotiations to "ratchet up" results where multilateral efforts have been disappointing. It could also serve as a regional laboratory for supranational policy experimentation. Finally, it could establish its own environmental protection mechanisms to com-pensate for absent or deficient structures at the global level.

Chapter 7 introduces a generalized theory of optimal environmental governance. Building on the analysis in chapter 6 of APEC's role in manag-ing environmental issues, the theory sets out guidelines for determining how to allocate responsibility for various environmental issues to governments at a range of geographic scales. The theory demonstrates, first, the need for a multitiered structure of environmental governance and, second, the importance of cooperation and competition across the various levels of government and among nongovernmental actors (businesses and NGOs) so as to improve the environmental performance at each jurisdictional level.

Chapter 8 surveys APEC's existing efforts to achieve sustainable development, concluding that APEC rhetoric about the environment is much more advanced than actual policy work. Current efforts are largely limited to information gathering and sharing. This level of cooperation is simply not enough. There is, moreover, little hope that things will improve at APEC's Vancouver Summit in November 1997, despite Canada's stated commitment to make environmental issues a key component of the Summit. Environmental attention in Vancouver appears likely to focus on the so-called FEEEP (food, energy, environment, economic growth, and population) initiative, a misguided long-range effort without an action program that is unlikely to result in a measurable improvement in environmental performance across APEC.

Finally, chapter 9 offers an environmental "action agenda" that would move APEC decisively from cooperation to coordination, from talk to action. The agenda, which promises to be both environmentally substantive and supportive of economic integration in the Asia Pacific region, builds on the theoretical and analytic work in the preceding chapters. It asks the following questions: What are the region's most serious harms? What is causing them? What might APEC do to address them? And what is the impact of deepening economic integration? The proposed agenda attends to the unique characteristics of APEC and its members. Substantial efforts have been made to ensure that the agenda has broad political appeal and is, in fact, practical and achievable.

We propose four substantive initiatives relating to climate change, energy and agricultural subsidies, sustainable fishing, and environmental standards. Given that the signatories to the Climate Change Convention are meeting in Kyoto in December 1997, APEC should promote cost-effective and flexible approaches to mitigate the buildup of greenhouse gases in the atmosphere that have the potential to contribute to climate change. In particular, APEC's members should support a *joint implementation* initiative as a way to promote North-South collaboration on projects to reduce greenhouse gas emissions.

Recognizing that while the ultimate aim of environmental policy should be to make the polluter pay, we suggest APEC begin by stopping "pay-the-polluter" programs. Specifically, APEC should lead a multilateral effort to reduce *agricultural and energy subsidies*. Such an initiative not only offers significant economic welfare gains but promises to reduce environmental harms resulting from the misallocation of resources for which subsidies are responsible. Moreover, since APEC's commitment to "full" free trade implies eliminating export subsidies and import controls, much of this proposal simply requires renewing and clarifying the Bogor commitment.

APEC countries should also consider introducing a regionwide *tradable fishing permit system* to return the Pacific fisheries to sustainability, thus ensuring a stable and secure supply of seafood for the region's citizens. In addition, consideration should be given to an *environmental standards* initiative that strengthens the enforcement of existing environmental regulations and encourages convergence or, where appropriate, limited harmonization of environmental product and process standards. Addressing standards in this manner would simultaneously address fears that environmental regulation will become a barrier to market access for developing countries and that high environmental standards will place developed countries at a competitive disadvantage.

To support the initiatives proposed, a number of institutional reforms will be required: the creation of an environment committee to oversee APEC's environment program, track key environmental indicators, and coordinate a regional capacity-building program; the establishment of an environmental advisory group charged with making proposals to APEC's leaders; and the development of an environmentally sensitive dispute mediation procedure. Much of the proposed action agenda will be self-funding or even result in an overall reduced need for government moneys. The proposed institutional innovations will, however, entail modest resource commitments; to this end a small APEC environment fund, to which APEC members could voluntarily contribute, would be required.

We conclude that economic integration and environmental protection can be achieved together, but only if APEC both responds to a difficult challenge and takes advantage of a unique opportunity. The challenge is to ensure that environmental issues do not become the battleground for competing conceptions of regional integration and globalization. If such skirmishes become widespread, economic openness is likely to be the casualty. Beyond the need to react to potential economy-environment conflicts, there is an important opportunity to strengthen the evolving Asia Pacific community. Specifically, by developing a mutual understanding of the seriousness of environmental issues and the elements of a common response, APEC's members can strengthen the social supports for continuing economic integration.

2

APEC's Economic Performance

Many APEC countries have experienced extraordinary economic growth in recent years. In fact, the emergence of the four Asian "tigers"—Hong Kong, Singapore, South Korea, and Taiwan—together with the group of newly industrializing economies (NIEs)—including Indonesia, Malaysia, and Thailand—has been one of the defining features of international economic affairs in the last three decades. Although less heralded, APEC's Latin American members have also been growing briskly and its developed members in North America and Australasia have been the most vibrant of all the world's developed economies. Understanding the dimensions and character of this economic "miracle" is essential to any effort to discern how the environment can be appropriately protected in the context of rapid growth and deepening economic integration.[1]

While the accomplishments of the APEC economies are undisputed, the source of the region's success remains hotly contested. Many commentators argue that East Asia's rapid economic growth is based primarily on the accumulation of factors of production: the expansion of employment, increases in education levels, and, most important, massive investment in physical capital (Krugman 1994; Kim and Lau 1994; A. Young 1994, 1995). Others argue that East Asia achieved superior growth because of improvements in technology and efficiency, measured as an increase in total factor productivity (TFP) (Swee and Low 1996; UBS 1996). The sources of the increase in TFP are the subject of a further dispute. Research-

---

1. While many other studies have focused on East Asia, Southeast Asia, or some other grouping of Asian economies, this chapter presents an APEC-aggregated analysis.

ers variously attribute the increase in TFP to superior government policies (World Bank 1993), cultural differences, or "convergence" with more industrialized economies (Barro 1991; Barro and Sala-i-Martin 1992). A number of other studies argue that East Asia's growth was trade led (Helliwell 1995; Page 1994; Pack and Page 1994). Others, not surprisingly, argue that East Asia's growth is attributable to a combination of these factors (ADB 1997; Frankel, Romer, and Cyrus 1996).[2]

Despite disagreement over the reasons for the region's recent stellar performances, commentators broadly agree that many of APEC's economies will continue to show high rates of growth and movement up the development ladder for some time to come. In fact, the dynamism of the Asia Pacific region—China, Southeast Asia, East Asia, Latin America, Australasia, and North America alike—has led journalists, academics, business leaders, and politicians to suggest that we are at the dawn of the "Pacific Century" (*Forbes*, 15 July 1996, 108; Rowher 1995, 98; Tay 1996, 190).[3]

Economic Trends

Five dimensions of APEC's economic performance over the last three decades deserve particular attention. First, and most prominently, a number of APEC economies have grown at unprecedented rates, with the result that the region is now the world's largest economic area. Second, this dramatic growth has been accompanied by the fastest rise of incomes for the greatest number of people ever seen in the world's history. Third, as APEC's economies have grown, their industrial composition has typically changed from resource- and agriculture-based industries to basic manufacturing and heavy industry, and then to high-tech manufacturing, finance, and service industries. Fourth, the volume of international flows—both trade and investment—has expanded at rates exceeding even the impressive rates of economic growth. Finally, and perhaps most important, the economic success of the region has been marked by increasing economic integration, evident not only in the high proportions of intraregional trade and investment but also in the evolution of border-spanning economic regions and APEC itself. This integration has been

---

2. The controversy over the sources of East Asia's growth plays out in the context of a broader debate over the causes of long-term growth. Growth theory has attracted renewed academic interest partly as a result of Romer's (1986) hypothesis that innovation is the key to sustained growth.

3. There are, however, a growing number of "Asia skeptics" who argue that we should not expect a Pacific century. See, for example, the *Independent* (14 April 1996) and the *Journal of Commerce* (24 July 1996).

primarily market driven and, to date, has been a fundamentally economic phenomenon with limited political dimensions (Bergsten 1997).[4]

APEC Economic Growth

In 1995, APEC's aggregate GDP was \$15.6 trillion,[5] with national economies ranging in size from \$5 billion for Papua New Guinea to \$7.1 trillion for the United States. APEC's share of the world economy is not only large, it is growing. Between 1977 and 1995, the GDP of the APEC countries increased from \$3.4 trillion to \$15.6 trillion in constant 1995 dollars, a staggering increase of 360 percent in less than 20 years. Over the same period, global GDP rose from \$7.5 trillion to \$29.2 trillion, an increase of 290 percent. As a result of the relatively faster pace of Asia Pacific growth, APEC's share of global GDP increased from 45.7 percent to 53.2 percent over this time. In brief, APEC's slice of the global economic pie is big and has been getting ever bigger.

These figures, based on market rather than purchasing power parity (PPP) exchange rates, mask the true distribution of global income (figure 2.1). When the data are adjusted to reflect PPP, the global income shares of the United States, Japan, and Europe drop. APEC's economies, excluding the United States and Japan, account for 23.4 percent of global PPP-adjusted GDP, compared to just 11.6 percent of nominal GDP.[6] Viewed this way, the APEC economies loom even larger and eclipse the European Union (EU) in terms of their share of GDP, even without the United States and Japan factored in.

An examination of recent country-by-country economic growth rates highlights the growing global significance of APEC's economies. Between 1991 and 1995, 9 of the 10 fastest-growing economies in the world were APEC economies, and all of the APEC countries, apart from Japan, were among the world's 25 fastest-growing economies. A comparison of APEC and EU growth rates starkly illustrates the comparative economic vibrancy of the Asia Pacific region. Figure 2.2 shows that with just two exceptions— Ireland in the case of the European Union, and Japan in the case of APEC—every APEC economy outperformed every EU economy between 1991 and 1995, highlighting the dynamism not only of APEC's Asian members but of its Latin American, North American, and Australasian

---

4. This stands in contrast to the creation of the European Union, where significant political integration has accompanied closer economic ties.

5. All monetary figures in this study are US dollars.

6. Much of this difference in GDP shares is attributable to the undervaluation of China's and Indonesia's GDP's under traditional analysis. China's and Indonesia's PPP-adjusted GDPs account for 9.8 percent and 2.4 percent respectively of the global total, compared to 2.4 percent and 0.6 percent of nominal GDP.

Figure 2.1 Share of global GDP: actual and purchasing power parity (PPP), 1995 (percentages)

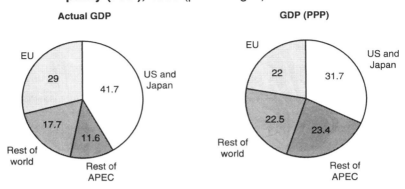

Actual GDP

EU 29

US and Japan 41.7

17.7

11.6

Rest of world

Rest of APEC

$29.2 trillion total

GDP (PPP)

EU 22

US and Japan 31.7

22.5

23.4

Rest of world

Rest of APEC

$31.2 trillion total

Note: GDP (PPP) statistics are 1994 figures but have been converted to constant 1995 dollars.

Sources: Authors' calculations at the Yale Center for Environmental Law and Policy; IMF, *International Financial Statistics Yearbook* 1996; Euromonitor, *International Marketing Data and Statistics* 1997; International Institute for Management Development (IMD), *The World Competitiveness Yearbook* 1996.

Figure 2.2 Economic growth: APEC vs. EU, 1991-95 (compound annual growth rate, percentages)

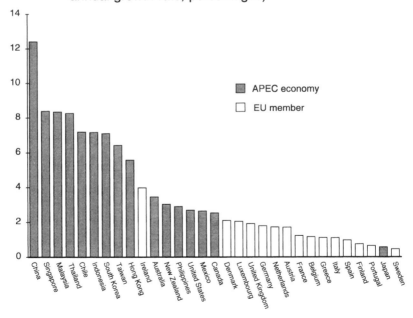

Note: Growth rate is computed on a local currency basis at constant prices.

Sources: IMF, *International Financial Statistics Yearbook*; IMD, *The World Competitiveness Yearbook* 1996.

Table 2.1 Real per capita annual GDP growth, 1965-95 (percent)

Country	Real per capita annual growth
South Korea	7.2
Singapore	7.2
Taiwan	6.2
China	5.6
Hong Kong	5.6
Malaysia	4.8
Thailand	4.8
Indonesia	4.7

Sources: Authors' calculations at the Yale Center for Environmental Law and Policy; IMF, *International Financial Statistics Yearbooks.*

members as well. Can there be any wonder why the United States (and Europe)[7] has turned its attention to the region to seek out new economic opportunities? APEC must now be reckoned with in every global economic calculus simply by virtue of its size. The European Union learned this lesson in 1993 when pressure from APEC helped to bring them to the table to conclude negotiations of the Uruguay Round of the General Agreement on Tariffs and Trade (GATT) (Bergsten 1995).

Rising Incomes across APEC

Behind the dazzling economic growth of many of the APEC nations lies a significant human story. While all of the APEC economies have experienced increases in real per capita incomes over the last three decades, several countries have seen particularly dramatic increases. In South Korea and Singapore, for example, real per capita income grew more than 700 percent between 1965 and 1995. Over the same period Taiwan, China, and Hong Kong logged more than a fourfold increase in real per capita income. And Malaysia, Thailand, and Indonesia each experienced real per capita income growth on the order of 300 percent.[8] This means, as table 2.1 shows, that each of these eight countries managed

---

7. Fearing that their limited economic engagement with Asia meant that lucrative business opportunities were being missed, European nations began a dialogue with Asian countries in 1996 through the Asia-Europe Meeting (ASEM) talks (*Daily Yomiuri*, 14 April 1996; *The Economist*, 9 March 1996).

8. Of course, if the baseline is the end of World War II, Japan's per capita income growth surpasses that of all these countries.

to sustain annual per capita GDP growth rates of between 4.7 percent and 7.2 percent for the last 30 years.

While achieving tremendous real per capita growth, the Asian tigers and NIEs have also successfully narrowed the gap between rich and poor. According to the World Bank (1993), not only did Asia's economies have the world's fastest growth rates between 1965 and 1990, but at the same time a number of them—including Hong Kong, Indonesia, Malaysia, the Philippines, and Singapore—achieved greater equalization of income distribution than any other developing country in the world. South Korea and Taiwan experienced more modest improvements in income equality simply because they had relatively equal income distributions to begin with.[9] In fact, these APEC economies are the only ones in the world that achieved both high growth and declining inequality in recent years.

Rapid economic growth, together with rising per capita incomes and declining income inequality, has meant that over the last three decades, hundreds of millions of Asians have been lifted from poverty (World Bank, *World Development Report 1996*). In China, for example, over 170 million of the 270 million living in absolute poverty in 1978 had been raised above the minimum poverty threshold by 1995. In Indonesia, the incidence of poverty declined from around 60 percent, or 70 million people, at the beginning of the 1970s to roughly 14 percent, or 26 million, in 1995. In Malaysia and Thailand, absolute poverty decreased from 49 percent and 57 percent, respectively, in 1970 to 10 percent and 20 percent, respectively, by 1995. Progress in reducing poverty has been accompanied by substantial increases in life expectancy and reductions in infant mortality, as shown in table 2.2.

Changing Industrial Composition

As APEC's members have grown they have also seen their industrial structures change dramatically. These changes, which have important environmental implications, have been most dramatic in APEC's Asian economies. The economic evolution of APEC's members can best be illustrated by examining three countries at different stages of development: Indonesia, South Korea, and Japan.

Indonesia represents a country in the early stages of industrialization (figure 2.3). In 1965, nearly 60 percent of Indonesia's GDP was accounted for by primary products. The last quarter century, however, has seen the steady relative decline of agricultural and forestry activities as manufac-

---

9. Comparatively little data are available on changes in income distribution in China, but recent figures indicate that the income share of the top 20 percent of the Chinese population increased from 37 percent in the early 1980s to 44 percent in 1995 (World Bank 1996a).

Table 2.2 Life expectancy and infant mortality in selected APEC countries

Country	Life expectancy at birth (years)		Infant mortality rate (deaths per 1,000 live births)	
	1960	1993	1965	1993
China	47	69	90	30
Hong Kong	66	63	27	7
Indonesia	41	63	128	56
Malaysia	54	71	55	13
Philippines	53	67	72	42
Singapore	65	74	26	6
South Korea	53	72	62	11
Thailand	52	68	88	36
Industrial economies	70	77	nc	nc

nc = not compiled.

Note: Industrial economics refers to nations of the world with a GNP per capita of $8956 or more in 1994.

Sources: UNDP, Human Development Report 1996; World Bank, World Development Report.

turing, wholesale and retail trade, mining, and finance have risen to take their place. Nevertheless, as figure 2.3 makes clear, even though agriculture has declined in importance, it has still grown in real terms.

South Korea has achieved a greater level of industrialization than Indonesia, and it is likely to cement its position among the ranks of the most-developed, highly industrialized countries within the next 10 to 20 years.[10] In 1960, agriculture was South Korea's largest industry, though manufacturing and wholesale and retail trade were already economically important (figure 2.4). By 1990, the South Korean economy centered on manufacturing, followed by the finance and insurance industry, a sign of significant modernization. Note that, as was the case for Indonesia, even industries in comparative decline, like agriculture, grew in real terms.

Japan serves as an example of one of the world's wealthiest and most highly industrialized economies (figure 2.5). In 1960, the Japanese economy, already comparatively highly industrialized, was dominated by manufacturing, wholesale and retail trade, and agriculture. By 1990, manufacturing was still the dominant industry, but less so than before. As a mark of its shift toward a postindustrial services economy, Japan's second-largest sector was finance, and its third-largest sector was community, social, and personal services.

The change in the relative importance of various industries reveals only part of the story. Just as important is how the composition of each industry

---

10. South Korea was admitted in 1997 to the Organization for Economic Cooperation and Development (OECD), the Paris-based "club" of the world's developed countries.

Figure 2.3 Industrial structure: Indonesia, 1965 and 1990

Contributions of each industry to GDP (percentages)

Industry	1965	1990
Agriculture, hunting, forestry, and fishing	58.9	21.5
Mining and quarrying	2.5	13.4
Manufacturing	7.6	19.9
Electricity, gas, and water	0.1	0.6
Construction	1.7	5.5
Wholesale and retail trade, restaurants, and hotels	12.3	16.9
Transport, storage, and communication	2.1	5.6
Finance, insurance, real estate, and business services	3.0	6.7
Community, social, and personal services	8.5	3.3
Production of government services	3.4	6.5
Total	**100**	**100**

Contributions of each industry of GDP[a]

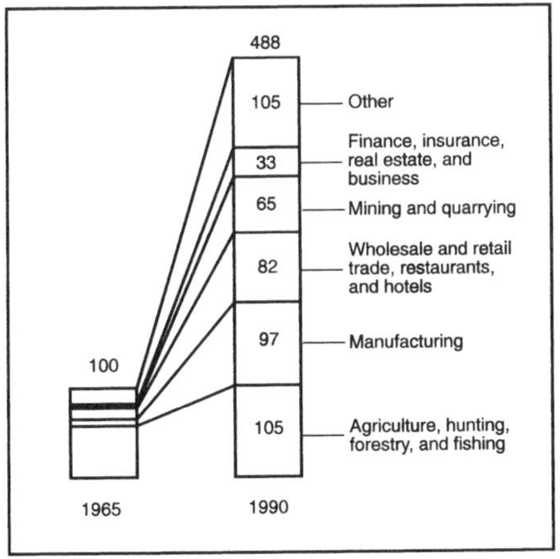

a. This figure indexes 1965 GDP to 100 and shows 1990 GDP calculated relative to that base year.

Sources: Authors; calculations at the Yale Center for Environmental Law and Policy; UN Yearbook of National Accounts Statistics; IMF, International Financial Statistics Yearbook.

Figure 2.4 Industrial structure: South Korea, 1960 and 1990

Contributions of each industry to GDP (percentages)

Industry	1960	1990
Agriculture, hunting, forestry, and fishing	38.0	9.2
Mining and quarrying	2.2	0.5
Manufacturing	14.0	29.5
Electricity, gas, and water	0.8	2.1
Construction	3.4	13.5
Wholesale and retail trade, restaurants, and hotels	12.9	11.2
Transport, storage, and communication	4.7	7.2
Finance, insurance, real estate, and business services	8.7	14.8
Community, social, and personal services	7.9	4.2
Production of government services	7.3	7.9
Total	**100**	**100**

Contributions of each industry of GDP[a]

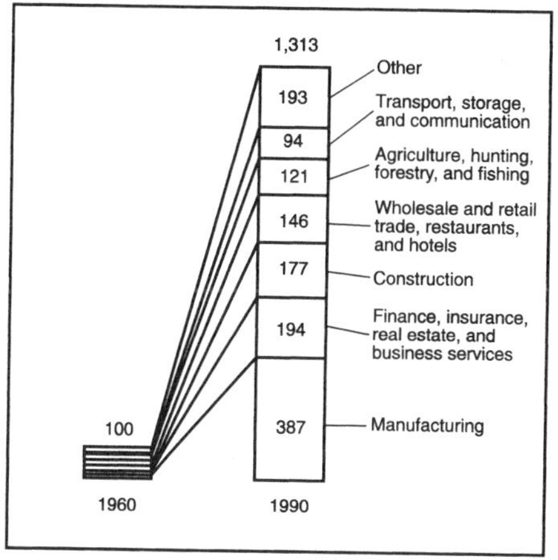

a. This figure indexes 1960 GDP to 100 and shows 1990 GDP calculated relative to that base year.

Sources: Authors' calculations at the Yale Center for Environmental Law and Policy; UN *Yearbook of National Accounts Statistics;* IMF, *International Financial Statistics Yearbook.*

Figure 2.5 Industrial structure: Japan, 1960 and 1990

Contributions of each industry to GDP (percentages)

Industry	1960	1990
Agriculture, hunting, forestry, and fishing	12.5	2.4
Mining and quarrying	1.7	0.3
Manufacturing	31.7	28.1
Electricity, gas, and water	2.3	2.6
Construction	5.3	9.6
Wholesale and retail trade, restaurants, and hotels	16.2	12.4
Transport, storage, and communication	8.3	6.2
Finance, insurance, real estate, and business services	8.9	15.8
Community, social, and personal services	10.1	15.3
Production of government services	3.0	7.4
Total	**100**	**100**

Contributions of each industry of GDP[a]

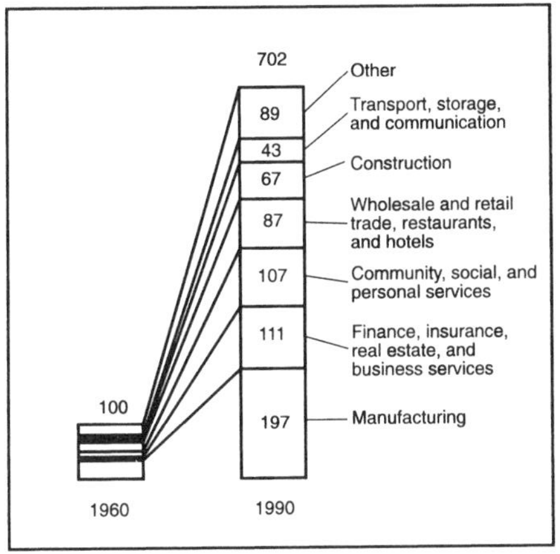

a. This figure indexes 1960 GDP to 100 and shows 1990 GDP calculated relative to that base year.

Sources: Authors' calculations at the Yale Center for Environmental Law and Policy; UN *Yearbook of National Accounts Statistics;* IMF, *International Financial Statistics Yearbook.*

Table 2.3 Structural changes in the Japanese manufacturing sector, 1955-90 (contribution of each subsector to total manufacturing output in percentages)

	1955	1960	1965	1970	1975	1980	1985	1990
Food	37.8	25.5	20.2	15.5	17.0	14.4	11.8	9.1
Textile	9.9	8.4	7.1	5.4	5.3	3.8	2.7	1.7
Chemical	1.6	2.3	2.9	4.1	5.0	5.9	7.4	9.1
General machinery	3.0	6.0	6.6	8.8	7.8	10.7	12.5	12.8
Electric equipment	0.5	1.3	1.8	3.2	4.4	8.5	14.8	21.6
Transport equipment	3.8	6.5	9.0	10.8	11.7	11.9	10.6	11.4
Oil and coal products	2.8	4.9	6.5	6.2	6.6	4.2	4.1	0.7
Glass/cement/ceramics	3.6	4.7	5.3	5.5	5.0	3.8	3.6	3.3
Primary metal	8.0	7.8	7.4	10.2	10.8	11.6	8.3	7.6
Metal products	2.7	3.8	5.6	6.4	5.0	4.7	4.9	4.8
Paper/pulp	1.4	2.9	3.2	3.0	3.0	2.7	2.5	2.6
Precision instrument	0.5	0.6	0.8	0.9	1.0	1.8	2.0	1.6
Other manufacturing	24.3	25.3	23.6	20.0	17.5	16.1	14.8	13.8
Total manufacturing	100	100	100	100	100	100	100	100

Source: O'Connor 1994.

has changed, a phenomenon best illustrated by examining the structural changes in the Japanese manufacturing sector over time. Figure 2.5—which shows that between 1960 and 1990 the manufacturing sector's contribution to total output changed little—hides the dramatic changes within the manufacturing sector itself (table 2.3). For example, between 1955 and 1990 the contribution of food fell from 37.8 percent to just 9.1 percent of total manufacturing output. Other industries, including chemicals, general machinery, electric equipment, and transport equipment, significantly increased their contribution to manufacturing output. These changes in industrial structure have important implications for the environment, since they determine the type and range of environmental problems that a country can expect to face.

Volume of Trade and Investment

The post-Bretton Woods international economic order has been characterized by increased openness to both trade and capital flows (Bergsten 1992; Jackson 1969, 1992), which can be attributed not just to progress made through multilateral institutions such as the GATT, the International Monetary Fund (IMF), and the World Bank, but also to domestic commitments in many countries to the liberalization of trade and investment regimes.

Figure 2.6 Share of global exports, 1965 and 1995 (percentages)

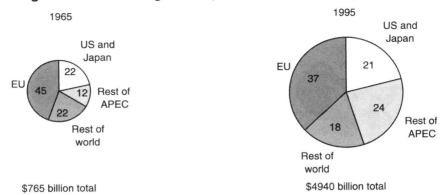

1965

US and
Japan

EU

22

45

12   Rest of
      APEC

22

Rest of
world

$765 billion total

1995

US and
Japan

EU

37

21

24

18

Rest of
APEC

Rest of
world

$4940 billion total

Note: Figures are constant 1995 dollars.

Sources: Authors' calculations at the Yale Center for Environmental Law and Policy; IMF, *Direction of Trade Statistics.*

Together with increased factor mobility arising from improved technology and communications, openness has provided the conditions for the expansion of both trade and investment volumes. APEC's economies have taken particular advantage of these conditions. They have expanded their export markets, on the one hand—often generating large trade surpluses—and attracted significant amounts of foreign direct investment (FDI) into their economies, on the other. While commentators disagree on how trade, investment, and economic growth are causally related,[11] there is no doubt that among many of APEC's members, expanding trade and rising investment flows have been accompanied by economic growth. Indeed, creating an export push and encouraging high rates of investment have been hallmarks of the Asian development model pursued by the tigers and the NIEs (World Bank 1993; Haggard 1995).

Trade

Between 1965 and 1995, a period during which global exports increased sixfold, APEC's economies significantly increased their share of world trade. During those decades, APEC exports grew from $262 billion to $2.2 trillion in constant 1995 dollars, an increase of 740 percent. If the United States and Japan are not included, exports jumped from $93 billion to $1.2 trillion, an increase of 1160 percent, equivalent to a compound annual growth rate of 8.8 percent. Over the same period, the European Union's exports expanded at an average annual rate of 5.7 percent. Thus, while

---

11. For discussions of the causal relationship between trade, investment, and growth see, for example, Rodrik (1994) and Harrison (1995).

Figure 2.7 Share of APEC's exports, 1965 and 1995 (percentages)

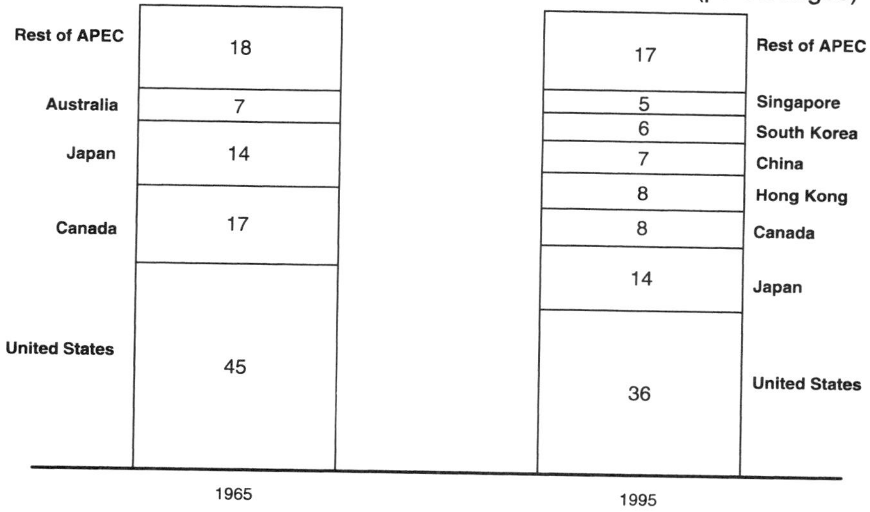

1965		1995	
Rest of APEC	18	17	Rest of APEC
Australia	7	5	Singapore
		6	South Korea
Japan	14	7	China
		8	Hong Kong
Canada	17	8	Canada
		14	Japan
United States	45	36	United States

Note: Figures do not include Taiwanese exports.

Sources: Authors' calculations at the Yale Center for Environmental Law and Policy; IMF, Direction of Trade Statistics.

the APEC economies accounted for only 34 percent of exports in 1965, by 1995 they claimed nearly half the world's exports (figure 2.6). The story is much the same on the import side of the trade equation.

Not only have APEC exports grown at a breakneck pace for the last 30 years, but the breadth of countries that contribute most significantly to APEC's exports has widened (figure 2.7). In 1965, four countries—the United States, Canada, Japan, and Australia—accounted for 82 percent of APEC's exports; each contributed at least 5 percent of APEC's total exports. By 1995, however, seven countries—the United States, Japan, Canada, Hong Kong, China, South Korea, and Singapore—were able to make that claim; if present trends continue, they are likely to be joined by Malaysia within the next decade.

Investment

While export growth stands as one of the most visible manifestations of the economic success of the APEC countries, the growth in foreign direct investment (FDI) also deserves attention. Investment flows are a crucial

Figure 2.8 APEC's share of global FDI inflows, 1985-95

Billions of dollars (1995 constant)

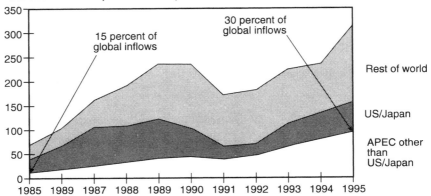

Sources: Authors' calculations at the Yale Center for Environmental Law and Policy; IMF, *Balance of Payments Statistics Yearbook.*

Figure 2.9 FDI inflows to selected APEC countries, 1985-94

Billions of dollars (1994 constant)

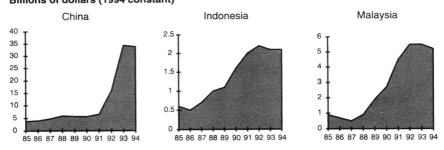

Sources: Authors' calculations at the Yale Center for Environmental Law and Policy; IMF, *Balance of Payments Statistics Yearbook.*

determinant of economic structure and performance.[12] FDI is also an important vehicle for the dispersion of environmental technologies.[13]

While global FDI flows have more than quadrupled in real terms since 1995, APEC's share of those flows has increased, showing that in the investment sphere APEC is also outpacing the rest of the world (figure 2.8). In 1995 the APEC economies, excluding the United States and Japan,

12. Ramstetter (1991), for example, has shown that there is a strong correlation between FDI and structural change in Asia.

13. Chapter 9, in discussing the contribution of FDI to the financing of sustainable development, explains the positive impacts that FDI has on the dissemination of environmental technologies and best practices.

Figure 2.10   FDI to APEC developing countries as a proportion of gross fixed capital formation, 1995 (percentages)

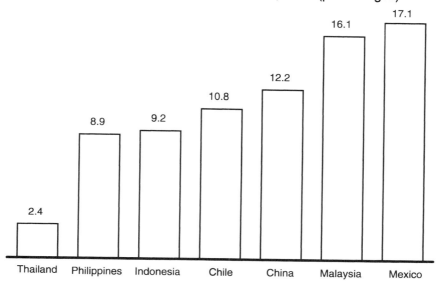

Note: Figures for Malaysia and Thailand are for 1994, and for China the figures are for 1993.

Sources: Authors' calculations at the Yale Center for Environmental Law and Policy; IMF, *Balance of Payments to Statistics Yearbook.*

received $95 billion in FDI. This represents 30 percent of global FDI flows, up from just 15 percent in 1985. The United States and Japan attracted a further $60 billion, bringing APEC's share of global FDI inflows to 51 percent.

A number of countries have been particularly successful in attracting FDI. As figure 2.9 shows, FDI to China increased from under $4 billion to over $33 billion (1994 dollars) between 1985 and 1994. In 1996, foreign investment in China topped $40 billion. Over the same period, Indonesia registered a threefold increase in FDI inflow, while Malaysia's FDI inflows increased from under $1 billion to over $5 billion annually.

Despite impressive growth, $95 billion worth of FDI may not seem significant, particularly when compared to the worldwide total invested capital of $18 trillion (Jaspersen, Aylward, and Sumlinski 1995). Nevertheless, FDI as a proportion of total gross fixed capital formation in fact looms large in a number of APEC's developing economies (figure 2.10). In Mexico and Malaysia, for example, one in every six dollars of gross fixed capital formation comes from overseas. In China, Chile, Indonesia, and the Philippines, FDI also contributes significantly to capital formation.

Foreign investment thus stands alongside expanded trade as a key factor in the ongoing growth of the Asia Pacific region.

Increasing Economic Integration

In addition to fueling APEC's growth, expanded trade and investment flows in the Asia Pacific region have reinforced the interdependence of APEC's economies (Watabe and Yamaguchi 1996). This interdependence can be seen both qualitatively and quantitatively by looking at the extent of intraregional economic activity.

Qualitatively, economic integration within APEC is evident in the rise of "region states" (Ohmae 1995) or "subregional economic zones" (SREZs) (Chia and Lee 1993). These are geographically contiguous areas separated by political boundaries that, by virtue of economic complementarity, geographic proximity, suitable infrastructure, and favorable economic policy, have become deeply economically integrated (Chia and Lee 1993). Such areas are generally characterized by a congregation of manufacturers, not by producers who have located there to take advantage of a ready supply of natural resources. While crossing national boundaries, these areas do not generally involve entire national economies (Pomfret 1996).[14]

Examples of such natural economic zones in the Asia Pacific are the region spanning the southern Chinese province of Guangdong, Hong Kong, and Taiwan; the SIJORI "growth triangle" covering Singapore, Johor in southern Malaysia, and Riau in northern Indonesia; and the northern "growth triangle" covering Medan in west Indonesia, Penang in northern Malaysia, and Phuket in southern Thailand. Although region states and SREZs are frequently characterized by official cooperation, government activities are usually a response to market forces and already growing private-sector linkages and activities.

Quantitatively, APEC's interdependence is demonstrated by the scope of intraregional trade flows. While intra-APEC trade has always been high, it has increased steadily over the last 30 years. In 1962, intraregional trade accounted for approximately 53 percent of the total trade in the APEC region. By 1994, this figure had reached 74 percent (J. Frankel 1997). Bora (1995), comparing intraindustry trade indices between 1980 and 1993, also found that the degree of intra-APEC trade had increased.

---

14. Ohmae's "region state" is more broadly defined than the SREZ concept. He includes economic areas that are wholly contained within, but not coterminous with, national boundaries, including the Silicon Valley/Bay Area in California; Japan's Kansai region, which includes Osaka, Kobe, and Kyoto; and the area comprising the cities of Fukuoka and Kitakyushu on the Japanese island of Kyushu.

High levels of intraregional trade have been accompanied by significant intraregional investment. Bora (1995) found that of all outward FDI emanating from the APEC region in 1992, 51.4 percent made its way to other APEC countries, up from 41.4 percent in 1980. These aggregate figures for APEC hide a more nuanced story (Bora 1996; Rowher 1995). In particular, Canadian and American investment in Mexico is very high. Japan invests heavily in the United States and the NIEs. Investment among the tigers is also high, as is FDI from the tigers to the NIEs, and vice versa. More recently, countries have been diverting a significant share of their investment away from the tigers and the NIEs to China.

Perhaps the most important feature of APEC's deepening economic integration is that it has been market driven (Lawrence 1996).[15] In the investment context, for example, the explosion of FDI in the 1980s occurred before the liberalization of investment regimes in the region. And in the trade context, absolute and intraregional levels of trade have been rising for several decades, long before intergovernmental cooperation began under the auspices of APEC. The private-sector-driven creation of SREZs is further evidence of the importance of the market and private enterprise in explaining Asia's economic integration. Acknowledging the central role of the private sector in the economic integration of the Asia Pacific—and in the creation of APEC itself[16]—APEC established the APEC Business Advisory Council (ABAC) in 1995 to advise the leaders and APEC forums about business-related issues and the business perspective on specific areas of cooperation.[17] In fact, APEC hopes that the private sector will continue to drive the process of regional growth and integration evidenced by the keenness of members to ground future APEC initiatives, where possible, on private-sector involvement and input.[18]

---

15. This is not to say that Asian governments have not intervened in the functioning of their economies. Japan, Korea, Singapore, and Taiwan have been particularly active in managing their economies. See World Bank (1993) for a discussion of the domestic policy interventions of East Asian governments between 1960 and 1990.

16. Business groups such as the Pacific Basin Economic Council (PBEC) were instrumental in advancing the policy process in the region that led to the creation of the APEC forum (Funabashi 1995).

17. The ABAC replaced the Pacific Business Forum (PBF), established by the leaders of APEC countries at Blake Island in 1993.

18. The commitment to engage the private sector in APEC's activities runs deep. It is best illustrated by the convening of a parallel summit for CEOs—the APEC Business Forum—by President Fidel Ramos in Manila in 1996.

What the Future Holds for APEC

Is the Asian miracle over? This question, which was recently posed by the *Economist* (1 March 1997, 23), has come to occupy the minds of many students of the region. While the prognosis for the long term is somewhat uncertain, and depends largely on the political and economic stability of China—as well as whether Hong Kong, South Korea, Singapore, and Taiwan can continue their growth, and whether Indonesia, Malaysia, the Philippines, and Thailand can emulate the success of the tigers—most APEC countries face bright economic prospects in the short term.[19] Trade liberalization will fuel much of the growth in the Asia Pacific. Gains are expected not just from the Uruguay Round agreements but from APEC's own commitment to achieve free trade in the region.

Prospects for Future Growth

Marcus Noland's (1996) study of APEC's economic prospects to the year 2003 concludes that Asia is likely to grow faster than the rest of the world, as it has in the past three decades. In even his worst-case scenario, Noland predicts that the APEC economies, excluding the United States and Japan, will account for 25.1 percent of PPP-adjusted global income in 2003, compared to 21.7 percent in 1993. In his more optimistic scenario, Asia's share of global income rises to around 30 percent. Noland also concludes that China will cement its place as the world's second-largest economy, behind the United States, at least in PPP terms.

Our analysis of the APEC economy backs Noland's conclusions. Using composite economic growth estimates from various sources, including the OECD and the Pacific Economic Cooperation Council (an APEC advisory body), we project that APEC's economic output in 1995 of $15.6 trillion will grow to $18.7 trillion by 2001, in constant 1995 dollars. This increase of $3.1 trillion is greater than the entire 1995 GDP of Germany, the world's fourth-largest economy (in PPP terms).

Predictions beyond the early years of the next century are fraught with uncertainty. The greatest variable is China. It remains unclear whether China will manage a successful transition to a market economy in which political and macroeconomic stability is secured, financial discipline and competition are increased (particularly vis-à-vis state-owned enterprises), the role of state-owned industry continues to decline, and property rights are appropriately created and allocated (Noland 1996; Goldstone 1996).[20] Additional uncertainty surrounds the role of China's central government

---

19. Recent projections by the World Trade Organization (*Bangkok Post*, 28 March 1997) and the Asian Development Bank (*Dow Jones Business News*, 17 April 1997) support the view that APEC's Asian economies will resume rapid growth despite a recent slowdown.

20. For a general discussion of some of the measures that countries in transition from plan to market should take, see Woo, Parker, and Sachs (1997) and World Bank (1996b).

(Noland 1996). Will its position be weakened by the increasing autonomy of regions such as Fujian, Guangdong, and Shenzen (van Kamenade 1997)? Will it lose macroeconomic control because of difficulties in collecting taxes and other government revenues? Will continued patronage to loss-making state enterprises deplete its coffers? The economic and political permutations concerning China are endless. This uncertainty regarding APEC's fastest-growing and third-largest economy makes it difficult to make credible long-term economic predictions about the region as a whole.[21]

Another question is whether the growth of Hong Kong, South Korea, Singapore, and Taiwan will slow as they industrialize further, in the same fashion as Japan's growth rate has dropped. Taiwan's growth already appears to have begun to slow over the last decade—its average growth rate in the 1990s to date has been around 6 percent, compared to 10 percent in the 1970s. Whether Malaysia, Indonesia, the Philippines, and Thailand will be able to build on their growth and continue their fast-paced development is also uncertain. The recent currency crisis, which sent Thailand and the Philippines to the IMF to ask for help, heightens concerns that growth in the NIEs may not be assured (*New York Times*, 1 August 1997).

Notwithstanding the difficulties associated with long-range forecasting, the Asian Development Bank (ADB) (1997, 118-27) has examined growth prospects for Asia up to 2025. Based on the assumption that countries maintain the natural and policy conditions recorded in 1995, the ADB foresees an annual per capita GDP growth from 1995 to 2025 of 4.5 percent in Southeast Asia and 6 percent in China. While the ADB forecasts for East Asia are more modest, it still estimates that per capita GDP in South Korea, Singapore, and Taiwan will grow by about 3 percent per year, providing East Asians with incomes on par with US citizens in the year 2025.

The Expected Benefits of Trade and Investment Liberalization

Why are APEC nations so enthusiastic about "free and open trade and investment" (APEC 1994a)? The answer is that—with their openness to trade and high trade to output ratios—they expect to profit handsomely from liberalization efforts.[22] One of APEC's primary goals, of course, has been to encourage deeper trade liberalization at the multilateral level (APEC 1993a, 1994a, 1995a, 1996). Using computable general equilibrium models, a number of studies have estimated the economic welfare gains that are expected to accrue from the Uruguay Round commitments. A

---

21. China is third-largest in nominal terms and second-largest on a PPP-adjusted basis.

22. As Bergsten (1995) suggests, APEC is "potentially the biggest trade agreement in history."

GATT (1993) study estimated, for example, that by 2005 global GDP would be $230 billion higher (in 1992 dollars) following Uruguay Round reforms than in their absence. A similar study by the OECD (1993) forecast an increase in global GDP of $274 billion (1992 dollars) by 2002.[23] And as global incomes rise, trade is expected to expand by more than 12 percent annually (GATT 1993). Given the openness and trade focus of APEC's members, they can be expected to be the beneficiaries of a significant portion of these welfare gains.[24]

In addition to encouraging multilateral trade liberalization—and perhaps as an alternative, if multilateral efforts falter—APEC has also focused on liberalizing trade and investment within the region.[25] These efforts are also expected to deliver significant benefits. Studies have shown that fully liberalized trade in the region could improve regional GDP by between $300 billion (Dee, Geisler, and Watts 1996) and $500 billion annually (Martin, Petri, and Yanagashima 1994), over and above the gains expected from the Uruguay Round reforms. Petri (1997) has also estimated that if barriers to foreign investment were reduced by half, regional welfare gains would be $60 billion annually. And if trade facilitation measures covering standards, competition policy, procurement, and regulation were also agreed upon, further gains of up to $440 billion could accrue (Dee, Geisler, and Watts 1996). With projected gains in the vicinity of $1 trillion per annum, it is easy to see why APEC's economies have focused on trade and investment liberalization, despite some disagreement over its pace.[26]

---

23. For further estimates of the economic welfare gains expected from the Uruguay Round see Francois, McDonald, and Nordstrom (1994) ($100 to $512 billion); Goldin, Knudson, and van der Mensbrugghe (1993) ($213 billion); Nguyen, Perroni, and Wigle (1993) ($212 billion); and Yang (1994) ($60 to $116 billion).

24. Schott (1994) believes the Uruguay Round models underestimate the potential welfare gains because they (1) omit certain key points of the negotiations, including commitments on government procurement and advances in relation to services and intellectual property rights; (2) fail to take into account the long-run dynamic effects of trade reform; and (3) incorrectly assume that in the absence of the successful conclusion of the Uruguay Round there would be no reversal of trade reforms already achieved.

25. There has been a spirited debate within APEC about how APEC liberalization will be applied to nonmembers. It appears that APEC's goal is "free trade in the area" (APEC 1994b, 54), not a "free trade area," reflecting resistance within APEC to the creation of a new preferential trading agreement (Bergsten 1997).

26. The most vocal critic of the pace of liberalization within APEC has been Malaysian Prime Minister Mahathir, who has said that it is "unrealistic and grossly unfair to coerce ... the less advanced member economies to undertake liberalization measures at a pace and manner beyond their capacity" (*Straits Times*, 24 November 1996, 21). Even Mahathir, however, concedes, "I have no problem with trade liberalization per se."

Conclusion

The picture in APEC is one of rapid growth and market-driven economic integration, not just in East and Southeast Asia but across the region. This trade- and investment-led growth has generated tremendous benefits—in particular, rising incomes and increasing income equality. There is, without a doubt, much to celebrate in the Asia Pacific region. As the next chapter shows, however, the favorable economic trends in the region have been accompanied by negative environmental ones. As APEC's members continue down the path of liberalization and integration, they must take steps to ensure that poor environmental performance does not ruin the party.

3

Environmental Problems Confronting
APEC's Members

From Santiago to Seoul, Manila to Mexico City, Bangkok to Beijing, the environmental problems of the Asia Pacific are legion.[1] Across the region, the environmental consequences of economic success—blackened skies, fouled water, sterile land, ravaged forests, depleted fisheries, and destroyed ecosystems—indisputably impose public health and ecological costs, representing real social welfare losses that must be offset against the material gains from economic growth.

Various studies have attempted to estimate the economic costs of environmental harms. Smil (1996) puts the annual economic losses from general environmental degradation and pollution in China—including losses caused by deforestation, degraded land, and destruction of wetlands, as well as health and productivity losses caused by pollution in cities—at between 5.5 and 9.8 percent of GNP. The Chinese Academy of Social Science (Smil 1996) similarly estimates economic losses on the order of 8.5 percent of GNP, or in excess of $30 billion annually. Other studies have found that the economywide costs of environmental harms amount to 3.3 percent of GNP in Mexico and 4.5 percent in India, a potential APEC member (Brandon and Homman 1995). Estimates place the economic costs of particulate and lead pollution in Jakarta alone at 2 percent of Indonesia's

---

1. Recent reports from APEC countries highlight the severity of environmental degradation across the region. Taiwan's Environmental Protection Agency recently reported, for example, that its environmental "misery index" was on the rise (Central News Agency [Taiwan], 17 April 1997), and the Philippines Department of Environment and Natural Resources concluded that the Philippines' environment was in a dismal state (*Straits Times*, 8 June 1997).

GNP (Ostro 1994; DeShazo 1996), with similar appraisals for Thailand (O'Connor 1994). Costs of this magnitude show that the environmental consequences of economic growth can be significant. Indeed, unless efforts are made to curb these losses, the net effect of development on social welfare, defined broadly, may not always be positive.[2]

Environmental Harms across the APEC Region

Serious environmental degradation and resource depletion are already apparent in many parts of the Asia Pacific. But the visible harms tell only half the story. Because environmental injuries often do not appear until conditions become crowded or certain thresholds have been exceeded, the continuation of current developmental, demographic, and behavioral trends means that further problems will likely emerge and threaten APEC's citizens and environment over time.

The APEC countries thus face a dual environmental challenge. They must attend to their existing set of pollution and resource problems so as to minimize the public health and ecological losses they are already experiencing.[3] And, at the same time, they need to find ways to forecast and mitigate the harms that will emerge as growth proceeds, new patterns of economic activity unfold, and critical thresholds are surpassed.

Land Degradation

In many APEC nations large populations eke out a living from a limited supply of productive land. High population densities in Asian countries— only 0.3 hectares of agricultural land per capita, compared with 1.6 hectares per person in the rest of the developing world and 1.4 hectares per person in OECD countries (ADB 1997, 206)—mean that even under ideal conditions, it would be difficult to produce enough sustenance. And conditions throughout the region are far from ideal. The agricultural productivity of large areas has fallen and some previously productive tracts of land have been rendered completely sterile. Soil degradation problems range from modest in some countries, such as the United States and Canada,

---

2. Standard economic theory teaches that if there are two distortions (e.g., trade restrictions and environmental externalities) in the global economy, the net effect on global welfare of reducing only one (e.g., trade restrictions, through liberalization) may not be positive (K. Anderson 1996; Daly 1993).

3. Actually, the goal should be to reduce the harms to *optimal* levels, at which further expenditure on pollution prevention or control would exceed the benefits to be obtained.

Table 3.1 Estimated extent of degraded land in selected APEC countries

Country	Total land (millions ha)	Degraded land (millions ha)	Percentage of total land
China	932.6	280.0	30
Indonesia	181.2	43.0	24
Philippines	29.8	5.0	17
Thailand	51.1	17.2	34
Vietnam	32.5	10.9	34

Source: Dent 1989.

to critical in nations such as China, Thailand, and Vietnam,[4] where, as table 3.1 shows, a third or more of the total land area is degraded.

Land productivity may fall for a number of reasons. In some cases, soil is exposed to wind or water erosion by deforestation, removal of vegetation, or other human activities. In other cases, poorly managed agricultural and industrial practices cause contamination and deterioration of the soil by physical and chemical means. About a third of the total land loss in the Asia Pacific region can be attributed to overgrazing by livestock (Oldeman, Hakkeling, and Sombrock 1990). Poor irrigation practices also account for a significant percentage of land degradation in the Asian region as a whole, resulting in widespread salinization (ADB 1997, 207).

Land degradation has many socioeconomic, public health, and ecological effects. Land degradation exacerbates poverty in many developing economies among communities that are poorly equipped to earn their livelihoods outside agriculture. Land degradation and conversion—in combination with population growth, rising incomes, and an attendant increase in caloric intake and changes in dietary structure (R. Johnson 1997)—are generating large requirements for investment in agricultural research to avoid increases in food prices and pressure on living standards for many poor people. In China, for example, despite strong growth in agricultural yields through the application of better technology and capital investments, grain prices have risen in recent years from well below to somewhat above world prices (Garnaut, Cai, and Huang 1996). Of course, as APEC countries become more integrated into the world economy, they will be able to import increasing amounts of food. Nevertheless, the pressure on a limited supply of land argues for care in managing this scarce resource.

In addition to creating problems relating to the distributional aspects of food supply, land degradation can lead to siltation of canals, reservoirs, and drainage systems across the region, resulting in greater maintenance

---

4. While not yet an APEC member, Vietnam is expected to be one of the first nations admitted when membership restrictions are lifted.

Table 3.2 Deforestation in selected APEC countries

| Country | Total forest area (1,000 ha) (1990) | Annual deforestation 1981-90 | | Total area deforested 1981-90 (percentages) |
		Area (1,000 ha)	Rate (percentages)	
Indonesia	109,549	1,212	1.1	11
Thailand	12,735	515	4.0	34
Malaysia	17,583	396	2.0	18
Philippines	7,831	316	4.0	34
Vietnam	8,312	137	1.6	15
Papua New Guinea	3,600	113	0.3	3

Source: FAO 1993.

costs and shorter operational life of water projects. Land degradation also results in declining incomes for agricultural populations, increased frequency of natural disasters like floods and landslides, and habitat destruction that translates into a loss of biodiversity (UNESCAP 1995, 17).

Deforestation

There has been a dramatic loss of forest cover in many APEC countries over the past four decades. In fact, Southeast Asia has the dubious honor of having the fastest rate of deforestation in the world, estimated at a 1.2 percent loss per year (FAO 1993). APEC countries also have the fastest rates of commercial logging, the highest volume of fuelwood removal, and the fastest rates of forest species extinction (UNESCAP 1995). As table 3.2 shows, in the period between 1981 and 1990, deforestation claimed more than a third of the forest area in Thailand and the Philippines. While the proportion of total forest cover lost in Indonesia and Malaysia was lower, high absolute levels of deforestation have been apparent. The UN Food and Agriculture Organization (FAO) (1994a) recently concluded that the Philippines, Vietnam, Malaysia, Thailand, and China have all exceeded or nearly exceeded the limits of forest sustainability.

Land clearing for mining and agricultural purposes, commercial logging and timber cutting for fuelwood, livestock grazing, and the construction of roads and dams represent the primary sources of deforestation in the APEC region. In Indonesia and Malaysia, for example, there has been large-scale clearing of forests for rubber plantations. In China, forests have been cleared to support expanded tea cultivation (UNEP/GEMS 1993).

Logging and the sale of forest products provide substantial employment and export revenues in many APEC countries. The Philippines, Malaysia, and Indonesia, for example, are major exporters of timber, with combined exports of $3.1 billion in 1995 (United Nations, *1995 International Trade Statistics Yearbook*). While the United States remains the world's largest exporter of logs, it has undertaken major replanting efforts (CEQ 1995).[5] Australia, Canada, and China are also engaged in major reforestation efforts.

Deforestation often causes grave ecological harm. Indiscriminate tree cutting results in hydrological disturbances that can cause inland water problems such as low stream flow and deterioration of water quality. A loss of ground cover also creates greater risk of soil erosion and desertification. Shrinking forests further exacerbate the problem of climate change by diminishing the stock of plant life that can absorb carbon dioxide from the atmosphere and thus partially offset the accumulation of greenhouse gases. Destruction of forest habitat also threatens forest species and can lead to a loss of biological diversity. The FAO estimates that plant species are lost at a rate of 1.0 to 4.3 percent per year because of tropical deforestation (FAO 1993).

Water Pollution and Scarcity

Many of APEC's Asian members suffer from severe problems of water quality and quantity. Pathogens and organic materials, emitted into local streams and rivers with the dumping of untreated sewage, create health hazards ranging from mild intestinal distress to life-threatening outbreaks of cholera. In Bangkok, for example, 10,000 metric tons of raw sewage flow into local rivers every day. As a result, fecal coliform levels in Bangkok sometimes rise to levels thousands of times higher than the World Health Organization (WHO) recommend for safe drinking and bathing water (UNESCAP 1995, 95). In South Korea, as recently as 1991, only a third of municipal wastewater went to sewage treatment plants (Ministry of Environment 1993).

Across APEC, solid and toxic wastes from the industrial, agricultural, and domestic sectors have caused further deterioration of surface water and groundwater quality. In Indonesia, for instance, concentrations of chromium, mercury, and cadmium exceed by more than a hundredfold the allowable limit set by the WHO (IIED 1994), reducing agricultural productivity and destroying fisheries as well as lake and river habitats.

Apart from contaminating water supplies, poor sanitary conditions make for greater exposure to pathogens in everyday life. Epidemics spread more easily and disease becomes commonplace—reducing the length and quality of life for millions and negatively affecting labor productivity. Various epidemiological studies have shown that improved sanitation facilities can cut back on the incidence of feces-borne diseases by more than 20 percent (Esrey et al. 1990). As figure 3.1 shows, the lack of access

---

5. In the United States, while the decline of primary growth forest remains a problem, timber growth (in secondary forest plantations) actually outstrips timber removal.

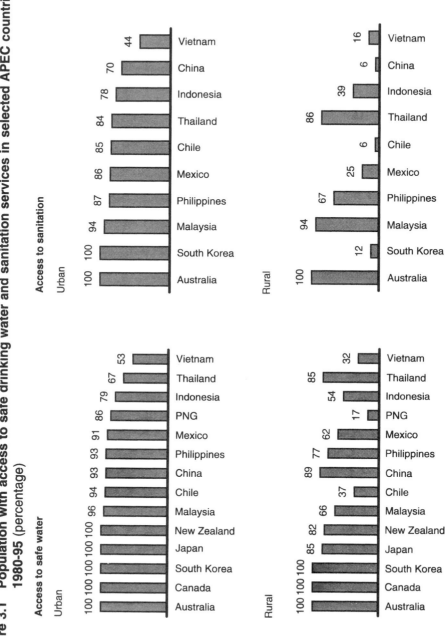

Figure 3.1 Population with access to safe drinking water and sanitation services in selected APEC countries, 1980-95 (percentage)

Access to safe water

Urban

Vietnam	53
Thailand	67
Indonesia	79
PNG	86
Mexico	91
Philippines	93
China	93
Chile	94
Malaysia	96
New Zealand	100
Japan	100
South Korea	100
Canada	100
Australia	

Rural

Vietnam	32
Thailand	85
Indonesia	54
PNG	17
Mexico	62
Philippines	77
China	89
Chile	37
Malaysia	66
New Zealand	82
Japan	85
South Korea	100
Canada	100
Australia	100

Access to sanitation

Urban

Vietnam	44
China	70
Indonesia	78
Thailand	84
Chile	85
Mexico	86
Philippines	87
Malaysia	94
South Korea	100
Australia	100

Rural

Vietnam	16
China	6
Indonesia	39
Thailand	86
Chile	6
Mexico	25
Philippines	67
Malaysia	94
South Korea	12
Australia	100

38

to safe water and sanitation services is more severe in rural than urban areas, and in the least-developed as opposed to more-developed countries. In some developing APEC nations, less than half the population has such access (WRI 1996).

Not only is water of poor quality in many parts of the APEC region, but it is also scarce. In many APEC countries, water demand outstrips supply. Engleman and Leroy (1993) suggest that water consumption is not sustainable when water resources fall below 1,700 cubic meters of freshwater per person. By this benchmark, a number of APEC nations will soon be facing water shortages. In particular, China will reach the sustainability threshold by 2025 and could face significant water shortfalls thereafter.[6] Singapore has already reached the Engleman-Leroy limit and has only been able to hold off a crisis by investing in a very elaborate pipeline system to bring supplies from neighboring Malaysia (UNESCAP 1995, 88). Apart from the social hardships it causes, water scarcity also imposes significant economic costs. In China, for example, water shortages cost the Chinese economy up to $1 billion per year (Smil 1996).

Water shortages in the APEC region are exacerbated by poor management of the limited supplies. The Asian Development Bank (ADB 1993) estimates that nearly three-quarters of the water available for public consumption in Hong Kong, Manila, and Jakarta is wasted before reaching the public. In Bangkok, Shanghai, and Singapore, more than one-third of the available water slips out of the supply system.

Air Pollution

Hundreds of millions of Asians and tens of millions of North Americans (particularly Mexicans) breathe highly polluted air. As figure 3.2 shows, 13 of 16 APEC cities surveyed have air pollution levels that exceed WHO guidelines for at least one pollutant. Of those cities, nine are located in developing countries. Not only are air pollution levels serious across the region, but the conditions seem to be worsening in many APEC countries. Particulate and ozone levels are on the rise. And while trends in sulfur dioxide and nitrous oxide emissions are not as uniformly negative, these pollutants remain a problem in most of the Asian members of APEC (Brandon and Ramankutty 1993).

Much of the air pollution problem can be attributed to the increased burning of fossil fuels caused by expanded industrial activity, a rapid increase in the number of cars,[7] and congestion (UNESCAP 1995, 140).

---

6. Water scarcity in China is "a function of heightened demand . . ., rapidly escalating levels of pollution, and the geographic patterns of water distribution" (Economy 1997, 126).

7. The past 30 years have seen a tremendous growth in the number of automobiles on the road in both developed and developing countries. In the United States, for example, total motor vehicle registrations increased from 90 million in 1965 to over 200 million in 1995.

Figure 3.2 Urban pollution in selected APEC cities, early 1990s

City	SO$_2$	SPM	NO$_2$	Pb
Christchurch, New Zealand	○	◍	—	—
Los Angeles, US	○	◍	◍	○
Montreal, Canada	●	○	—	—
New York, US	○	○	○	○
Sydney, Australia	○	○	—	—
Tokyo, Japan	○	○	○	◍
Vancouver, Canada	○	○	—	—
Bangkok, Thailand	○	●	○	◍
Beijing, China	●	●	○	○
Guangzhou, China	●	●	—	—
Jakarta, Indonesia	○	●	○	◍
Kuala Lumpur, Malaysia	○	◍	—	—
Manila, Philippines	○	●	—	◍
Mexico City, Mexico	●	●	◍	◍
Seoul, South Korea	●	●	○	○
Shanghai, China	◍	●	—	—

● Serious pollution   ◍ Moderate to heavy pollution
○ Low pollution   — Insufficient data

Notes: (1) SO$_2$ = sulfur dioxide; SPM = suspended particulate matter; NO$_2$ = nitrogen dioxide; and Pb = lead. (2) "Serious" refers to situations in which WHO guidelines are exceeded by more than a factor of two; "moderate to heavy" refers to situations in which WHO guidelines are exceeded by up to a factor of two (short-term guidelines exceeded on a regular basis at certain locations); and "low" means that WHO guidelines are normally met, but that short-term guidelines may be exceeded occasionally.

Sources: WHO and UNEP 1992; Seager 1995.

The problem is made worse by the use of poor quality fuels such as unwashed coal or leaded gasoline, as well as by inefficient energy consumption practices. In many parts of the Asia Pacific region, exposure to indoor air pollution is as serious as exposure to outdoor pollution (UNESCAP 1995, 141). In China, for example, many families heat and cook by burning coal briquettes or biomass in poorly ventilated braziers.

Poor air quality can have devastating public health impacts.[8] Respiratory distress and diseases such as pneumonia, bronchitis, asthma, and

During the same period, registrations in Japan jumped from 6 to 67 million and in Thailand from 140,000 to 5 million; in China registrations increased from 900,000 in 1975 to 10 million in 1995 (AAMA 1997).

8. This fact is recognized in both developed and developing countries. In June 1997, for example, President Clinton decided to sharply tighten US air pollution standards for particu-

emphysema have reached very high levels in a number of cities in the APEC region. In China, the government estimates that respiratory disease now accounts for 26 percent of all deaths (WRI 1996). In Mexico City, particulates contribute to an estimated 6,400 deaths per year, and almost a third of all children have unhealthy levels of lead in their blood (Bartone et al. 1994). The World Bank has concluded that if particulate levels in APEC's developing countries met WHO standards, between 2 and 5 percent of all deaths in urban areas with excessive particulate levels could be averted (World Bank, *1996 World Development Report*).

Solid and Hazardous Waste

Solid and hazardous waste generation plagues densely populated and fast-growing countries. While high volumes of waste can sometimes be indicative of deeper environmental problems, most waste issues can be effectively dealt with through appropriate management regimes. In APEC's developed countries, municipal solid waste is not an especially critical issue. However, rising volumes challenge even the ability of the most-developed countries to manage their waste. In Tokyo, for example, garbage is building up in mounds in Tokyo Bay, threatening both the shipping and fishing industries (WRI 1996, 23).

Many of APEC's developing countries lack the capacity to dispose of wastes properly. Not only is comparatively little waste collected, but it is disposed of haphazardly. In Bangkok, for example, between 20 and 50 percent of municipal solid waste goes uncollected (Bartone et al. 1994). Uncollected garbage blocks drainage channels in many Asian cities, increasing the risk of waterborne diseases. Poor waste practices can also lead to vermin-generated disease or to air pollution from open burning of garbage. In many APEC countries waste gets sent to poorly designed, unlined landfills, causing ecological degradation and posing health risks to local inhabitants as well as to populations of itinerant scavengers.

Hazardous waste presents a more complex problem due to its highly toxic effects and steeper cleanup costs. The early stages of economic development often seem to be accompanied by rapid increases in the level of toxic wastes generated, while more-developed countries find ways to continue to increase industrial output with declining per capita levels of toxic by-product. China, for example, generates 50 million tons of hazardous waste each year, a much higher level of hazardous waste per person than South Korea or Japan (ADB 1997; UNESCAP 1995). Across the Asia Pacific, large corporations appear to be improving their hazardous waste management and disposal, but small and medium-sized enterprises—unable to pay for appropriate hazardous waste management—

lates and ozone (smog), despite concern over costs, arguing that the more strict rules will bring health benefits to 125 million Americans (*New York Times*, 26 June 1997).

remain an important source of dangerous waste, particularly in APEC's developing countries.[9]

Finally, despite multilateral efforts (notably, the 1989 Basel Convention) to regulate trade in hazardous wastes, black-market waste dealers continue to operate, taking hazardous materials from countries with strict standards (and high disposal costs) to ones with more lax rules (and lower costs).

Depletion of Fisheries

Pacific fisheries are rapidly being depleted (FAO 1994b). In fact, the World Resources Institute (WRI 1996) estimates that nearly all the Pacific fisheries are overfished and at risk of depletion. As figure 3.3 shows, all of the fish stocks in the northwest Pacific are fully fished, overfished, depleted, or recovering. In the northeast, western central, southwest, and southeast Pacific rates of overfishing and depletion exceed 50 percent.[10]

The APEC region is the world's largest producer of seafood, accounting for 50.6 percent of the world's total marine catch (APEC 1995b). But the dramatic increases in fish landed in the 1980s (hundreds of percent growth in China, Australia, and New Zealand) cannot be sustained (WRI 1996)[11]— there simply are not enough fish in the ocean. Unsustainable fishing practices are also likely to have dramatic economic impacts. A Philippine government-commissioned study recently found, for example, that 120,000 Filipino fishermen would lose their livelihoods by the year 2000 unless access to fishery resources were restricted (*Straits Times*, 28 June 1997).

While one answer to the decline in fisheries on the open seas is aquaculture, this method of seafood production creates its own environmental harms. In particular, coastal mangrove habitats are often destroyed, and in some cases threatened or endangered species are lost. In both Thailand and the Philippines, for example, more than 200,000 hectares of mangrove forests have been cleared in the last 30 years (GESAMP 1993). The loss of these mangroves changes drainage patterns, nutrient availability, and the frequency of tidal inundation, dramatically altering the coastal habitat (UNEP/GEMS 1993).

---

9. Along the US-Mexico border, for example, most multinational corporations handle their hazardous waste quite carefully while local manufacturing operations engage in illegal "backdoor" dumping (Esty 1996a, 35).

10. A recent sign of the severity of the depletion of the Pacific fisheries is the report that fishing by Taiwan, South Korea, Indonesia, New Zealand, Japan, and Australia has brought southern bluefin tuna to the brink of extinction (Central News Agency [Taiwan], 30 July 1997).

11. Malaysia's recent efforts to improve fishing yields by using fish-attracting devices are indicative of the difficulty in sustaining high-yield growth (*The Star*, 31 July 1997).

Figure 3.3 State of exploitation of Pacific fisheries, 1992[a]

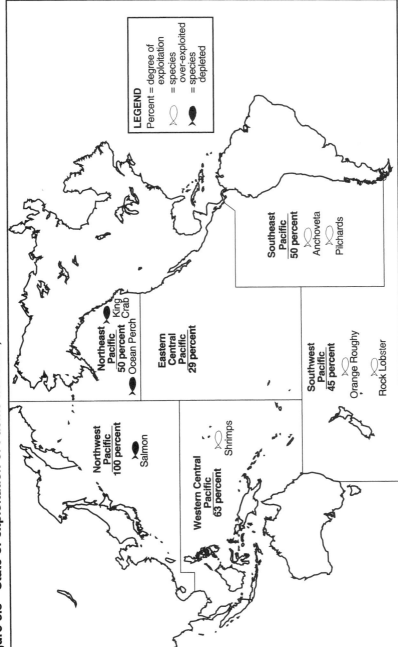

a. Percentage of stocks fully fished, overfished, depleted, or recovering.

Source: Seager 1995; WRI 1996.

43

Marine and Coastal Pollution

Marine and coastal pollution, apart from contributing to the death and contamination of fishing stocks, also causes a host of ecological problems, including habitat destruction and algal bloom. Nearly half of all marine pollution originates from land-based discharges from rivers or direct discharges (Weber 1993).[12] In fact, it is estimated that 80 percent of the pollutants in the Yellow Sea and South Sea off the Korean peninsula come from inland activities via Korean rivers (Government of Korea 1994). Airborne emissions that originate from industrial activity on land are another major source of marine pollution.

Coastal pollution is responsible for significant coral reef damage, particularly in Southeast Asia (Weber 1993). Sometimes called the marine equivalent of tropical rain forests, coral reefs not only support coastal fishing and protect biological diversity, but they are also a protective barrier for coastlines.

"Red tide," a form of algal infestation, is also caused by marine pollution. By severely depleting oxygen levels in coastal waters and rivers, red tide causes the mass death of aquatic creatures—at a significant economic cost—and causes shellfish poisoning, which can be hazardous to humans. The economic impact of red tides can be serious. A four-day tide in Manila Bay in 1990 caused fish and shellfish prices to drop by 75 percent, inflicting an estimated loss of $2.4 million on Filipino fishers (UNESCAP 1995, 125). Red tides have also recently caused difficulties in Australia, Hong Kong, and China.

Acid Rain

Acid rain—caused primarily by sulfur dioxide and nitrogen oxides emissions from the burning of fossil fuels—is already a major problem across APEC. Acidification can render lakes and rivers uninhabitable, kill trees and forest ecosystems, and damage man-made structures. Because it traverses national boundaries, acid rain threatens to become a significant source of political and environmental tension among APEC nations.

Large quantities of highly acidic rain spill from the midwestern United States into eastern Canada. Canada has long complained about the acidification of its lakes and forests, the damage to its agricultural produce, and the corrosion of its buildings. But with the signing of an acid rain agreement with the United States in 1992 and the introduction of tradable sulfur dioxide (SO_2) emissions permits under the 1990 US Clean Air Act, SO_2 emissions in the United States have fallen from a recent high of 22.8

---

12. In the Philippines, ocean pollution as a result of land-based sewage discharges is threatening more than a hundred resorts with closure (Reuters, 9 July 1997).

million tons in 1989 (CEQ 1995).[13] The opposite pattern holds across much of the Asia Pacific. China's emissions now exceed 20 million tons per year and are rising rapidly (UNEP, *Environment Data Report 1996*). Chinese acid rain not only harms southern and eastern China but also is responsible for significant acid deposition on South Korea and Japan. Until recently, the Chinese rejected any suggestion of their responsibility for acid rain in Korea, Taiwan, and Japan, even though numerous studies have shown that a significant percentage of the acid rain falling in this region can be traced to Chinese power plants and industrial facilities (see figure 3.4). Signs of acid rain problems have also started to emerge in the Philippines, Thailand, and Malaysia.

Without action to reduce acid rain, future Asian prospects are grim. One analysis predicts that SO_2 emissions in Asia will more than double between 1990 and 2010, rising to as much as 76 million tons by the year 2010 (Foell and Green 1990). And another study estimates that in Northeast Asia alone,[14] emissions will rise from 15 million tons in 1990 to 40 million tons by 2020 (Streets 1997). The World Energy Council (WEC) estimates, moreover, that without measures to curb emissions, acid deposition in parts of China and Southeast Asia could soon exceed the critical load limits for most agricultural crops by a factor of 10 (WEC 1993).

Ozone Layer Depletion

A thin layer of ozone gas in the stratosphere approximately 12 to 50 kilometers above the Earth's surface protects the planet from harmful ultraviolet radiation emanating from the sun. This ozone layer is threatened by the release of a family of chemicals, including chlorofluorocarbons (CFCs), that break down ozone molecules. CFCs can persist in the upper atmosphere for hundreds of years (UNEP/WMO 1994); it is estimated that one CFC-derived chlorine atom can destroy up to 100,000 ozone molecules before leaving the stratosphere.

The discovery of a large "ozone hole" the size of the continental United States over Antarctica in the mid-1980s galvanized public and political concern over CFCs and the depletion of the ozone layer. Negotiations to limit the release of CFCs and other ozone-layer-depleting chemicals commenced and resulted in the 1985 Vienna Convention on Ozone-Depleting Substances, the 1987 Montreal Protocol on Substances that Deplete the Ozone Layer, and several later amendments to the protocol. Together, these instruments mandate a phaseout of ozone-layer-damaging

---

13. The 1990 US Clean Air Act mandates a reduction of 10 million tons of SO_2 by 2000.

14. Northeast Asia is defined to include Japan, South Korea, North Korea, and northeast China.

Figure 3.4 Acid rain in the APEC region

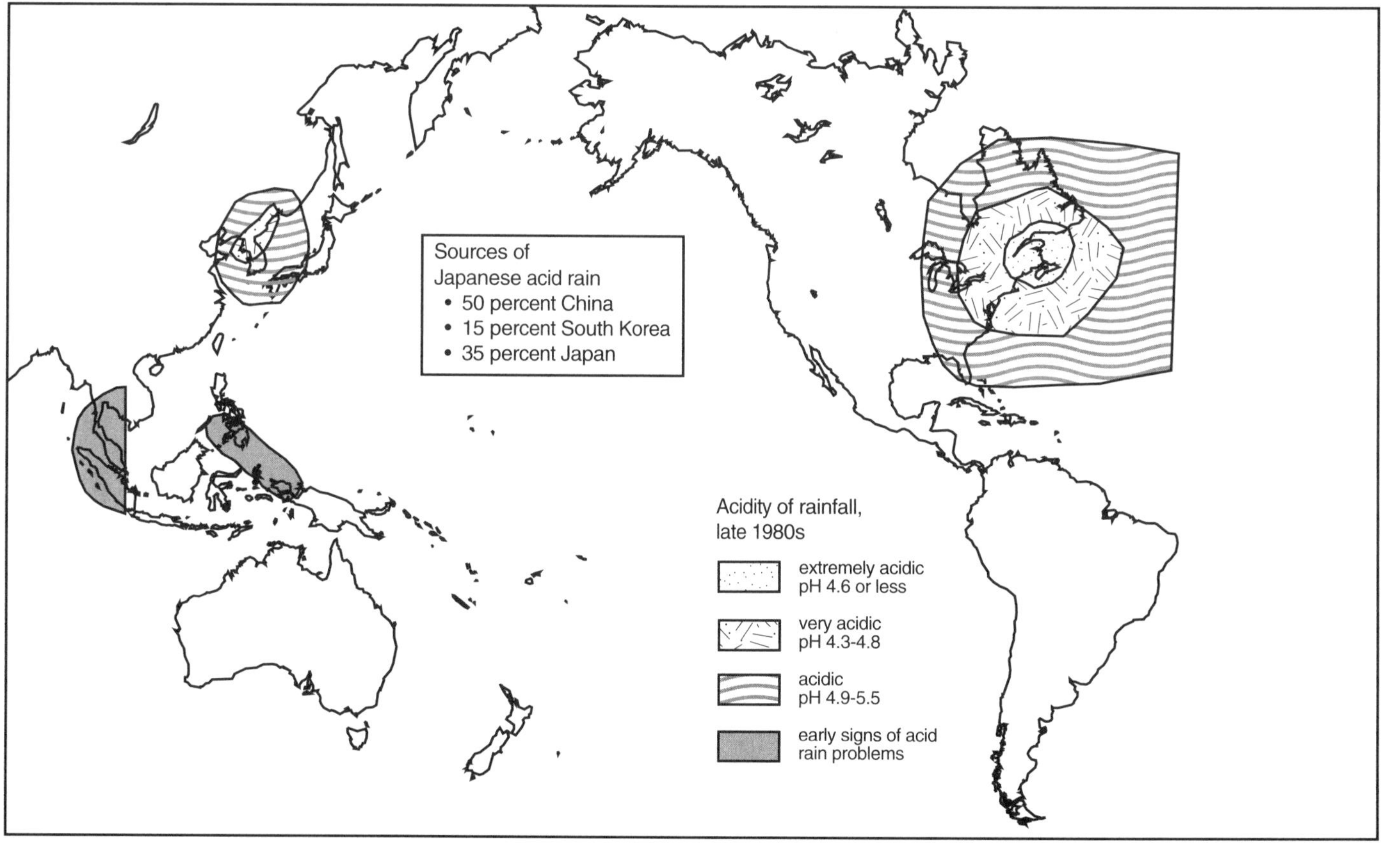
Sources of
Japanese acid rain
• 50 percent China
• 15 percent South Korea
• 35 percent Japan
Acidity of rainfall,
late 1980s
extremely acidic
pH 4.6 or less
very acidic
pH 4.3-4.8
acidic
pH 4.9-5.5
early signs of acid
rain problems

Source: Seager (1995).

products that were once widely used in refrigeration, plastic foam production, electronics, aerosol sprays, and a number of other applications.[15]

Heightened exposure to ultraviolet radiation, which occurs with a thinned ozone layer, has been associated with higher incidence of skin cancer, cataracts, weakened immune system responses, and increased outbreaks of infectious diseases (UNESCAP 1995, 144). Studies estimate, for instance, that every 1 percent depletion of the ozone layer increases the incidence of nonmalignant melanoma by 2 percent (WMO 1994). Already, APEC nations near the ozone hole have seen a dramatic jump in skin cancer rates. New Zealand, for example, witnessed a 22 percent increase in cancer incidence from 1980 to 1991 (UNESCAP 1995, 144). In addition, increased ultraviolet exposure could harm the world's agriculture. One recent study predicted that if the Montreal Protocol did not succeed in reversing the trend of ozone layer thinning, wheat crop yields might drop by as much as 5 percent, potatoes by 21 percent, soybeans by 20 percent, and squash by 90 percent (UNEP/GEMS 1992).

As a result of actions taken to meet obligations imposed by the Montreal Protocol, CFC production fell 76 percent between 1988 and 1995.[16] As figure 3.5 shows, CFC and halon consumption has fallen sharply across the developed-country members of APEC. But in most developing countries, CFC production and consumption of ozone-depleting chemicals continues to increase, in many cases significantly. Because of the long atmospheric lifetime of CFCs and because developing-country consumption continues to rise, the hole in the ozone layer has not yet healed. In fact, the ozone hole over Antarctica has increased in size since the mid-1980s, and in 1996 the average size of the hole was 22.3 million square kilometers, larger than the whole of North America (NASA 1996).

While some progress is being made, the verdict on the Montreal Protocol is still out (Brack 1996; Jacobson and Brown Weiss 1997). Reductions in developed-country CFC production and consumption have been achieved, but compliance with the treaty is uneven. In particular, it is not yet clear whether industrializing economies will take the measures required to meet their CFC phaseout commitments.

Climate Change

The accumulation of greenhouse gases (carbon dioxide, methane, and nitrous oxide) in the atmosphere threatens to warm the earth's surface

---

15. Under the Montreal Protocol, developed countries are required to phase out consumption and production of CFCs, halons, and related compounds by 1996, and hydrochlorofluorocarbons (HCFCs) by 2030. The corresponding dates for developing countries are 2010 and 2040, respectively.

16. Much of the success can be explained by the fact that the cost of the transition to CFC alternatives was less than expected, and indeed in many cases alternative technologies and production processes proved to be less expensive than CFCs (French 1997).

Figure 3.5 CFC and halon consumption in the APEC region

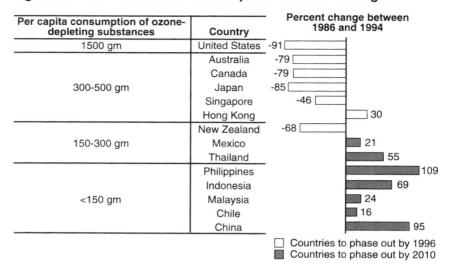

Per capita consumption of ozone-depleting substances	Country	Percent change between 1986 and 1994
1500 gm	United States	-91
300-500 gm	Australia	-79
	Canada	-79
	Japan	-85
	Singapore	-46
	Hong Kong	30
150-300 gm	New Zealand	-68
	Mexico	21
	Thailand	55
<150 gm	Philippines	109
	Indonesia	69
	Malaysia	24
	Chile	16
	China	95

☐ Countries to phase out by 1996
▨ Countries to phase out by 2010

CFC = Chlorofluorocarbon.

Sources: UNEP (*Environment Data Report*); Seager 1995; Brack 1996.

and to produce other climatic changes (IPCC 1995). Although the rate, magnitude, and regional effects of climate change remain uncertain, it is clear that the atmospheric concentrations of greenhouse gases (GHG) have grown significantly—by nearly 30 percent (WRI 1996)—since preindustrial times. The Intergovernmental Panel on Climate Change (IPCC), a UN-sponsored colloquium of scientists from around the world, concluded recently that "these trends can be attributed largely to human activities, mostly fossil fuel use, land use change, and agriculture," and that "the balance of evidence suggests that there is a discernible human influence on global climate" (IPCC 1995, 3, 5).

The greatest contribution to GHG emissions is from energy production and use. The burning of fossil fuels alone accounts for 80 percent of CO_2 emissions worldwide. Deforestation adds to the concentration of CO_2 in the atmosphere by reducing the stock of trees, which act as carbon "sinks."

As figure 3.6 shows, APEC countries accounted for 46.7 percent of total global GHG emissions in 1992. In fact, four of the six largest GHG emitters are APEC countries. The United States stands today as the world's largest emitter of greenhouse gases, accounting for almost 22 percent of global emissions. China is the second largest with approximately 12 percent of global emissions, and Japan is the fourth largest with approximately 5 percent (WRI 1996).

Figure 3.6 APEC's contribution to global CO_2 emissions

Global CO_2 emissions, 1950–92

(Millions of tons)

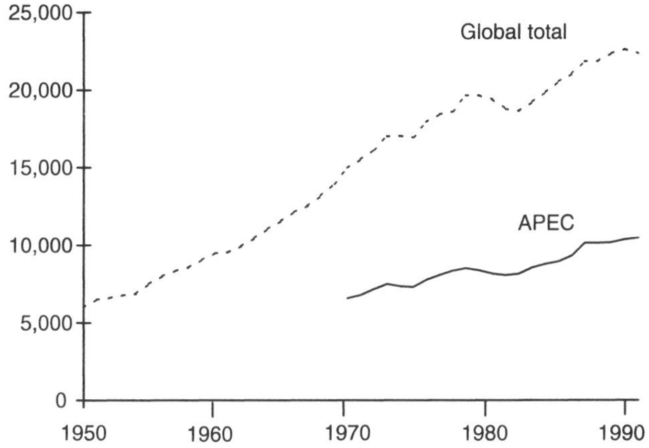

Source: WRI 1996.

APEC country CO_2 emissions, 1992

Country	Emissions (millions of tons)	Percentage of global total	Global rank
United States	4,881	21.8	1
China	2,668	11.9	2
Japan	1,094	4.9	4
Canada	410	1.8	6
Mexico	333	1.5	13
South Korea	290	1.3	16
Australia	268	1.2	17
Indonesia	185	0.8	23
Thailand	113	0.5	31
Malaysia	70	0.3	40
Singapore	50	0.2	50
Philippines	50	0.2	54
Chile	35	0.2	64
New Zealand	26	0.1	68
Papua New Guinea	2	0	118
Total	10,475	46.7	

Figure 3.7 Predicted global CO$_2$ emissions, 1990-2020

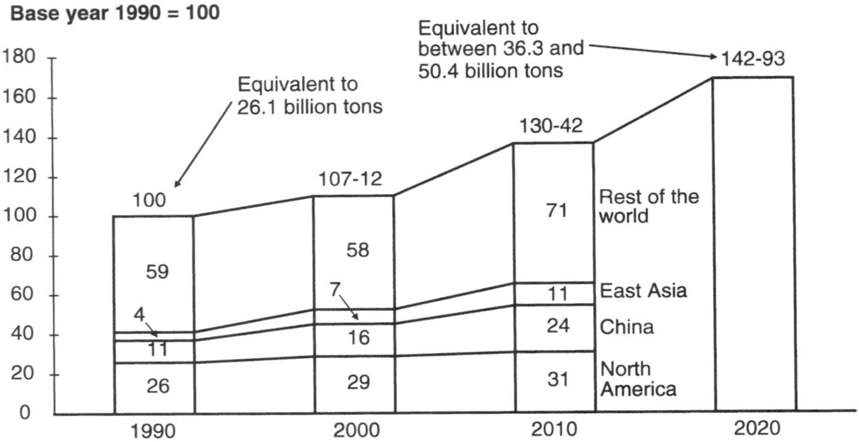

Base year 1990 = 100

Sources: WEC 1995; IEA 1995b; US Department of Energy 1995.

Global GHG emissions are predicted to rise significantly over the next 25 years (see figure 3.7). Studies by the World Energy Council (WEC 1995), the International Energy Agency (IEA 1995a), and the US Department of Energy (1995) forecast that global emissions will rise by between 30 and 42 percent by 2010 and by as much as 93 percent by the year 2020. China— with its rapid economic growth fueled largely by coal burning—will likely double its GHG emissions by 2010 (WRI 1996) and is expected to surpass the United States as the world's largest emitter by 2020 (Esty and Mendelsohn 1995).

Increased levels of greenhouse gases in the atmosphere could cause a variety of climate change effects. Current modeling suggests that global mean temperatures will rise by between 1°C and 3.5°C by 2100, with a midrange estimate of 2°C (IPCC 1995, 6). The IPCC scientists further predict that thermal expansion of the oceans and melting of glaciers and ice sheets will cause a rise in sea level of 15 cm to 95 cm by the year 2100, with an increase of about 50 cm as the midpoint projection (IPCC 1995, 6). Climate change may also cause changes in rainfall patterns, the frequency and severity of storms, hydrological cycles, and soil moisture (IPCC 1995, 6). These effects could translate into changes in agricultural productivity, the prevalence and patterns of diseases, and the exposure of people to severe weather.

Current greenhouse effect modeling suggests that the regional impacts from climate change may be quite disparate (IPCC 1995). No area of the world seems more likely to suffer adverse effects than Asia. Topping, Quershi, and Samuel (1990) observe that a one-meter rise in sea level would put 126,000 km^2 of land in China under water and would threaten coastal environments around the Pacific Rim. Southeast Asia appears especially vulnerable to sea level rise since 70 percent of the population lives in low-lying areas that are susceptible to flooding, and inhabitants of this region depend significantly on fishing and agriculture that may be disrupted by climate change. Moreover, under a number of climate change scenarios scientists predict changes in precipitation from Asian monsoons (IPCC 1995, 6), deeply affecting weather patterns and hence agriculture in the region.

Biodiversity Loss

Biodiversity loss in the APEC region can be attributed to destruction of habitats by farming, infrastructure construction, deforestation, land degradation, and water pollution (ADB 1997, 207). These problems are exacerbated by the pressures of poverty and population growth, and they are especially serious in the region's tropical areas.

Apart from their capacity to "sequester" carbon and thus mitigate the effects of climate change, tropical forests are valuable as a source of biodiversity. More than half of all known species live in rain forests, and Harvard biologist Edward O. Wilson (1992, 278) calculates that some 50,000 of these species are becoming extinct annually, largely due to human activity. While there is great debate over how serious a problem the loss of biodiversity is,[17] there is no doubt that Asia is one of the regions most dramatically affected by species loss.

The APEC nations constitute some of the most biologically diverse places on the planet. Of the world's 11 "megadiversity" countries (McNeeley et al. 1990), four—China, Malaysia, Indonesia, and Australia— are APEC members. In addition to being biologically diverse, the APEC countries also have among the highest incidences of endangered species. Of the 18 global "hot spots"—locales where native species are numerous *and* where a large proportion of those species are particularly threatened— identified by Myers (1988, 1990), 6 are in APEC countries: peninsular Malaysia, northern Borneo in Indonesia, the Philippines, southwestern Australia, California and Oregon in the United States, and central Chile.

Table 3.3 shows a country-by-country analysis of the number of endangered species in the region. The greatest number of threatened plants are in Australia and the United States, while the largest number of threatened mammals and birds are in Indonesia and China. It is worth noting that the figures listed in table 3.3 do not include species that have already become extinct. Estimates of plant diversity in the Philippines alone place

---

17. Cooper (1994) argues that loss of biodiversity is a relatively small problem since most of the species being lost are insects. In contrast, Kellert (1996) argues that species loss is a fundamental threat to human existence and life as we know it.

Table 3.3 Threatened plants and higher vertebrates in the APEC countries

Country	Plants	Mammals	Birds	Reptiles	Amphibians	Total species	Percentage threatened
						Number of threatened species	
Australia	2,024	38	39	9	3	16,733	12.6
United States	2,262	27	43	25	22	20,591	11.6
New Zealand	232	1	26	1	3	2,699	10.0
Chile	284	9	18	0	0	5,557	5.6
Malaysia	522	23	35	12	0	13,691	4.3
Mexico	833	25	35	16	4	23,472	3.9
Taiwan	95	4	16	0	0	3,883	3.0
Philippines	159	12	39	6	0	9,748	2.2
South Korea	33	6	22	0	0	2,978	2.0
Brunei	40	9	10	3	0	3,662	1.7
China	350	40	83	7	1	34,166	1.4
Japan	41	5	31	0	1	5,827	1.3
Singapore	19	4	5	1	0	2,343	1.2
Indonesia	70	49	135	13	0	25,315	1.1
Thailand	68	26	34	9	0	13,897	1.0
Papua New Guinea	88	5	25	1	0	12,796	1.0
Hong Kong	5	1	9	2	0	2,213	0.8
Canada	12	5	6	0	0	3,664	0.6

Source: WCMC 1992.

the number of currently listed threatened species, 159, as one-tenth of the number of plants that may have already become extinct. Furthermore, it is now estimated that major ecosystems in the Indo-Malayan regions have lost almost 70 percent of their original vegetation. This is especially tragic in Malaysia, where forests are believed to harbor an estimated 25,000 species of flowering plants (UNESCAP 1995, 60).

The tangible benefits of biodiversity are keenly debated. The case for emphasizing the maintenance of biological and genetic diversity can be divided into three strands (Caldwell 1996). First, some scientists argue that our imperfect understanding of life and the interrelationships of various animals and plants makes species preservation imperative. Second, other biodiversity advocates note that "bioprospecting" can yield economic benefits, including the commercialization of important scientific advances in chemicals and pharmaceuticals. A more emotionally charged version of this argument suggests that in destroying species, we risk losing a potential cure for cancer or other diseases. Finally, Kellert (1996) argues that human life is defined by and enriched through our connection to nature and, thus, the diversity of the species on the planet represents an important independent virtue. Others emphasize a similar moral aspect of genetic preservation, suggesting that humanity ought to avoid "playing God," and should therefore preserve all species.

Environmental Harms: A Geographic Taxonomy

The seriousness of the environmental harms that APEC members confront and to which they contribute cannot be dismissed lightly. Later chapters in this study consider the underlying causes of these harms (chapter 4) and the roles that APEC must play to ensure that they are addressed (chapter 6). In this regard, thinking about environmental harms as falling into one of three geographic categories—local/national, regional, or global—proves to be useful.

Local or national harms, for example, include land degradation, pollution of internal water resources, lead and particulates in the air, and problems of waste management. *Regional harms* are those that traverse national borders, spilling over onto neighboring countries or onto the regional commons; they include pollution of shared airsheds and bodies of water. Some regional harms affect all or most APEC members, such as the depletion of the Pacific fisheries. Other regional harms affect a subset of APEC countries. For example, China's sulfur dioxide emissions cause acid rain in South Korea and Japan. Likewise, acid rain from United States industrial emissions affects Canada.[18] Finally, *global harms* arise when emissions blanket the earth affecting all nations regardless of the origin of the pollution. Depletion of the ozone layer and the buildup of greenhouse gases that may cause climate change represent the paradigmatic global issues.[19]

Of course, not all harms fit neatly into these three geographic categories. Some environmental problems have multiple dimensions. Deforestation, for example, has both local and global effects. At a local level, deforestation contributes to soil erosion, land degradation, and water pollution. At the global level, deforestation reduces the world's supply of carbon sinks that can mitigate the effects of greenhouse gas emissions. In addition, some harms do not fit easily into a particular geographic category. For example, there is disagreement about whether species loss is a purely local harm (since species and habitats in other countries remain unaffected) or

---

18. Another environmental harm involving just a subset of APEC's members involves air pollution in Malaysia caused by the burning of forests in Indonesia. This air pollution has disrupted Malaysian air traffic and caused health problems in Malaysia and Singapore (*Straits Times,* 5 August 1997 *New York Times,* 25 September 1997).

19. In the case of transboundary—regional or global—harms, a large portion of the harm can often be attributed to a small set of countries that play oversized roles because of their particular demographic heft, resource endowments, or rogue behavior (Esty 1998). These "pivotal states" (Chase, Kennedy, and Hill 1996) deserve special attention from policymakers because of their capacity to shape regional or global security. From an ecological perspective, a number of the most important actors—the United States, China, Indonesia, Mexico, and Japan—are APEC members. The presence of a critical mass of states whose behavior can dramatically affect the magnitude of environmental harms (or efforts to abate harms) around the world makes APEC an especially valuable forum for environmental diplomacy.

whether species should be considered part of the global commons, making their loss a world-scale problem.[20]

Notwithstanding the difficulty of categorizing all environmental harms as falling exclusively within one of the categories suggested alone, a differentiation based on the geographic locus of the harms proves useful for several reasons. First, the optimal policy response and level of required governmental intervention varies depending on the geographic scope of the harm (Esty 1996b). As the discussion in later chapters makes clear, the scope of the jurisdictional response should match the scale of the harm in question.

Second, the geographic scope of the harm is a primary determinant of the attention that national governments pay to a particular harm. As we explain in chapter 4 (under "structural failures"), the more localized the effects of an environmental harm, the sooner the problem yields to rising income levels as investments in environmental protection become affordable and citizens demand action from their governments. Regional and global harms do not tend to abate as incomes rise, since some part of the pollution costs falls on citizens in other countries about whom national governments care very little. Thus, categorizing harms based on their geographic locus helps us to understand why transboundary environmental harms are difficult to address—and require special efforts at collective action. Indeed, it is in providing a structure for the required overarching cooperation that APEC can play a vital role.

Conclusion

As a recent Asian Development Bank study (ADB 1997, 30) notes, "Asia's environmental performance has not matched its remarkable economic progress during the past 30 years." This conclusion holds true for APEC as a whole, in spite of considerable environmental progress in its developed nations. As a result, public health and ecological costs have become a significant offset against the social welfare gains achieved through economic growth. And the problem is probably worse than it looks since many environmental harms will appear only as conditions become more crowded and critical ecological thresholds are exceeded.

APEC could play Nero and fiddle while Rome burns, but to do so requires an assumption that either the panoply of environmental problems

---

20. The difficulty in categorizing a particular harm as either local, regional, or global arises when we focus narrowly on the *physical* effects of an environmental harm. In chapter 7 we extend our analysis, arguing that the geographic reach of a harm should be determined by reference not only to its *physical* effects but also to its *economic* and *psychological* effects. Thus, because loss of a species may emotionally affect citizens all around the world—a psychological effect—biodiversity is arguably a global problem.

identified are not real or serious, or someone else can or should respond. As the data presented in this chapter make clear, a belief that Asia Pacific pollution and resource issues do not deserve attention rests on counterfactual premises and would be irresponsible.

While conceding that environmental problems are real and serious, skeptics might, however, ask why APEC should be called upon to act. Shouldn't national governments be held responsible? Aren't there international bodies already at work on these issues? The answer to these questions is—yes, but only in part. As we explain in detail in chapter 6, APEC is better positioned than any other body to respond with regard to some— particularly regional-scale—problems. On other issues, APEC may be positioned to reinforce actions taken by governments at the local/national or global levels. And to the extent that economic integration creates a demand for coordinated action on noneconomic issues, including environmental policy, APEC's core mission cannot be accomplished without an environmental program.

The opportunity is clear: improved environmental performance will allow the APEC economies to grow while mitigating environmental degradation and the associated social costs of pollution harms and resource depletion. But so too is the risk: inattention to public health and ecological harms will continue to propel fast-growing APEC countries down an unsustainable path toward local, regional, and global pollution and resource crises.

4

Underlying Causes of Environmental Harms Facing APEC

Addressing the environmental harms confronting APEC's members requires an understanding of their underlying causes—market and government failures. Economic theory tells us that the free market can be expected to produce an efficient and welfare-maximizing level of resource use, production, consumption, and environmental protection if the prices of resources, goods, and services capture all of the social costs and benefits of their use. The corollary of this principle is that if private costs—which are the basis for market decisions—deviate from social ones, then there will be "market failure," resulting in allocative inefficiency in general, and suboptimal resource use and pollution levels in particular. Unfortunately, market failures are a hallmark of the environmental domain. Prices in the marketplace often do not capture the social costs (or benefits) of pollution (or pollution control) or the scarcity value of common resources. As a result, economic actors are able to spill onto others all or part of the environmental costs they generate.

Some market-failure-driven problems could be addressed by appropriately allocating, enforcing, and vindicating environmental property rights. But in other cases, the resources are inherently "open access" or "common" or otherwise not amenable to a resolution based on property rights. In these circumstances, government intervention will be required to avoid the allocative inefficiency of, and welfare losses from, market failures. But governmental regulatory efforts often go awry as well, resulting in suboptimal environmental results. Moreover, in their pursuit of goals in other policy areas—like energy and agriculture—many governments have adopted policies that have deleterious effects on the environment. In the context of rapid economic growth, demographic factors—such as expanding populations and urbanization—often magnify the harms attributable to market and government failures. Designing an optimal APEC environmental policy requires first understanding these various failures, next sorting out which problems are best dealt with at the regional level, and then carefully tailoring a strategy to respond to them.

Market Failures

The breadth and depth of environmental problems reflects the ubiquity of market failures. Certain failures in particular are responsible for many environmental harms: (1) externalities or pollution spillovers, (2) over-exploitation of open access or common resources, (3) intertemporal misallocation of resources reflecting the inability of future citizens to participate in decisions made today that will affect the world they inherit, and (4) failures arising both from the absence of perfect information assumed to underlie smoothly functioning markets and from the uncertainty and complexity that are dominant features of environmental decision making.

Externalities

Externalities—situations in which consumers or producers can spill pollution harms onto others without paying for them—represent the core environmental market failure (Baumol and Oates 1988; Stiglitz 1988). Externalities arise because the social costs and benefits associated with the use, production, and consumption of resources, goods, and services are not properly aligned with the private costs and benefits that determine individual and corporate behavior (Hanley, Shogren, and White 1997). The ability to disregard some of the costs of pollution leads to a misallocation of resources and insufficient incentives for pollution control, resulting in inappropriately high levels of pollution. In designing policy responses to market failures, it is important to separate out several distinct categories of externalities.

Negative and Positive Externalities

Externalities may be either negative or positive. *Negative externalities* arise when some part of the costs of an activity are not borne by those who produce or consume the good or service in question. For example, when a cement factory in Sydney emits pollutants into the atmosphere they may cause visibility problems, may affect the health of local residents, and may also contribute to global warming—all costs that are not factored into the price of cement, because they do not have a direct impact on the production process. As long as the costs of cement production do not reflect the full costs to society—and externalities remain uninternalized—the factory will not operate with optimal economic or environmental efficiency.

Positive externalities, conversely, arise when the full benefits of an activity are not internalized by the regulating jurisdiction. For example, when Indonesia grants timber companies logging concessions, it does so in return for revenues that supposedly reflect the value of the timber to be cut. But the value of forests in supporting biodiversity, together with the value of the trees as carbon "sinks," is generally not reflected in the price of the concessions, because those who benefit from these forest amenities—citizens around the world—are not involved in the transaction. In other words, the price the government (and thus the Indonesian public) receives for use of its environmental resource—the forest—does not reflect the full social value of the resource as judged from a worldwide perspective. As a result of the disconnect between the social value and private value of the resource, the price of the concession is lower than it should be, and the resource is overconsumed.

Regular Externalities and "Super Externalities"

We find it useful to distinguish between regular and "super" externalities. *Regular externalities* are those that arise in situations in which harms are not paid for by the producer or consumer of a good but the damage caused is limited in geographic scope to a single political jurisdiction. In these cases, regulators could internalize the externality if they chose to, and a welfare-maximizing government will have an incentive to do so. In other cases, however, the geographic scope of the harm crosses political boundaries, spilling over onto other countries or onto the commons, beyond the jurisdiction of any nation. We call these spillovers *super externalities*. They represent a qualitatively more difficult policy problem because no single jurisdiction has an incentive to regulate such harms optimally, as viewed from an overarching perspective.

To understand the difference, consider a steel mill in South Korea that emits particulates, sulfur dioxide (SO_2), and carbon dioxide (CO_2) into the atmosphere. The particulates are likely to cause local visibility problems and inflict respiratory distress on those immediately downwind. The local government in the jurisdiction where the plant is located has an incentive to address these problems because its own citizens are the ones who pay the price for the harms that are being externalized by the mill. The government is well positioned to intervene to internalize these costs and to force some degree of pollution control to ensure that the mill's local benefits exceed the local costs.

To the extent that the SO_2 emissions fall on downwind Korean citizens, the national government will have some incentive to address the harm and to optimize the level of pollution abatement required. But because some of the emissions drift beyond the Korean border, the government will not have the full spectrum of environmental costs in mind when it makes its regulatory decisions about how much pollution control to require. Indeed, some of the sulfates travel hundreds of miles downwind and fall on citizens of Japan. And the CO_2 released blankets the planet, contributing to the global greenhouse effect. The public health and ecological costs inflicted by these transboundary harms are unlikely to be factored into the regulatory calculus of the jurisdiction in which the plant is located. When some of the cost bearers of pollution or beneficiaries of regulation lie beyond the jurisdiction of the regulating authority, there is no reason to believe that the harms will be internalized; thus, they become super externalities.

These cross-border harms are especially hard to handle in the international environmental policy context because agreements between jurisdictions to optimize pollution control spending from a comprehensive viewpoint are often not in place. Indeed, to the extent that South Korea would have to bear the full costs of any acid rain or greenhouse gas controls undertaken within their jurisdiction, they are unlikely to properly invest in SO_2 and CO_2 emissions controls (from which they will get limited benefits) absent collective action.

In sum, uninternalized externalities represent the most common and threatening type of market failure in the environmental context. Whether a particular pollution spillover is likely to be addressed by government intervention—and thus not cause a market failure—depends very much on whether the harm is within the scope of a single regulating jurisdiction. In the case of regular externalities, there are many reasons why the government may not optimally control the emissions, but at least it has an incentive to do so. When the emissions span several regulating jurisdictions or the entire world, there is an increasing likelihood that the government whose facility is causing the harm will choose not to act, because its own cost-benefit calculus does not justify intervention.

Psychological and Economic Spillovers

While spillovers of physical pollution are the paradigmatic externality, they are not the only type. When people suffer psychological distress as a result of another's choices about resource use or environmental protection, economists describe the welfare loss as a *psychological externality* (Cooper 1994).[1] For example, when a decision was made to dam the scenic Franklin River in the Australian state of Tasmania in the early 1980s, Australians across the country felt aggrieved and demanded that steps be taken to

---

1. These spillovers are also sometimes referred to as "nonuse" or "preservation" externalities (Stewart 1992). We might also call them "moral" or "values" spillovers because the external harm suffered often arises from a sense of what the harm bearer considers morally acceptable.

prevent the proposed construction of the hydroelectric project (Hall 1992).[2] Similarly, the deaths of endangered sea turtles at the hands of Thai and Filipino shrimp fisherman inflict real psychological welfare losses on American animal rights activists. Whether the externality is physical or psychological, the economic effect from a welfare perspective is the same.[3] Whenever costs or benefits are not accounted for in the use or consumption decision, a misallocation of the resources in question will result.[4]

A final important category of spillovers is *economic* or *competitiveness externalities.* As traditional barriers to trade are reduced or removed and international competition becomes more intense, differences in various domestic policies, including environmental standards, become more significant in determining competitiveness and hence the pattern of trade and investment flows. By affecting competitiveness, environmental standards alter a country's terms of trade—a change that has associated effects on exchange rates, employment levels, and growth. These competitiveness pressures may induce "regulatory competition" among jurisdictions as governments work to make their location attractive to industry, both to lure investors who intend to construct new facilities and infrastructure and to prevent their present industrial base from relocating overseas to take advantage of lower environmental compliance costs. In some circumstances, competitiveness pressures will induce governments to regulate efficiently and the competition will thus be welfare enhancing (Tiebout 1956; Revesz 1992). But in other cases, competition among horizontally arrayed jurisdictions may precipitate a welfare-reducing "race toward the bottom" in which countries lower their environmental standards to suboptimal levels, fail to enforce existing rules, or refrain from raising their standards.[5]

---

2. After a legal action testing the validity of the federal government's decision to designate the area a protected World Heritage area failed, the project was ultimately abandoned (*Commonwealth of Australia v. The State of Tasmania* [1983] 46 A.L.R. 625).

3. While economists accept the welfare effects of psychological spillovers, they note that in practice, such externalities are hard to measure. In particular, they fear that without a way to measure such harms, those who are claiming psychological injury can easily exaggerate their losses. But this problem of "moral hazard" is a methodological problem, not a theoretical one.

4. Psychological externalities are gaining more prominence as people increasingly demand that their psychological welfare—reflected in their preferences for conservation—be factored into decisions with environmental effects. Psychological externalities also underscore the sharp cultural differences—particularly noticeable among APEC's diverse members—about which environmental harms are important and which provide a legitimate basis for regional cooperation when there is no physical spillover. We take up these issues in chapter 7.

5. Because the race-toward-the-bottom dynamic arises as a result of competition among jurisdictions, it may also be thought of as a government failure.

Problems of the Commons

Market failures often arise when goods are "public" or when resources are commonly owned (Cornes and Sandler 1986). Public goods, such as the atmosphere, are recognized by two defining criteria: consumption of the good by one person does not reduce the amount available to anyone else and no member of the public can be excluded from consumption of the good (Samuelson 1954; Hanley, Shogren, and White 1997). Commonly owned resources—resources that, arguably, are held by governments in trust for the public (Sax 1970, 1980)—such as national parks, lakes, and rivers, while not undepletable in the same way as public goods, are characterized by the absence of a clear allocation of ownership rights to individuals.

In the case of both public goods and commonly owned resources, the "tragedy of the commons" often leads to suboptimal environmental results (Hardin 1968; Cooper 1994; Vogler 1995). Because the costs of overusing such resources are borne collectively while the gains are enjoyed privately, individuals have an incentive to exploit shared resources to a greater extent than if they had to pay for their use. The lack of ownership also creates a disincentive for private actors to preserve the resource, since doing so may impose costs but not benefits on the actor, as others are free to continue their consuming or polluting. Thus each individual, acting rationally, will seek to "free ride" on the conservation efforts of others.

A number of regional environmental challenges reflect problems of the commons. For example, the depletion of the Pacific fisheries can be attributed to the fact that each fishing nation—indeed each fishing boat—has an incentive to land as many fish as possible, even though when every other country and every other boat does the same, stocks are depleted, and everyone's capacity to make a living and enjoy the full benefit of the resource is diminished. The same dynamic exists with regard to resources of the global commons, such as the atmosphere. Since countries and their polluting entities do not pay for greenhouse gas emissions into the atmosphere, no one has an incentive to undertake expensive pollution control to mitigate possible climate change effects when any benefits will be dissipated in the face of others who are not exercising similar restraint.

Intertemporal Market Failures

A further set of allocative inefficiencies arise in the context of pollution or resource management problems that stretch across time (Brown Weiss 1993). Indeed, as mentioned earlier, many environmental harms only become apparent over time as certain critical thresholds are exceeded or as conditions become more crowded. Activities that seemed not to cause harm in the past may one day produce serious and apparently sudden environmental damage. Because for some environmental problems the time delay may stretch out over decades or even centuries, the optimal allocation of rights to pollute, and the responsibility to clean up, over time may be hard to determine, particularly since future citizens are not present today to affect the decision process by casting their "market" votes. The prospect of intertemporal resource misallocations is heightened by the tendency of politicians to have a short-term focus. As discussed below, because politicians have what economists call high "discount rates," they put little value on harms that will accrue in the future, beyond their own term of office.

Uncertainty and Information Problems

Each of the three market failures identified above—externalities, problems of the commons, and intertemporal misallocations of resources—is exacerbated by a lack of information about how much harm pollution is causing. Even if one were to establish, for example, a mechanism to internalize environmental externalities, there would remain a great deal of debate over just how much should be paid for the harm caused. The owners or guardians of environmental resources often do not know the benefits they receive from these resources, nor do polluters and resource users always know the extent of the harms caused by their activities. Not only is there difficulty in measuring the harms, but there is additional uncertainty created by honest dispute over the value of environmental amenities. How much is it worth to protect a scenic view? What price should be put on a human life saved?

The Central Role of Property Rights

In many respects, the environmental market failures discussed above—in particular, externalities and problems of the commons—can be attributed to a lack of clear property rights (Rose 1994; Hammer and Shetty 1995; Hanna, Folke, and Mäler 1996). In fact, if property rights over all environmental resources were clearly defined and enforced (Demsetz 1967), and if the transaction costs involved in buying them were low, then a free market for environmental resources would produce environmental-harm-internalizing, welfare-maximizing (Coase 1960), and fair outcomes.[6] Under such conditions, disputes about pollution spillovers and resource ownership could be addressed through a framework of tort and contract law. The problem, however, is that property rights in the environmental domain are frequently undefined, poorly delineated, or difficult to vindicate.

---

6. "Fair" in this context refers only to the issue of respecting property rights. A broader fairness issue—whether the initial endowment of rights is equitable—remains open.

Undefined Property Rights

That property rights in public goods and community-held resources are frequently unspecified largely explains the problem of the commons identified above (Snape 1994). Defining rights in relation to waterways, the air, or other public goods is inherently difficult, given their diffuse and incorporeal nature. These resources cannot be easily "privatized," because of the difficulty of excluding nonowners from use.[7] Although some resources, including national parks and lakes, are not strictly "public," they nevertheless have a long tradition of being held in common. It would be possible to define and allocate property rights in such resources—for example, by selling a national park to private property holders—but this "efficient" result is unlikely to be satisfactory to the citizens who believe that such resources are their patrimony. While the absence of well-defined rights with respect to shared resources is common to all APEC members, it is a particularly acute problem in China and Vietnam, where many facilities and much property are collectively owned.

Poorly Delineated Property Rights

Further confusion arises over the rights and responsibilities that attach to property ownership. Most private property systems are grounded on the owner's right to use his or her property, the right to exclude others from the land, and the power to transfer title to others. Ownership, however, also implies a responsibility to respect the rights of neighboring citizens and other property owners. Courts and legislatures across the APEC region have attempted to resolve the tension between rights and responsibilities, but a number of issues remain unresolved or unclear. Does ownership mean that landholders have a right to engage in polluting activities? Or do neighbors have a right not to be polluted? What degree of harm triggers the right to insist on protection from spillovers? How should governments deal with situations in which harms are diffuse or unidentifiable? How do the responsibilities of property owners change as activities that were once thought to be harmless are recognized as causing damage? Who holds the rights with regard to behavior that has little effect in uncrowded circumstances, but that inflicts injuries when repeated by thousands or millions of people under more crowded conditions? In the absence of clear property rights, status quo behavior often goes unchallenged. This "default rule," under which polluters pollute with impunity and resource users consume with abandon (Esty 1996b,

---

7. Despite the significant technical problems in defining and allocating property rights, some successful efforts have been made. For example, the 1990 Clean Air Act amendments effectively created "rights" to air in the United States, through the allocation of tradable emissions permits for SO_2.

582-85), benefits actors who have the weight of prior and continuous activity on their side, even when these activities cause harm to others.

In a number of APEC countries, further problems arise because of uncertainties surrounding traditional common property rights. For example, in countries like Indonesia, Malaysia, and the Philippines, the uncertain duration of community land tenure does not encourage long-term stewardship of property and resources but rather extraction of maximum short-term value from the land and the spilling of harms onto others (Brandon and Ramankutty 1993; Lynch and Talbott 1995). In other APEC countries, the existence of native title to land creates uncertainty vis-à-vis more recently established common law property rights. For example, in Australia, the recent determination by the High Court that native title and pastoral leases can coexist on the same land has fueled debate over property rights.[8]

Difficulty in Vindicating Property Rights

Even where the ownership of environmental resources is clear, the property rights at issue may not be enforceable or vindicable at law. Much of the problem can be explained by examining the relative stakes of polluters and pollutees—and determining who bears the costs of action or inaction. Polluters benefit when they can push wastes from a smokestack or effluent pipeline onto society at large. The "victim" of these emissions is a diffuse public, in which each individual in most cases suffers only minor harms— rarely enough to justify counteraction.

Because of the high cost of vindicating one's property rights through legal action or the political process, most individuals simply accept their losses. In the face of diffuse harms caused by politically powerful and well-organized polluters who are unafraid of lengthy and expensive litigation, emissions often go unaddressed even when they clearly violate property norms and rights.

The difficulties involved in enforcing and vindicating rights are further complicated when the source of the harms is an actor in another jurisdiction. In these cases, which we have called super externalities, the absence of an overarching legal regime (Ellickson 1979) makes recovery even more difficult and gives further license to polluters and consumers of public resources.[9] In sum, in the absence of appropriate mechanisms for the

---

8. See *Wik Peoples v. State of Queensland and others* (1996) 141 A.L.R. 129.

9. While there may be a norm of customary international law that proscribes transboundary environmental spillovers (Sands 1994a), international litigation based on customary law is unlikely to be successful (Bodansky 1995). Many of the remedies available through domestic legal channels, moreover, are unavailable in the international arena, including punitive damages, criminal fines, and injunctive relief. And as Stone (1993, 69-70) notes, there are "various jurisdictional and doctrinal problems: jurisdiction is noncompulsory, trials are

vindication of property rights, a Hobbesian state of nature prevails, leaving the strong free to seize common resources and to pollute without restraint. This outcome is neither economically efficient nor fair (Esty 1996b, 584).

Government Failures

Some resource issues and environmental harms could be addressed by establishing and strengthening mechanisms for the determination, adjudication, and enforcement of property rights. Many environmental harms are not, however, amenable to property rights solutions; in other cases, the obstacles to establishing an appropriate property rights regime appear insurmountable. This creates a need for governmental intervention to protect the environment (Stiglitz 1988; Baumol and Oates 1988).[10] Governments can take various actions to align private and social costs, such as imposing pollution charges or taxes, subsidizing emissions contracts, or promulgating regulations to restrict socially harmful behavior (Pigou 1920; Hahn and Stavins 1992). Unfortunately, just as the market fails and delivers suboptimal environmental outcomes, so too government efforts to protect the environment frequently fall short (Hammer and Shetty 1995). Not only do governments fail in their environmental endeavors, but their policy choices in nonenvironmental areas often have unintended negative effects on pollution or resource management. The list of government failures does not end with policy failures—both environmental and nonenvironmental—but includes public choice problems and structural failures.

Policy Failures

There are a number of different ways in which poor policy choices may lead to bad environmental results or even create new environmental harms. First, suboptimal outcomes may result simply because environmental policy is extremely complex and because governments lack the capacity or resources to perform regulatory functions adequately. Second, policies in certain sectors of the economy—in particular, energy, agriculture, and transportation—may have important derivative impacts on the environment. And finally, a government's development policy may give inappropriate priority to growth at the expense of environmental goals.

---

complex and time-consuming, and recovery is, in all events, unlikely. Irreversible damage may proceed far faster than the legal system that is pursuing it."

10. While this view is widely accepted, some commentators doubt that governments can ever design and implement regulatory policies that counteract market failure; they label this proposition the "nirvana fallacy" (Demsetz 1969; Menell 1992).

Incapacity and Regulatory Complexity

Many of the public health and ecological problems in APEC countries can be traced directly to environmental policy failures that derive from the inherent complexity of environmental policymaking and the regulatory incapacity of many nations. Environmental policymaking involves a large number of steps—problem identification, data collection, fate and transport analysis, epidemiological and ecological studies, risk assessment, policy design and alternatives development, cost-benefit analysis, implementation and enforcement, and evaluation—each of which requires a degree of technical knowledge and sophistication (Esty 1996b).

At each stage of the process, a lack of regulatory capacity—insufficient human resources, inadequate technical and scientific infrastructure, and insufficient financial resources for policy implementation, monitoring, or enforcement—can cause policymaking to go wrong (OECD 1996). With respect to water resources management, for example, the environmental agencies of China and most members of the Association of Southeast Asian Nations (ASEAN) lack skilled staff, suffer from a shortage of equipment to monitor discharges, and possess inadequate enforcement powers (UNESCAP 1995, 104). Insufficient monitoring capacity or human and financial resources also hampers urban air pollution control in many APEC countries (UNESCAP 1995, 153). Industrial pollution goes virtually unregulated in many developing APEC nations. In Thailand, for example, as late as 1989, a mere 700 staffers were available to monitor and enforce emissions and effluent standards at more than 50,000 industrial plants (Siwabut 1992). Forest management across APEC also suffers from regulatory incapacity (UNESCAP 1995, 44).

In a number of APEC's developing countries, furthermore, responsibility for environmental protection is fragmented among a number of government agencies and departments. Even when responsibility has been consolidated into one agency, "bureaucratic resistance on the part of the long-dominant economic ministries to any encroachment on their authority" (O'Connor 1994, 53) makes serious regulation difficult. This problem helps to explain why, as discussed below, a number of APEC's developing members appear to be placing too high a priority on economic development and growth, to the detriment of the environment.

Sectoral Policy Spillovers

In many cases environmental damage results from spillovers caused by policy choices made in other economic sectors. Whether these harms arise from government decisions that affect the quality of the environment directly—such as transportation planning choices that ignore air pollution effects—or indirectly as a result of the incentives placed before private-sector actors—such as price supports that induce farmers to grow on environmentally sensitive marginal lands—very real environmental impacts can be traced to unsound government policymaking in the nonenvironmental realm. Poor energy, agriculture, and transportation policies are especially significant causes of environmental harm across APEC.

Some of the most serious policy failings arise from subsidies[11] that distort price signals and lead to inefficient resource use and pollution (World Bank 1997; Panayotou 1993; Munasinghe and Cruz 1995; Earth Council 1997; de Moor 1997). Not only are many subsidies environmentally harmful, but they also cause economic welfare loss and disrupt efforts to promote freer trade. Although the extent of the problem is, in many cases, well documented and the solution (elimination of the subsidy) well known, entrenched political forces make policy rationalization difficult.

Energy production is subsidized in many ways, including through direct government grants, tax breaks to producers or distributors, rebates to consumers, and restrictions on competing energy sources and imported fuels. Whatever form subsidies take, the result is that prices paid by consumers do not reflect the true economic costs of energy consumption, never mind the full social (including environmental) costs of production and consumption. The outcome is overconsumption of energy, persistent inefficiencies in the use of energy, blunted incentives for conservation, and unnecessarily high levels of pollution.

Subsidies for coal in Australia, Canada, China, Japan, and the United States cause more of this fuel to be burned than would otherwise be the case. Such preferential treatment leads to higher levels of emissions of greenhouse gases, sulfur dioxide, and particulates, as well as to landscape and habitat destruction from coal mining. Subsidies for diesel fuel and gasoline in many APEC countries result in worsening carbon dioxide emissions, carbon monoxide pollution, the release of lead, and nitrous oxide emissions.

Agricultural subsidies for logging, fishing, crop and livestock production, and agricultural inputs also wreak havoc on the environment in Asia (World Bank 1997; Roodman 1997). Below-cost timber sales in Australia, Canada, Indonesia, Malaysia, and the United States accelerate deforestation and cause siltation of streams, soil erosion, and increased flooding. In the multibillion-dollar fishing industry, massive subsidies in some countries to fishers for fuel, equipment, and income support create sig-

---

11. Defining *subsidies* has proved to be notoriously difficult. The broadest definition captures both explicit and implicit subsidies and includes direct government payments to producers or consumers (cash subsidies); government guarantees, interest subsidies, or soft loans (credit subsidies); reductions of tax liabilities (tax subsidies); government equity participation (equity subsidies); government provision of goods and services at below-market prices (in-kind subsidies); government purchases of goods and services at above-market prices (procurement subsidies); and implicit payments through government regulatory activities that alter market access or prices (regulatory subsidies) (Clements, Hugounenq, and Schwartz 1995).

nificant overcapacity, promote overfishing, and threaten the long-run viability of coastal communities and oceanic ecosystems (Stone 1997; Associated Press, 2 June 1997). Below-market-cost grazing fees for livestock on public lands in Australia, Canada, and the United States encourage overgrazing and land degradation.

Many APEC countries also subsidize public irrigation projects and drinking water systems, encouraging overconsumption of water and discouraging conservation. Falling water tables, deterioration of water quality, and, in some places, salinization of water supplies result. Subsidies for pesticides and fertilizers lead to chemical-intensive agriculture that causes groundwater contamination, public health problems for farmworkers, chemical exposure, food safety concerns, the emergence of pesticide-resistant insects, degradation of water quality, and deterioration of ecosystems.

The transportation sector is another policy realm with significant environmental policy spillovers (E. Frankel 1997). Most important, private vehicular use is subsidized by publicly funded roads and automotive fuel priced well below the true environmental costs. More cars driving more miles means more smog, particulates, oxides of nitrogen (NO_x), and greenhouse gas emissions, as well as damage to habitats arising from road construction.

In cataloging the harms that can be attributed to subsidies, almost all of the major environmental problems currently facing APEC's members appear. The implication is clear: before launching a move to adopt the much-vaunted "polluter pays" principle, "pay-the-polluter" programs need to be stopped.

Misguided Development Choices

One of the primary contributors to environmental injury in developing countries is the choice of development strategies that give short shrift to environmental concerns (Bello and Bullard 1997). Indeed, many APEC nations seem to have opted for a "pollute-now-pay-later" approach to development (O'Connor 1994), based on the belief that a period of "darkness" and heavy pollution is the necessary price for industrial development and economic modernization. Those pursuing this course often cite Japan's development pattern as their model.[12] After World War II, the Japanese government placed overriding priority on industrialization and export promotion (World Bank 1993), with the effect that by the late 1960s, pollution was so severe and widespread that Japan gained a reputation as a "wasteland of pollution" (Fujisaki 1995).[13]

---

12. South Korea and Taiwan, in particular, appear to have followed the Japanese model (Bello 1993).

13. Of course, the model of Eastern Europe, where the legacy of toxic wastes now represents a significant drag on future economic prosperity, can also be described as conforming to this "developmentalist" path (Esty 1997a).

A development strategy that always places growth ahead of environmental protection is, however, economically irrational. First, it falsely assumes that there are no environmental investments worth making in the early stages of development. On the contrary, at every stage of economic development there are environmental investments whose benefits vastly exceed their costs (Esty 1997a). In fact, it is the poorest countries that can least afford to overlook low-cost, high-return pollution control opportunities. The World Bank found, for example, that an investment of just $20 million to reduce water pollution from the top 100 dischargers in Manila would result in labor productivity improvements and reduced risk to fisheries valued at $150 million a year (cited in ADB 1997, 239). Thus, while some pollution is likely to accompany industrial growth and a target of zero emissions would be unwise at any level of development, every country has the opportunity to put itself on a development trajectory that is sustainable and that minimizes the environmental effects of economic growth.

Second, the pollute-now-pay-later approach does not take into account that some environmental harms either are irreversible, such as biodiversity loss, or will be more expensive to clean up later, such as disposal of heavy metals and bioaccumulative toxins in waterways. Finally, because many capital investments are expected to contribute to economic activity for long periods of time, it is often expensive to change direction once a particular policy course has been set. China's commitment to power generation through hundreds of small-scale, highly polluting, coal-burning power plants may meet short-term economic needs. But this policy is likely to be demonstrably suboptimal for a richer China 20 years from now, when these highly polluting power plants are only halfway through their life cycles. Indeed, the net present value of expenditures to retrofit existing pollutive plants and factories will, in many cases, be substantially more expensive than it would have been to install the appropriate environmental technologies in the first place.

Public Choice Problems

In discussing efforts to formulate policy, we have assumed that governments know and act on the desires of their citizenry for environmental protection. But it is clear that in many cases, APEC's member governments do not faithfully and accurately reflect the environmental preferences of their citizens. Failures to follow public preferences fall under the rubric of "public choice" problems.

Unrepresentative Governments

In a number of APEC countries, the translation of public preferences into regulatory outcomes is not a first-order goal of the political leaders.

Particularly in China, and to a lesser extent in Indonesia and Malaysia, the wishes of the citizenry appear to have taken a back seat to the attainment of other objectives, primarily rapid economic development and perpetuation of the ruling regime. As a result, human health and the environment have suffered.

Where democratic traditions are absent or weak, not only may governments fail to accurately reflect citizen preferences, but those preferences may themselves be distorted by a lack of accurate environmental information. In particular, citizens living under such regimes may have low expectations about environmental and health standards simply because of a paucity of information about harms, as well as the absence of vigorous public debate about whether and how harms can and should be addressed.[14] Thus, there exists a strong correlation between sound environmental policies and the presence of a free press and a right to free speech, as well as the existence of environmental groups and other nongovernmental organizations (NGOs) (Andersson, Folke, and Nyström 1995).[15]

Interest Group Manipulation

Even in APEC countries that have representative governments, public choice problems persist. In fact, decisions concerning environmental protection and resource use are particularly susceptible to special interest manipulation because the costs of pollution control are more concentrated and tangible than the benefits. This asymmetry in the concentration of regulatory costs and benefits means that polluters have a systematic incentive to intervene in the political process (Ackerman 1985) and are often easily organized to do so. Mobilizing the diffuse public for large-scale political activity, in contrast, presents a much greater challenge (Buchanan and Tullock 1962; Olson 1965; Noll 1989).

Interest group influence takes many forms, including lobbying, campaign contributions, and publicity campaigns. In other cases, the special interest influence can be attributed to payoffs, outright bribery, or other special relationships between political and business leaders.[16]

Short-Run Focus

Many environmental problems, as noted above, are marked by long time lags before harms emerge. The resulting tendency to focus on the benefits

---

14. O. Young and Demko (1996) highlight the importance of public education to make people aware of environmental issues.

15. While the presence of democratic traditions is generally an indicator of the degree of representativeness of government, it does not always predict environmental performance. Singapore, for example, has a system of government that many consider undemocratic, in which there is only nominal opposition to the ruling party. Nevertheless, Singapore has done a very good job of dealing with many of its most pressing environmental problems.

16. Parnwell and Bryant (1996) attribute these problems to "crony capitalism."

of economic activities (jobs, new factories, etc.) and to disregard not-yet-apparent issues is exacerbated by another public choice problem—the disconnect between the time horizons, or "discount rates," of politicians and those of the general public (Viscusi 1995). Specifically, politicians, concerned about the next election (Downs 1957), often give little weight to costs or benefits that arise in the future (Esty 1996b, 599). This problem systematically biases decision making against addressing harms that will only emerge in full force some years hence.

Structural Failures

While every APEC government succumbs to some extent to policy and public choice failures, they all try to address environmental issues that affect their citizens. But when environmental harms fall, in part, beyond a nation's borders—creating super externalities—governments have a reduced incentive to take the problem seriously, as well as a reduced capacity to respond appropriately. Fundamentally, there exists a structural mismatch between the scale of their jurisdiction and the geographic scope of the harm.

Nations have little incentive to take transboundary harms seriously because they are primarily concerned with the welfare of their own citizens, not welfare generally. This focus on national rather than global welfare leads governments to ignore positive or negative environmental effects on others.[17] Environmental policies turn on cost-benefit analyses that disregard the preferences of those beyond the government's jurisdiction, no matter that in some cases, the "omitted voices" may have a big stake in the policy outcome (Graham and Wiener 1995).[18] Thus, while US coal-fired power plants and industrial facilities cause acid rain in Canada, US regulators have no incentive to consider the effects on Canadian cities and citizens. Disregard for effects beyond one's own borders skews the policy calculus, yielding a more than optimal level of industrial activity. Benefits that accrue outside the jurisdiction where the activity is taking

---

17. In the trade arena, the world community has come to realize that a broad focus on global welfare is preferable to a narrow focus on national welfare. The successful reconfiguration of international trade from a zero-sum "beggar-thy-neighbor" game into one in which the aim is to increase global welfare is, in fact, one of the major successes of post–World War II international relations (Lawrence, Bressand, and Ito 1996; Jackson 1969). The trade regime may thus provide a useful model for addressing super externalities.

18. The problem of omitted voices occurs not only across space but also across time. To the extent that future generations are not able to have their views heard and counted, their interests, which may be deeply affected by current policy decisions, will receive insufficient attention. And while some analysts suggest that the interest of people in protecting their children will prevent a bias in decision making toward the present, a considerable body of work (Diamond 1977; Brandts and de Bartolome 1988; Brown Weiss 1989) suggests that bequest motives are insufficient to protect the interests of future citizens.

place similarly will be ignored. Unable to capture the biodiversity and carbon sequestration benefits of its forests, Malaysia's decisions about how much timber to cut reflect only the national benefit of lumber sales while disregarding the nonmonetizable value of standing trees. The level of tree cutting is set at the national rather than the worldwide optimum.

In addition to having little inclination to respond to their own transboundary transgressions, countries are limited in their ability to respond to harms inflicted on them that emanate from outside their borders, since the principle of national sovereignty limits the regulatory competence of countries to activities arising solely within their geographical bounds. Territorial sovereignty, often exalted as the cornerstone of international relations, fails as a governing principle in a world of ecological interdependence (Pallemaerts 1994; Esty 1997c). Canadian regulators are unable to address harms from US coal power plants, though they know that the acid rain originating in the United States causes billions of dollars' worth of damage in Canada. The only way that progress has been made is through collective action, namely, the conclusion of an Acid Rain Treaty between the United States and Canada. Similar acid rain problems exist between China and Japan. Japan has been forced to address the problem by paying for the installation of scrubbers on the offending Chinese power plants. Without clear property rules and an overarching legal regime to enforce them, China (the polluter) seizes the property rights. Japan (the victim) is reduced to paying the Chinese not to pollute.

The structural mismatch between the scale of the jurisdiction and the geographic scope of the harm exists whenever damages (or benefits) spill over from one country to another, from a country to a commons, from a commons to a country, or from one user of a commons to another. In each case the dynamic is the same: there is a systematic disincentive for the regulating authority to take into account costs and benefits that either are borne by or accrue to citizens of other countries or citizens outside their jurisdiction.

Relationship Between Income, Scope of the Harm, and Abatement

Structural mismatches help to explain why, although localized pollution harms improve as countries become wealthier, regional and global harms tend not to. Specifically, it appears that as incomes rise, environmental problems follow one of three distinct patterns of abatement, which turn primarily on the geographic scale of the harm and, to a lesser extent, on the visibility, severity, and temporal immediacy of the injury (figure 4.1).

In the first category, environmental conditions improve monotonically as incomes grow (figures 4.1a and b). The downward sloping harm-income curve—evident, for example, in improved access to clean water and sanitation services (Shafik and Bandyopadhyay 1992) and in falling concentrations of lead and cadmium in waterways (Grossman 1995)—

Figure 4.1 Relationship between income and abatement of harms

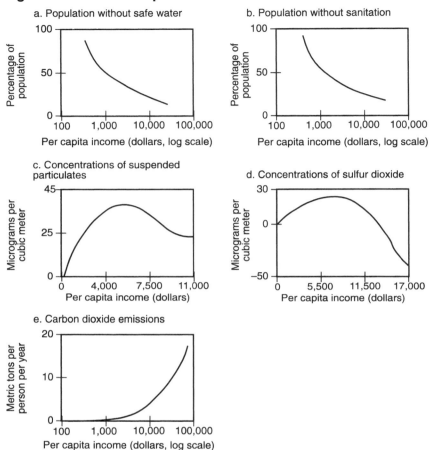

a. Population without safe water

b. Population without sanitation

c. Concentrations of suspended particulates

d. Concentrations of sulfur dioxide

e. Carbon dioxide emissions

Sources: Shafik and Bandyopadhyay 1992; Grossman and Krueger 1993.

occurs when problems are plainly apparent, serious, and highly localized in the public health harms and costs they impose. Governments recognize the benefits to their constituents of action. They understand that even if the costs of providing improved environmental infrastructure are significant, the gains to their citizens may be even bigger (and quickly appreciated by the voting public). This particular pattern—where the costs and benefits of action fall within the territory of the regulating authority—yields a high probability of action by local or national governments without outside intervention. Environmental investments are likely to be made commensurate with the financial and technical resources available. Policy intervention will probably begin even at the earliest stages of development, because some investments will immediately deliver benefits that exceed their costs.

A second set of environmental problems does not improve monotonically with income but instead follows an inverted-U relationship between income and environmental conditions (figures 4.1c and d). In these cases, environmental quality deteriorates in the early stages of economic growth, but improves at higher income levels. A number of studies have found that basic air and water pollution often fit this pattern. A number of studies, for example, have found that particulates and sulfur dioxide levels worsen in the early stages of development, peak at GDP per capita levels (PPP-adjusted) of between $5,000 and $8,000, and decline thereafter (Shafik and Bandyopadhyay 1992; Grossman and Krueger 1993, 1995; Grossman 1995; Selden and Song 1994; Islam 1996). These studies have reached similar conclusions with regard to water pollutants, including fecal coliform and arsenic.

The logic behind this environmental "Kuznets curve" is quite straightforward (Kuznets 1955).[19] In the early stages of industrialization, countries are poor; deciding they cannot afford much environmental protection, they make tradeoffs between pollution and growth that favor economic expansion. As a country becomes richer, however, its capacity for investment in pollution prevention and control becomes greater. Not only are resources available for these investments but a wealthier public is likely to demand them more insistently, strengthening the environmental regime and improving performance (Radetzki 1992; Crowley and Findlay 1996). Moreover, highly polluting industries are likely to emerge in the early stages of development, with cleaner production activities coming on line over time.

The kinds of problems that follow the inverted-U harm-income relationship are likely to be somewhat less localized in their impacts—the harms may be spread over a wider area and may not be felt immediately. While this pattern of more diffuse costs generates a less clear cost-benefit logic to national investments in pollution prevention or control, the fact that the harms accrue to the country's own citizens ultimately provides a sufficient basis for acting.

Based on their empirically derived inverted U-curves, Grossman and Krueger (1995, 370) conclude that there is "no evidence that economic growth does unavoidable harm to the natural habitat." Yet even Grossman (1995, 43) recognizes that this statement is too sweeping, because some types of pollution continue to rise "with national output throughout the entire range of income levels." Thus, the third income-abatement pattern (see figure 4.1e)—an ever-rising level of harm—reflects a set of environ-

---

19. Kuznets showed that an inverted-U relationship existed between income inequality and level of development.

mental problems that do not appear to lessen with wealth. This pattern emerges when a harm is largely externalized—spatially or temporally—beyond the jurisdiction responsible for deciding on the level of abatement and there is thus a structural mismatch between the scope of the harm and that of the regulating authority. Emissions of carbon dioxide, for example, continue to rise as higher levels of GDP per capita are achieved, albeit at a decreasing rate (Shafik and Bandyopadhyay 1992; Selden and Song 1994). The fact that CO_2 emissions rise irrespective of income can be explained by the distribution of cost bearers and beneficiaries—in particular, the diffusion of the harms caused and the concentration of the burdens to be borne by investments in abatement.

Quite clearly, when a large portion of the harm from an environmental problem drifts across borders, the regulatory cost-benefit calculus will be skewed. Specifically, the benefits of pollution prevention or control (much of which accrue to those beyond the jurisdiction's borders) will never justify the costs (which will have to be fully borne by those within the jurisdiction). Thus, in dealing with the carbon dioxide emissions that blanket the globe and that may contribute to climate change at some point in the future, no jurisdiction has much of an incentive to control its emissions unilaterally. As a consequence, rational action on the part of each actor will yield demonstrably suboptimal results overall. With regard to transboundary pollution harms, no country chooses to undertake the appropriate environmental actions, preferring instead to free ride on the actions of others, producing, in game theory terms, a "lose-lose" Nash equilibrium.

Once the three types of income-abatement relationships identified above are understood, several important policy implications emerge. First, those environmental harms with the most immediate and serious impacts on local communities will likely be attended to as soon as incomes rise and as long as governments are reasonably diligent and capable in their environmental activities.

Second, there are a range of other harms that are also likely to respond to higher incomes, although only after a period of worsening degradation during the earlier stages of development. These are not as clearly and closely connected to local habitats or health, and are therefore not the most pressing policy priorities. The shape of the curve—and thus the magnitude and duration of the harm—can, however, be affected by policy-makers. In particular, with an increased awareness of environmental harms, the development of environmental technologies, and the opportunity to learn from their richer counterparts, APEC's low-income countries should be able to make the inverted-U shape turn down earlier, abating harms at lower income levels. The inverted-U curve might also be made flatter, reflecting a lesser degree of accrued harm, if countries were to respond appropriately to the various sources of environmental harms.

Figure 4.2 APEC population, 1950-2025 (millions)

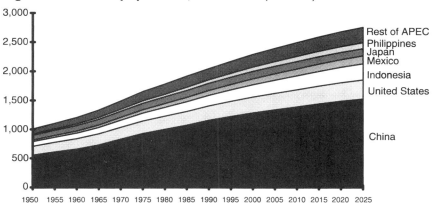

Note: Figures for 2000-2025 are estimates.
Source: UN 1994.

Such policies would require, among other things, properly defining property rights, internalizing externalities, reassessing development-first practices, removing subsidies, strengthening environmental policymaking capacity, and informing the public about the harms they face.

Third, where environmental problems do not yield to increases in income—as is the case for many transboundary harms—only collective action will overcome the incentive for free riding and ensure that all those playing the "game" can escape the lose-lose outcome (Carraro and Siniscalco 1995). As chapter 6 argues, there exists an important need for international structures—like APEC—to facilitate the requisite policy coordination. This conclusion flows directly from standard economic theory and garners support from even the most devoted free traders in the economic literature (Bhagwati 1993a; Cooper 1994; Nordhaus 1994).

Demographic and Economic Magnifiers

A number of studies have identified population pressures, urbanization, poverty, and industrialization as critical underlying causes of environmental degradation (Brandon and Ramankutty 1993, 28-29). These economic and demographic factors are not, however, independent causes of environmental harms but rather magnifiers of market and policy shortcomings (Hempel 1996).

In 1995, APEC's population was about 2.2 billion people—38 percent of the global total. China alone represented 1.2 billion people. By 2025, according to United Nations estimates, APEC's population is expected to be 2.8 billion (figure 4.2). At that time, six APEC members—China, the

Figure 4.3 Urban and rural population growth in APEC, 1950-2025 (millions)

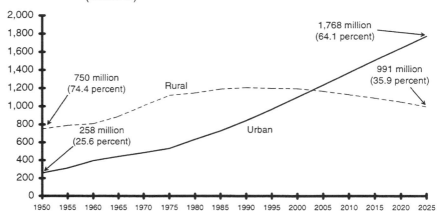

Note: Figures for 2000-2025 are estimates.
Source: UN 1994.

United States, Indonesia, Mexico, Japan, and the Philippines—will have populations exceeding 100 million people. Rising populations inevitably cause resources to be spread thinner and can result in serious environmental stress.

By 2025, much of APEC's population will have moved from rural to urban areas. As figure 4.3 shows, between 1995 and 2025, demographers expect APEC's urban population to almost double from 965 million to over 1.75 billion. China's urban population is forecast to increase by 125 percent to over 830 million. UN projections suggest that the proportion of APEC's Asian population living in urban centers will increase from 37.2 percent today to 59.1 percent. Rapid urbanization will create megacities in many APEC countries (figure 4.4). By 2010, APEC will be home to 11 urban centers with populations greater than 10 million. The rural population will fall from a peak in 1995 of 1.2 billion to about 990 million.

Although poverty levels continue to fall across the Asia Pacific region, 150 million APEC citizens are still likely to be living in dire poverty in 2010. As we noted earlier, the pressures of day-to-day life under conditions of severe deprivation often translate into short-term thinking and environmentally harmful actions.

Industrialization also heightens the environmental policy challenge. As countries develop, they experience an evolution in their industrial structure, with a corresponding change in the composition of the ecological and public health problems they face. In early stages of development—when countries are reliant on resource-based industries and light industrial activity—countries find themselves preoccupied with land degrada-

Figure 4.4 Global distribution of megacities, 1970-2010

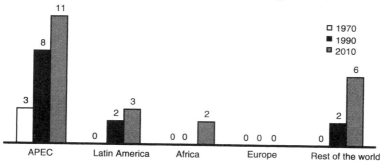

Note: Figures for 2010 are estimates.

Source: UN 1994.

tion, water scarcity, and water pollution. Later, as they move into heavier industries—such as metals processing, petrochemicals, cement, and glass—they face issues relating to air pollution, toxic chemicals, and heavy metals. Finally, as production shifts to industries with lower pollution intensity—electronics, advanced machinery, and services—nations are confronted with a new set of challenges, particularly problems arising from consumption of polluting goods such as cars.

These demographic and economic factors—population, urbanization, poverty, and industrialization—often interact to further magnify environmental stresses. Smoke from home cooking using biomass fuels, for example, may be of little consequence in uncrowded rural villages. But in densely populated urban areas, the same behavior may cause serious air pollution. Similarly, problems in urban centers arising from exposed sewage and poor water sanitation facilities will increase as urban populations multiply, if governments fail to develop sewage and sanitation infrastructure at a rate that keeps pace with this demographic change. Experience in many APEC countries demonstrates that where increasing population is coupled with widespread poverty, increased deforestation and unsustainable land management can be expected as citizens are forced to make environmentally damaging choices to ensure their own short-term survival.

Moreover, because many of APEC's economies are industrializing very rapidly, they are faced with new sets of environmental challenges before they have been able to attend to existing problems. Both Thailand and Indonesia, for example, have just entered the most pollution-intensive phase of their development with major investments in petrochemicals and metals processing. Yet they still face serious pollution problems from past resource-intensive industries, such as timber and mining. And at the same time, both countries are also experiencing rapid growth in "advanced" industries, such as electronics and transport equipment, that create significant hazardous waste and toxic chemical problems. The telescoping of the development process creates multiple overlapping environmental demands (Beckerman 1992) and compounds the policy challenge of achieving sustainability.

While population pressures, urbanization, poverty, and industrialization can increase the scale of environmental harms, the real culprits remain market and regulatory failures. Indeed, the experience of the northeastern United States, Japan, and Singapore—all of which have undergone industrialization, and all of which have high population densities and a significant degree of urbanization but comparatively modest environmental problems—demonstrates that good government policies that address underlying market failures can alleviate environmental harms.

Conclusion

While significant efforts have been made to understand the drivers of Asia Pacific economic growth, much less attention has been devoted to analyzing the sources of the region's environmental harms. But progress in addressing the pollution and resource issues that plague APEC members cannot be achieved without an understanding of these causes.

- Most environmental harms can be attributed to one of four *market failures*: externalities, problems of the commons, intertemporal trade-offs, and imperfect information.

- Many of the environmental harms caused by market failures—in particular, externalities and problems of the commons—can be overcome by appropriately allocating, defining, and vindicating *property rights* and, where necessary, strengthening the rule of law.

- When property rights solutions are not readily available or are impractical, government intervention to mitigate market failures will be required. Governments, however, frequently succumb to various types of *government failures*:
  - *Policy failures:* In regulating to protect the environment, governments frequently regulate suboptimally. Moreover, government policies in nonenvironmental areas often have unintended environmental consequences, creating or exacerbating environmental harms.
    - *Incapacity and regulatory complexity.* Since many harms across APEC persist because of regulatory incapacity, improving environmental policymaking and program implementation should be a goal for national governments and supranational bodies. Regulatory complexity can be addressed by APEC-wide exchange of data, science,

risk analysis, cost-benefit studies, policy options, and program evaluations.

■ *Sectoral policy spillovers.* Eliminating agricultural and energy subsidies and reforming policies that distort transportation incentives offer the promise of significant environmental and economic gains.

■ *Misguided development choices.* APEC's members need to revise their development strategies to reflect the welfare effects of environmental harms. By strengthening their project appraisal capabilities so that the economic value of environmental assets is appropriately measured, APEC's developing countries will find that many environmental investments are both economically and environmentally attractive.

■ *Public choice problems:* Better environmental policy and improved environmental outcomes in APEC countries require diligent efforts to ensure that policy choices reflect and represent informed public preferences. This entails open debate in APEC countries about existing circumstances and policy alternatives, a process enhanced by a free press, an active NGO community, and an informed public.

■ *Structural failures:* Collective action is required to respond to the structural mismatches that undermine national incentives to respond to regional and global harms. APEC can play a role in facilitating the requisite cross-jurisdictional cooperation.

Unless pollution spillovers are externalized, commons problems are addressed, and government policies that distort resource prices are reformed, APEC's economic goals will be hard to achieve. Allocative inefficiency will be widespread and the integrity of the emerging regional economic system will be compromised. The market and governmental failures enumerated above must be addressed not only to abate environmental degradation but to improve the efficiency of markets across the Asia Pacific, an objective that underlies APEC's efforts to liberalize trade and investment.

5

Tensions at the Economy-Environment Interface

As the preceding chapters make clear, serious environmental harms across APEC threaten to directly undercut the welfare gains achieved through economic growth (chapter 3). Furthermore, widespread uninternalized externalities, unmanaged common resources, and price-distorting and environmentally damaging government policies (all of which are responsible for serious environmental harm) undermine the efficient functioning of market forces and further reduce social welfare (chapter 4). Another important reason to address environmental issues arises from the range of tensions at the economy-environment interface that threaten to spill over into the economic realm and make countries back away from trade and investment liberalization—or, worse, erect new protectionist barriers. Given that the increasing openness of national economies has been central to the economic vitality of the Asia Pacific region, a retreat from further liberalization could leave many citizens in APEC's developing nations in poverty and may, more broadly, derail economic progress across the region.

At stake is the political will to proceed with further economic integration. In many APEC countries, both developed and developing, the political forces in favor of trade liberalization face constant challenges from those who see expanded international trade as a threat to national sovereignty as well as to traditional economic structures and values. In the United States, in particular, majority support for new trade and investment initiatives cannot be taken for granted (Nader 1993; Perot 1993).

These tensions also endanger the delicate trade bargain between developed and developing countries.[1] The industrializing nations of APEC

---

1. As Tay (1996, 193) notes, many (e.g., Khor 1992) in the developing world "believe [they] have paid too high a price for that bargain. They seek to re-open some of the past discussions, and to question the entire basis of international trade."

have benefited enormously from their access to export markets, and they recognize the need to open their own markets in return. But many officials in the South fear economic domination from the larger and better established enterprises of the North; they are concerned about rising protectionism, especially in the form of hidden nontariff barriers, in the United States and their other export markets. Conversely, business and government leaders in APEC's developed nations recognize the significant opportunity represented by the large and growing markets of APEC's developing members. Thus, although they worry about a flood of cheap imports, they have been willing to promise to keep their markets open, minimize the use of trade disciplines, and work within the multilateral framework to resolve trade disputes, in return for the removal of the remaining substantial trade barriers in developing countries (and Japan) (Bergsten 1996).

Political support for further economic integration might be undercut by any one of a number of strains at the economy-environment interface. The central tensions include

- a conflict between developing-country desires for market access commitments, including guarantees that environmental standards will not be used to exclude their products, and developed-country insistence on maintaining regulatory sovereignty and the right to set their own environmental standards;

- disputes over the appropriateness of using trade measures to reinforce multilateral environmental agreements or of applying trade sanctions unilaterally to achieve extrajurisdictional environmental objectives;

- disagreement over the legitimacy of competitive advantages accruing to nations with lower environmental standards;

- controversy over the benefits of freer trade and economic growth more generally, with some environmentalists rejecting these goals as inevitably leading to more pollution and the depletion of scarce resources; and

- discomfort in some nations at the prospect of deepening economic relationships with countries whose behavior, including environmental performance, dips below what they regard as baseline standards.

These tensions are not new. They have, however, gained prominence as a result of deepening economic integration across APEC. The primary effect of integration—as many small and medium-sized economies have realized—is a considerable loss of autonomy over fiscal and monetary policy, as international markets impose external disciplines on economic policy (OECD 1997; Cooper 1994; Greider 1997). A similar loss of autonomy over environmental decisions occurs in the context of regional integration and globalization (K. Anderson 1995a; Rodrik 1997). Increasing interdependence has also put new economic issues—competition and antitrust rules, tax codes, and environmental standards—at the top of foreign and trade policy agendas.

The increased scrutiny given to what have traditionally been "domestic" policies can be attributed to two factors. First, as barriers to trade are removed and international competition becomes more intense, differences in domestic policies become more significant in determining trade and investment flows and the pattern of industrial location (Lawrence, Bressand, and Ito 1996; Lawrence 1996; K. Anderson 1996). This competitiveness pressure explains complaints by organized labor about "social dumping" and by environmentalists about "eco-dumping," and the demands that there be baseline standards for all participants in a free trade area to ensure "fair" trade (Bhagwati 1993a).

The second reason for increased scrutiny of domestic policies is that economic integration brings countries into closer contact with each other, creating a sense of community and giving rise to pressures for common standards that define the bounds of behavior for all those operating within (and benefiting from) that community (Esty 1996b, 638-48; Rodrik 1997, 29-44). Of course, it is often difficult to disentangle the source of demands to reduce social policy differentials. Most such demands arise because of both competitiveness concerns, which may in part be protectionist, and a sense that all members of a community should adhere to communitywide baselines of behavior.

The scrutiny given to behind-the-border policies is heightened in APEC, where values are diverse and policy differentials are wide, creating the potential for significant acrimony. Globalization and regionalization have thus unleashed forces upon APEC's members that have created an increasing interest in each other's domestic environmental policies and in how these policies are used directly or indirectly to influence the environmental behavior of other countries. This interest is unlikely to subside as integration deepens (OECD 1997).

Market Access and the "New Protectionism"

An important tension in APEC arises from the competing demands of its less- and more-developed members: the former seek guaranteed access to developed-country markets, while the latter want to be able to set their own health and environmental standards at whatever level of risk they independently deem appropriate (OECD 1996; Arden-Clarke 1993).[2] The

---

2. A second dimension of concern about market access and protectionism involves private-sector rather than government behavior. In particular, tensions may arise if voluntary eco-labeling schemes or environmental management certification systems (such as ISO 14000) become default environmental product and process standards either because consumers come to expect products to carry eco-labels, or because companies require their suppliers

belief among some countries, notably Indonesia and Malaysia, that they are reducing their trade and investment barriers faster than they would otherwise choose to compounds the strain. These countries accept the faster pace of liberalization on the basis that the United States and Japan will ensure continuing and improved market access and thus greater export opportunities. Developed countries, while aware of this concern, are faced with domestic demands that environmental standards not be weakened in the name of market access.

A stronger version of the concern about market access is the fear in developing countries that environmental standards might be a guise for protectionism.[3] In a number of countries, including the United States, some environmental interests have been "captured" by, or have colluded with, domestic industries seeking to operate in less-than-open markets (Crowley and Findlay 1996; Low and Safadi 1992; Oxley 1993; Palmeter 1993; Van Grasstek 1992). Wariness about coalitions of the "green and greedy" (Oye and Maxwell 1994) is not unfounded. In a number of cases, industrialists and environmentalists have proposed higher domestic environmental standards, countervailing duties, or import restrictions on goods and services produced in countries where process standards are less strict than those at home.

The difficulty in these cases lies in separating legitimate environmental objectives from overly stringent health and environmental standards that are designed to protect industry. In January 1997, for example, the Australian government decided to retain its ban on imports of uncooked Canadian salmon even though a draft inquiry had found that such imports did not put Australian salmon stocks at risk of contamination. The decision no doubt turned, in part, on pressure from the Australian salmon industry (André Dua, *The Australian*, 13 January 1997). Cases such as these exemplify the tension between market access and environmental standards that looms large as a source of potential friction within APEC. APEC countries thus need—and APEC is well positioned to provide—a procedure by which they can ascertain whether health and environmental standards are based on a sound scientific inquiry, appropriately designed to reflect community preferences, and well tailored to address the ecological or public health challenge, or whether they are a product of protectionist influence.[4]

---

to have ISO 14000 certification. These concerns may sharpen if the standards adopted are perceived to be biased, inappropriate, or otherwise flawed—no matter that they are voluntary and private-sector driven. (For a discussion of ISO 14000 in the APEC context, see Roht-Arriaza [1996].)

3. Developed countries are by no means the only nations with standards that raise such concerns. South Korea, for example, has effectively used health (or "sanitary and phytosanitary") standards to prevent agrifood products from entering its domestic market (Smithers and Dua 1994).

4. Esty (1994a, 117-27) spells out an environmental "legitimacy" test, designed to separate bona fide environmental policies from those motivated by protectionism.

Trade Measures as "Sticks"

Many developing countries are uncomfortable with the use of trade measures to achieve environmental goals (Hudec 1996). They fear that the use of trade policy as a "stick" will be arbitrary and almost always wielded by the strong against the weak.[5] In particular, they object to the use of trade restrictions to enforce multilateral environmental agreements (MEAs).[6]

But even more upsetting to developing countries has been the unilateral use of punitive trade measures—in particular, import bans—by the United States to achieve extraterritorial environmental objectives. The US ban on imports of Mexican tuna caught using purse seine nets, which also killed dolphins, stands out as a celebrated case in point.[7] More recently, the United States raised the ire of Thailand and Malaysia by banning imports of shrimp caught using fishing techniques that threaten endangered sea turtles.[8] While the United States is attempting to negotiate a resolution with the aggrieved parties, Thailand has decided to go ahead with a complaint it filed at the WTO.[9]

Developing-country anxieties are shared by many free trade advocates, who worry that the use of trade measures to advance environmental goals will weigh down an already fragile trading system (Bhagwati 1993b).

---

5. These fears are not groundless. Trade sanctions often appear to be somewhat arbitrarily imposed by powerful nations on weaker ones. US sanctions against Taiwan (but not the more egregious violator China) for failing to control trade in rhinoceros horns and tiger bones as required by international endangered species protection agreements provide one example of this phenomenon. The failure of Austria's attempt to label and tax timber from unsustainably managed plantations and forests in the face of threatened retaliation by ASEAN countries provides further evidence that power, more often than principle, drives the use of trade measures.

6. The reluctance of developing countries to submit to trade disciplines in MEAs may reflect, in some cases, the absence of any serious intention by the signatories of adhering to the commitments they have made. Alternatively, among some countries the aversion to using trade measures in support of environmental goals may derive from a fear that they will have trouble meeting the goals set.

7. Two GATT dispute resolution determinations concluded that the US measure violated trade rules. In separate "tuna-dolphin" decisions (one in a case brought by Mexico and the other by the European Union), GATT "panels" concluded that the US tuna ban violated GATT's Article III national treatment requirement, and that while Articles XX(b) and (g) were designed to protect human or animal life and exhaustible natural resources, parties could not take advantage of these exceptions to justify "extrajurisdictional" actions (Esty 1994a, 268-69).

8. Trade bans such as this have dramatic economic impacts. Thai shrimp exports are forecast to fall to 40 billion baht in 1997, down from 51 billion in 1995 (*Bangkok Post*, 26 June 1997).

9. Thailand has been joined in its action by Malaysia, India, and Pakistan (*Bangkok Post*, 26 March 1997). ASEAN, furthermore, recently decided not to sign an agreement with the United States to protect sea turtles, choosing instead to sign their own protection pact (*Bangkok Post*, 14 March 1997).

Why, they ask, must the trade regime do the bidding of environmental policy? Shouldn't pollution control and resource management aims be pursued with environmental policy tools?

Many environmentalists fear the opposite result. In particular, they worry that new trade agreements might impose disciplines on the use of trade measures employed to promote participation and compliance with international environmental agreements. They see economic integration and market access commitments as a backdoor mechanism by which trade goals will be positioned ahead of environmental ones. While other tools are available to affect environmental policy choices in other countries,[10] environmental advocates believe that the alternatives will be ineffective (e.g., eco-labeling) or, in practice, unavailable (e.g., resources for education or funding to induce compliance).

In contrast, trade measures, or the threat thereof, have been demonstrably successful. Both China and India hinted that they might not sign the Montreal Protocol, but each ultimately joined the worldwide effort to protect the ozone layer when spurred by the prospect of curbs on their trade (as well as the promise of funding to support the acquisition of CFC substitutes) (Brack 1996). Similarly, Taiwan, facing sanctions from the United States for failing to uphold the Convention on International Trade in Endangered Species (CITES) controls on trafficking in rhinoceros horns and tiger bones, dramatically improved its endangered species protection program (*Los Angeles Times*, 19 March 1995). In addition to supporting the use of trade provisions in MEAs, many NGOs advocate the use of unilaterally imposed trade sanctions.[11]

In the absence of a dispute mediation procedure that defines the legitimacy of, and boundaries for, trade measures aimed at changing the environmental behavior of other countries, APEC's economic vision remains constantly at risk. Aggrieved parties—either those subject to sanctions or those who feel that a trading partner is failing to uphold environmental obligations—may walk away from their trade commitments or the liberalization process more generally.

Competitiveness and "Race Toward the Bottom" Concerns

Many American industries complain that stringent US environmental standards place them at an unfair competitive disadvantage vis-à-vis companies operating in countries with lax environmental standards. They

---

10. Esty (1994a, 132) provides a comprehensive list of possible tools.

11. Charnovitz (1993, 50), for example, observes: "treaties do not appear like magic spirits. . . . Thus, those arguing that unilateral action is inappropriate have the burden of demonstrating the feasibility of [alternatives]."

demand a "level playing field" (Cooper 1994; S. Richardson 1992; Char-novitz 1995). Environmental advocates, in turn, worry that these competitiveness fears will trigger a regulatory "race toward the bottom" as countries seek to attract new industrial activity to their jurisdiction or prevent domestic industries from migrating to countries with lower environmental standards ("pollution havens") by "lowering" their environmental standards.

Developing countries, for their part, see the call for "fair" trade as protectionist, as well as intruding on their national sovereignty (Haas 1993). They object to being held to standards they perceive to be too strict given their level of development, environmental preferences, endowments, and assimilative capacity.[12] Differences in environmental standards are part of comparative advantage, they argue. Moreover, such differences are what make gains from trade possible.

Who is right? Most empirical studies seem to suggest that competitiveness and productivity suffer little from stringent regulations (Kalt 1988; J. Richardson 1993; Repetto 1995), and there is little evidence of industrial flight to countries with lower environmental standards (Dean 1992; Low and Yeats 1992; Jaffe et al. 1995; Eskeland and Harrison 1997). Yet politicians do fear the effects of regulation on competitiveness, and there is ample anecdotal evidence to support their conclusions (Esty 1994a, 21-23). Moreover, some recent analyses (Han and Braden 1997; van Beers and van den Bergh 1997) conclude that strict environmental regulation *will* affect competitiveness. Low standards in some jurisdictions might thus engender a welfare-reducing race toward the bottom.[13]

The empirical data must furthermore be taken with a grain of salt. Races toward the bottom are often difficult to spot because jurisdictions rarely lower environmental standards or remove environmental regulations that are already on the books. Instead, competitiveness concerns create a "political drag" (Esty 1994a) on environmental policymaking.[14]

---

12. Where differences in standards legitimately reflect points of comparative advantage, they need not be—indeed, should not be—"leveled." But in other circumstances, variations in standards may reflect not natural advantages but rather artificial ones akin to manipulated exchange rates. In such cases, policy intervention is justified to avoid triggering a competitiveness-driven race toward the bottom in environmental regulation. We unpack the call for "level playing fields" and the related demand that trade be "fair" in greater detail in chapter 7.

13. Some observers (e.g., Revesz 1992) argue that "regulatory competition" actually improves welfare, since competitiveness pressures force governments to operate more efficiently. But Esty (1996b) has shown that the market for industrial location in which jurisdictions compete is far from perfect and thus will often deliver inefficient and welfare-reducing outcomes.

14. A good example of the effect of political drag, or what Zarsky and Hunter (1997) call being "stuck in the mud," is the European Union's failed attempts to implement a carbon tax because of the fear that its members' competitiveness would suffer if the United States did not follow suit (Esty 1994a).

Governments relax their enforcement of existing standards (Barron and Cottrell 1996), quietly promise to turn a blind eye to environmental harms, or choose not to raise standards. In each of these instances, empirical studies face the nearly impossible task of measuring something that does not happen.

In any case, the political reality of concerns over competitiveness cannot be denied. No issue retained more bite throughout the NAFTA approval process (Esty 1994b; Abbott 1995). If the current US debate over the extension of fast-track negotiating authority and the accession of Chile to NAFTA are any guide, the environmental competitiveness issue appears to have intensified (Richard Gephardt, letter to Democrat congressional colleagues, 26 February 1996).[15]

Resolving the tension between competitiveness concerns and fears on the part of developing countries that environmental standards will be inappropriately imposed on them will require a carefully structured bargain. APEC is ideally situated, as we argue in chapter 9, to provide the policy coordination required to manage this tension while at the same time facilitating the expansion of trade and investment.

Resource Depletion and Pollution Caused by Trade-Led Growth

Some environmentalists see economic integration as a step in the wrong direction. They fear that trade and investment liberalization promotes economic growth, which leads inexorably to more pollution and the unsustainable consumption of resources (K. Anderson 1993). In particular, environmentalists who adhere to the "Club of Rome" or "limits to growth" worldview, which emphasizes population expansion and the likelihood of resource shortages (Meadows 1972), see all economic growth as harmful (Alker and Haas 1993; Andersson, Folke, and Nyström 1995). For them, there can be no reconciliation with free traders. Trade means growth, and growth means inevitable and irreversible environmental despoliation.[16]

Fortunately, the theories forecasting limits to growth have been shown to be largely overblown.[17] Real-world experience suggests that, in fact,

---

15. In NAFTA, the conflict of unfair competitive advantage versus legitimate comparative advantage was ultimately resolved through an "Environmental Side Agreement," a commitment by all parties to enforce their own standards more vigorously—a precedent that may be useful for APEC.

16. This view is embraced by both developed- and developing-country NGOs (Eder 1996, 117).

17. At the opposite end of the spectrum are a new generation of environmental optimists who see few environmental problems as either real or ultimately threatening (Easterbrook 1995).

the environmental effect of economic growth can be either negative or positive (OECD 1994). Whether economic growth is sustainable turns in large measure on whether the scale effect of expanded activity (which leads to increased pollution and consumption or resources) overwhelms (1) the income effect of growth (which provides more resources for investment in environmental protection and creates a wealthier public that demands greater attention to environmental quality); (2) the technology effect (which occurs as countries get richer, invest in research and development, and acquire newer, less-polluting plants and equipment); and (3) the industrial evolution effect (which arises as nations develop and their economic base evolves toward a cleaner high-tech and services-based economy).

Most environmentalists today accept the view that development can be sustainable. The "sustainable development" paradigm holds that economic growth can be environmentally beneficial if policymakers ensure that pollution control efforts advance in tandem with expanded production and consumption, and some portion of the material gains from growth are devoted to environmental protection. But despite the potential for good that many environmentalists see in economic growth, many fear that the world's current growth trajectory is unsustainable, especially in APEC.[18]

The demands of environmentalists for a course correction have elicited a strong response from countries in the developing South. Malaysia, Indonesia, Singapore, and others argue that they have a fundamental right to development. For support, they point to Article 8 of the Stockholm Declaration, which says that "economic and social development . . . are necessary for the improvement of the quality of life," and Principle 3 of the 1992 Rio Declaration, which recognizes the "right to development."[19] The leaders of APEC's industrializing economies resent what they see as attempts by the industrial North—and especially environmentalists, whom they regard as "eco-imperialists"—to retard their economic development and their progress toward prosperity. They are backed by an influential group of domestic politicians, advisers, academics, business leaders, and journalists who, armed with the confidence provided by recent economic success, have been forthright in expressing their views. Nevertheless, most officials accept the model of sustainable development. And many of APEC's developing countries have, in fact, strengthened their domestic environmental regimes in the last decade to reflect their commitment to sustainability.

---

18. This view has been forcefully articulated at the People's Summits in Osaka and Manila, held in parallel with the Leaders' Summits.

19. The United States took a "reservation" on this point at the Rio Earth Summit and thus rejects the notion of any right to development.

But the agreement of most environmental NGOs and most developing countries on sustainable development as the goal—despite the more strident views on either side—does not diminish the seriousness of the tension outlined above. Because environmental groups in the United States represent such an important swing constituency in trade debates, their views cannot be ignored (Esty 1997b). Without an effort to address this tension, US participation in future trade liberalization agreements cannot be guaranteed—with potentially dire global consequences.

Discomfort with the Policy Choices of Trading Partners

Citizens in APEC's developed countries are increasingly expressing discomfort with the environmental policy choices of certain other countries—an unease that grows as economic integration makes these countries more important trading partners or competitors. This discomfort has received its strongest expression in the United States, where people ask whether they really want cheap imports if the goods are produced under conditions that they consider morally unacceptable. Should they accept Thai shrimp, the harvesting of which causes the death of endangered sea turtles? And do they want Chinese toys made in factories that expose workers to toxic chemicals, dramatically increasing the workers' risk of developing cancer?

Such questioning of the moral content of trade, however, raises serious concerns in the developing world, where countries strongly believe that social policy should not be dictated to them. National sovereignty, they assert, is the cornerstone of international relations.

As we discuss in the chapters that follow, economic integration to some extent creates a sense of community that, in turn, gives citizens a basis for demanding that others with whom they are dealing meet shared, community-determined environmental values. As the sense of community grows over time, and as the level of economic interaction broadens and deepens, the scope of the demands that citizens feel free to impose on each other may also expand. This process of parallel social integration will not always be smooth, but it will be necessary if countries wish to deepen their economic ties. It will test the developing-country expectation that "domestic" environmental policy should be immune to external pressures, a belief that misunderstands the imperatives of deepening economic integration. And it will challenge the developed-nation view that their moral preferences should be accepted by others. In sum, in the absence of a political foundation to undergird the push for economic integration, the fundamental mission of APEC—trade and investment liberalization—may grind to a halt.

Conclusion

Each of the above tensions—relating to market access, the use of trade measures, competitiveness concerns, the effect of trade-led growth on the environment, and unease with trading partners' social choices—is serious. And each has the potential, if not carefully managed by APEC, to cause countries to back away from their commitment to freer trade or, less likely, to quit the international trading regime altogether. The missed opportunity to achieve social welfare gains would be a high price to pay for inattention to environmental issues, particularly when the tensions are plainly apparent and, as we argue in chapter 6, APEC is well positioned to respond.

6

Why APEC Must Act

Environmental problems matter. They detract from the gains from growth;
they reduce the allocative efficiency of the economic system; and they
threaten the prospects of continuing trade and investment liberalization
and economic integration. What, if anything, can APEC do? And why
should APEC act rather than national governments or existing international organizations?

First, as a regional grouping of Pacific Rim nations, APEC represents
the optimal institutional response to regional-scale pollution and resource
management problems—no other forum covers all of the relevant actors in
this geographic space. Second, the environmental performance of national
governments and international organizations frequently falls so short of
the mark that APEC has an important role to play in strengthening the
results at other levels in the multitiered environmental governance structure. APEC's economic and political clout, its diverse membership, and
its flexible modes of decision making, in particular, create important
opportunities for intervention by APEC to compensate for deficiencies at
the local/national and global scales.

Thus, both economic theory and policymaking practice provide the logic
for an APEC environmental management program. But even if they did
not, market-driven economic integration across the Asia Pacific, together
with the decision to promote that integration through the APEC forum,
creates an imperative for environmental action. As we argue in this chapter,
economic integration cannot be sustained without attention to social
issues, including protection of the environment. Thus, the pattern of economic integration becomes an important factor in determining the appro-

priate level at which environmental issues should be addressed.[1] While the APEC "community" that currently exists is weak, deepening integration will, over time, fuel the process of community building and create an increasingly powerful need and basis for coordinating responses to environmental issues across APEC.

APEC'S Environmental "Value Added"

APEC members confront a wide spectrum of environmental problems at the local/national, regional, and global levels. The primary case for an APEC environment program lies in its capacity to respond to regional super externalities, including the depletion of Pacific fisheries, acid rain, pollution of shared air and watersheds, and destruction of the Pacific coastal habitat.

But serious institutional weaknesses in both national and global environmental programs create further opportunities—even requirements—for APEC.[2] More specifically, regional cooperation could reinforce environmental policymaking at the national level, where regulatory incapacity presents a serious obstacle to optimal environmental policymaking, particularly among APEC's developing countries. While increased wealth may, over time, reduce these shortcomings, the capacity-building process could be accelerated by APEC-level collaboration. Countries with more sophisticated regulatory regimes could help less-developed APEC members to overcome their technical and scientific limitations.

Among APEC's more-developed nations, cooperation on common environmental problems could save money and achieve economies of scale in environmental protection by dividing up the necessary analytic work and sharing data, science, risk assessments, cost-benefit analyses, and policy approaches. An APEC environmental program might also facilitate information exchanges between governments and nongovernmental organizations (which would help to enrich environmental policy debates) as well as between governments and the public (which would allow people to better understand environmental protection issues and options).

In addition, APEC might compensate for deep flaws in the global environmental management structure. While the structurally optimal response to problems at the worldwide scale would be the creation of a Global Environmental Organization (GEO), political obstacles make this institutional reform unlikely in the short term. Until such obstacles can be

---

1. In chapter 7, we develop a theory of *optimal environmental governance* that establishes guidelines for determining which jurisdictional level is best equipped to respond to a particular environmental issue.

2. In making up for deficiencies at other levels—national and global—APEC is, in the language of economists, a "second-best" institutional response.

overcome, APEC can act as an intermediate institution supporting better global environmental management. In particular, collective strategic interventions by APEC countries could "ratchet up" multilateral environmental efforts in much the same way that the organization has influenced multilateral trade efforts. APEC could also serve as a smaller-scale— 18-country—testing ground for future global collaborative environmental action. Moreover, regional environmental management could provide institutional structures that can both compensate for the absence or inefficacy of regulatory structures at the global level in the short run and provide institutional experience for new structures of global management in the long run. In addition, an APEC environmental regime might bring together countries that otherwise would not collaborate, most notably helping to bridge the North-South divide that is so troublesome in the international environmental domain.

Optimal Responses to Regional Harms

As we observed in chapter 4, environmental problems (or benefits) often span more than one political jurisdiction, and optimal environmental policy responses are thus unlikely to be adopted. Such structural mismatches explain, at least in part, the failure of efforts to respond to transboundary acid rain, depletion of Pacific fishery stocks, destruction of the marine ecosystem around the Pacific Rim, US-Canada competition for salmon, toxic contamination of the Great Lakes between the United States and Canada, and pollution of the Mekong River delta. In each of these cases, the incentive to disregard the costs and benefits that accrue to those beyond one's own constituency—the "super externality" problem—leads to inadequate regulation.

In a few instances, APEC neighbors have recognized their interdependence and have developed cooperative responses to regional environmental threats (UNESCAP 1995; Caldwell 1996; ASEAN 1992; Boer, Ramsay, and Rothwell 1997). The United States and Canada, for example, concluded an Acid Rain Treaty in 1991, albeit after a decade of bitter Canadian complaints about their acidified lakes and dying forests. The United States and Mexico have also developed a Border Environmental Plan. And while China continues to balk at suggestions that it is financially responsible for Japan and Korea's acid rain problems, Japan's payment for scrubbers on Chinese power plants has slowed the growth of acidic deposits in East Asia (Evans 1994).[3]

---

3. Japan has recently signed a bilateral agreement with China in which it undertakes to provide around $30 million in funding to abate environmental harms, including the SO_2 emissions that contribute to Japan's acid rain (*Asia Pulse*, 7 July 1997; BBC Summary of World Broadcasts, 2 July 1997).

Efforts to protect the coastal and marine environment in the region have also advanced slowly. The ASEAN countries adopted an action plan under the Regional Seas Program of the UN Environment Program (UNEP) in the early 1980s to promote marine protection in Southeast Asia. Australia, New Zealand, Papua New Guinea, and the South Pacific Islands have developed an action plan designed to protect coral reefs and fisheries off their coasts. In addition, APEC itself has made sustainability of the marine environment one of its priorities, although (as we discuss in chapter 8) little has been done to advance this concern.

Shared waterways and water resources have also been focal points for regional cooperation. For example, Thailand, Vietnam, and their neighbors have concluded an agreement on Cooperation for the Sustainable Development of the Mekong Basin. The bilateral International Joint Commission of the United States and Canada oversees transboundary environmental issues with special emphasis on the management of the international waterways of the Great Lakes.

The most comprehensive efforts to address regional environmental harms among APEC countries are those of NAFTA's members. The North American Commission for Environmental Cooperation (CEC), established under the Environmental Side Agreement to NAFTA, offers particular promise.[4] Notably, the NAFTA regime incorporates a number of important environmental innovations: a structured system of outreach to NGOs, an environment-oriented dispute settlement mechanism, and procedures to regularize meetings among environment ministers (P. Johnson and Beaulieu 1996).

Despite these modest successes in various corners of APEC, little concrete progress has been made in a number of important areas. For example, even though Japan is transferring pollution control technologies to Chinese power plants, acid rain continues to pour down across East Asia. Acid rain is also becoming a problem in Southeast Asia. On the marine front, although cooperative efforts under UNEP's Regional Seas Program are now well established, the joint activities have been primarily limited to assessment, monitoring, and planning (Caldwell 1996). Destruction of the coastal environment shows no sign of abating, and fishing stocks in many of the Pacific fisheries continue to decline precipitously.

The opportunity to tailor environmental policies to the appropriate geographic scale would be especially valuable in addressing the regional environmental problems described above. The challenge for APEC countries is to curb free-riding and cost-externalizing behavior. In this regard, efforts to clarify who holds the property rights to contested or common regional resources might return substantial dividends. APEC might, for example, develop a scheme of market-based tradable fishing rights that,

---

4. For a review of the CEC's trilateral environmental efforts, see its most recent annual report (1996). See also Executive Office of the President of the United States (1997).

by limiting the total oceanic fishing catch, could help to return the Pacific fisheries to sustainability.[5] It might also provide a mechanism to ensure that Malaysia, Singapore, Brunei, and the Philippines get compensation for the harms they have suffered from smoke caused by Indonesian forest fires, a problem especially in the summer of 1997. By developing a regime that governs regional pollution spillovers and common resource use, an APEC environmental program would help to build a base of environmental norms to guide the resolution of disputes involving transboundary harms.

We do not wish to overstate the importance of regional externalities in making our case for APEC involvement. The number of truly regional physical spillovers is limited. As a consequence, the argument for an APEC environmental regime depends, in part, on the effectiveness of regional environmental collaboration in improving both national responses to localized harms and international responses to global challenges.

The Regional Contribution to National Environmental Policymaking

An APEC environmental program offers the prospect of enhancing national environmental efforts and lowering regulatory costs in a variety of ways. Regional cooperation offers special promise for APEC's developing countries, which need to strengthen their environmental program to improve their performance. But even the APEC countries with sophisticated environmental regulatory regimes in place could benefit from regional collaboration.

Capacity Building

Many of APEC's less-developed countries have received, and continue to receive, significant support to build their institutional capacity for environmental protection. The Asian Development Bank, the UN Development Program, the UN Environment Program, the World Bank, the Global Environment Facility, other international bodies, and bilateral aid donors have all invested in capacity building. The Australian Agency for International Development, the Canadian International Development Agency, the Japan Fund for the Global Environment, and the United States-Asia Environmental Partnership are all engaged in environmental training and technology development on a bilateral basis. Many developed-country NGOs are also involved in capacity building. For example, the Japan Fund for the Global Environment reports that Japan-based NGOs are involved in over 50 environmental projects in APEC countries (personal communication with Tatsuya Eguchi, 19 March 1997). While valuable, these efforts are generally uncoordinated, unfocused, not comprehensive, and of limited scope. Hence they have failed to address the

---

5. See chapter 9 for a more detailed discussion of this potential initiative.

capacity-constraint problems of APEC's industrializing countries in a systematic fashion.

The existing efforts also suffer from other fundamental problems. First, in many cases, insufficient commitment by both host countries and donor agencies obstructs success (World Bank 1996c). Second, donors often dominate capacity-building efforts (Baser 1996), resulting in a lack of host country "ownership" of projects (Needham 1997). Third, pressure to show immediate results compromises the need to engage in long-term capacity building (P. Morgan and Qualman 1996). Fourth, there tends to be an overreliance on technical assistance without appropriate training of, and knowledge transfer to, local personnel.

While regional cooperation is not required to support Asia Pacific capacity building, APEC-level collaboration could deliver significant benefits (statement of Sidek Bin Saniff, Singaporean minister of the environment, 9 June 1997) and should be pursued on a voluntary basis.

The question, of course, is how APEC would succeed in capacity building where others have failed. First, as members of a nascent economic community, APEC members have an incentive to develop a shared capacity to address environmental problems. As we noted earlier, inadequate environmental programs in one or more countries within a trading relationship, especially when the countries are moving toward deep integration, can create competitiveness sensitivities and trigger welfare-reducing strategic behavior in environmental policymaking. In turn, the fear of regulatory races toward the bottom can chill enthusiasm for freer trade. Quite simply, the momentum for economic integration depends on all parties to the trade regime having functioning national environmental programs. APEC's trade and investment liberalization goals will therefore be considerably advanced by an appropriate program of environmental outreach. The consequences of not having such a program could be dramatic; without adequate environmental footings the APEC liberalization process may come to a point where it cannot proceed further without collapsing in rancor over tensions created by divergent environmental standards and values (see chapter 5).

Second, because APEC includes countries from the North and South, East and West, the potential for capacity "arbitrage"—in which experience about how to develop capable people and institutions, as well as an environment that supports better regulation, is transferred from developed to developing countries—will be great. Finally, APEC comes to the capacity-building challenge fresh. It can jettison past approaches that have failed and build on those that have worked.

Collaboration on Common Problems

Regional collaboration might also be attractive to APEC's more advanced members as a mechanism for cutting their environmental regulatory costs, especially because so many of the problems they face are common to most or all APEC countries (Esty 1994c). Because environmental policy-making is technically complex, there exist real economies of scale in regulatory activities (Kimber 1995). By avoiding needless duplication of technical tasks in every country, an APEC environmental program would allow regulators in APEC countries to spend scarce government resources more effectively. One such task is determining the safe level of pesticide residues in food, on which the United States spends more than $100 million per year (Esty 1994a); there are many other areas where a division of regulatory labor would be useful.[6]

While countries can—and usually do—undertake their own technical analysis and scientific work in relation to these issues, regional collaboration on common issues offers the prospect of both better and more cost-effective policymaking. At a time when budgets for environmental protection are limited, even shrinking, as governments try to rein in national deficits, countries should welcome the opportunity to streamline their regulatory programs through joint efforts.

Improving Information about Environmental Harms

Collaboration on common problems on the part of APEC countries would offer further benefits if it were accompanied by a standardized regionwide data collection and tracking program (UNESCAP 1995; Hammer and Shetty 1995). Improved communication is particularly important in the APEC context, where cultural and social diversity have traditionally limited information exchange and dialogue—especially between the Asian and Western members of APEC (Ryan 1997), and sometimes even among the Asian countries themselves (Funabashi 1995).[7]

Quite apart from the benefits of improving the data available to regulators, it is crucial that citizens across APEC be provided with information about the nature and extent of ecological and public health problems. As we saw in chapter 4, one of the major sources of suboptimal environmental policy in APEC countries is the failure of governments to reflect accurately the preferences of the citizenry. These public choice problems are partly caused by the absence of readily accessible environmental information, particularly among APEC's developing members. Environmental literacy varies widely across APEC. In Singapore, for example, depletion of

---

6. Collaboration on risk assessments need not result in each country adopting the same regulatory response or identical environmental standards. Richer countries can choose to put in place tougher standards than poorer nations. Not only would each APEC country be free to make its own political determination about how best to respond to harms analyzed jointly, but the policy design, implementation, and enforcement would remain the exclusive province of individual jurisdictions.

7. Information relevant to environmental problems should be regarded as a "public good" and thus made available to any country seeking environmental solutions.

the ozone layer topped the list of public concerns in a recent poll, while in China nearly half of the government officials and business people recently surveyed did not even know what the ozone layer was (UNESCAP 1995, 574).

Many of these problems could be addressed if APEC were to develop a program to monitor local/national, regional, and global environmental "indicators."[8] Such a program would provide visible benchmarks for gauging progress in pollution prevention and control, as well as in resource management. The ready availability of comparable cross-country data would highlight weak environmental performance and might shame governments into implementing policies that are more ecologically friendly and reflect public preferences. This initiative would also provide citizens across the Asia Pacific region with the kind of information they need to reach a deeper understanding of environmental issues and to judge the relative performance of their own governments.[9]

Global Gains from Regional Management

The global environmental regime is deeply flawed (Hurrell and Kingsbury 1992; Haas, Keohane, and Levy 1993; Victor, Raustiala, and Skolnikoff 1997).[10] The UN Environment Program (UNEP), lacking political and financial support and hobbled by its location in Nairobi, verges on collapse. Global environmental management thus falls to a tangled web of UN bodies,[11] ad hoc commissions, individual treaty secretariats, and multilateral funding agencies.

This haphazard structure produces poor results. First, despite the considerable number of international institutions, many serious problems get little or no attention—and certainly nowhere near the level of policy focus needed to fully internalize environmental costs and benefits. Second,

---

8. Environmental indicators are quantitative or qualitative measures of environmental performance that can be tracked over time (Hammond et al. 1995).

9. Of course, a well-informed public is only the first step toward better environmental policies. Minimizing public choice distortions ultimately requires functioning democracies, representative governments, and far-reaching political reforms to combat special interest manipulation of the political process—changes that fall outside the ambit of a narrowly tailored agenda of regional environmental management.

10. In a recent report, UNEP itself concluded that "global governance structures and global environmental solidarity remain too weak to make progress a world-wide reality. . . . The gap between what has been done thus far and what is realistically needed is widening" (UNEP 1997).

11. In addition to UNEP, the UN Development Program (UNDP), the Commission on Sustainable Development (CSD), the UN Food and Agriculture Organization (FAO), the World Health Organization (WHO), and the International Atomic Energy Agency (IAEA), among others, all claim parts of the international environmental mandate.

because the roles and responsibilities of the existing international institutions are not clearly defined, there is widespread duplication of efforts. The issue of "trade and the environment," for example, highlights the problem of overlapping mandates. UNEP, the Commission on Sustainable Development (CSD), the Organization for Economic Cooperation and Development (OECD), the UN Conference on Trade and Development (UNCTAD), and the World Trade Organization's (WTO) Committee on Trade and the Environment (CTE) all have "trade and environment" programs. Coordination across these bodies has been minimal and tensions among them have been high, thereby limiting policy progress. On the issue of climate change, the same story emerges: work is being done by the OECD, UNEP, the World Bank, the Intergovernmental Panel on Climate Change (IPCC), and the Climate Change Treaty Secretariat. With so many competing and clashing groups and interests, the whole that emerges is much less than the sum of its parts.

Another structural flaw arises from the ambiguous mandates given to various international environmental bodies. Because of the diversity of views across the international scene, the lack of seriousness of many countries with regard to transboundary harms, and the capability of laggards (the least-committed nations) to determine the level of action (Susskind 1994),[12] progress is slow on many issues and nonexistent on even more.

Third, there is a lack of coordination among the existing international bodies, exacerbated by their geographic spread around the globe. UNEP is located in Nairobi, the World Bank in Washington, the UN Development Program (UNDP) in New York, UNCTAD in Geneva, the Climate Change Treaty Secretariat in Bonn, and the Vienna Convention on Ozone-Depleting Substances Secretariat in Montreal. Coordination is made more difficult by the fact that these bodies are fiercely protective of their regulatory turf and have often been unable to work efficiently and effectively toward common goals (Keohane 1996). Disputes among the World Bank, UNDP, UNEP, and other stakeholders, for example, have hampered the operation of the Global Environment Facility (GEF) and nearly led to its collapse at the time of the Rio Earth Summit (Fairman and Ross 1996). More broadly, the various components of the international environmental regime fail to compare harms, set common priorities, coordinate efforts, rationalize budgets, and consequently achieve the greatest result at the lowest cost.

Finally, the ad hoc, case-by-case approach to global environmental problem solving squanders the limited political capital available to address transboundary pollution and resource issues. Each new multilateral effort con-

---

12. Multilateral action generally requires "consensus," which often gets translated into a demand for unanimous support. Thus, agreements tend to be watered down and their language left vague.

sumes enormous amounts of time and energy in initial negotiation—to get agreement on the scope and nature of the problem, determine what action is required, identify who will act, and settle on who will pay. Thus, precious little political capital remains to implement, enforce, and evaluate outcomes.

The logical response to the inefficiency and ineffectiveness of current international environmental management efforts would be the creation of an umbrella Global Environmental Organization (Esty 1994a; 1994c; 1997c). But creation of a GEO does not seem politically feasible, at least in the short to medium term.[13] Without a major trauma to highlight the world's ecological interdependence and the need for a new institutional regime to govern global environmental issues,[14] fears about the loss of sovereignty to a global environmental agency and doubts about the wisdom of creating a new international body—at a time when so many international organizations are performing poorly—override the logic of a comprehensive and coherent international environmental management structure.

Given the dim prospects for reform at the global level, APEC offers a compensating mechanism to improve international environmental policy outcomes. In some respects, an APEC environmental program could substitute for the missing global regime. The invaluable experience it could provide in collaborating on a supranational level would also reassure skeptics and thus facilitate development of a GEO down the road.

"Ratcheting Up" Multilateral Efforts

By acting in a coordinated fashion, the APEC countries may be able to change the dynamics of multilateral environmental negotiations. Both theory and practice demonstrate that changing coalitions or introducing new ones can alter negotiated outcomes (Dixit and Nalebuff 1991). Because APEC represents a broad coalition of countries—diverse from the standpoints of both culture and of economic development—the likelihood of hitting on new approaches or unanticipated ways to make progress is heightened.[15] Moreover, any common position would carry great weight in international policy debates. In short, APEC's involvement in the international arena can "change the game" (Brandenburg and Nalebuff 1996).

---

13. Although Germany, Brazil, Singapore, and South Africa proposed the creation of an overarching international environmental body (*Wall Street Journal*, European ed., 20 June 1997) at the June 1997 "Rio + 5" meetings at the United Nations, a GEO still seems some years off.

14. The world community came to grips with its economic interdependence only after the Great Depression and World War II dramatically illustrated the world's economic connectedness and the need for cooperation on a global scale—catalyzing the creation of the Bretton Woods economic institutions.

15. Of course, this same diversity makes agreement on a unified APEC position potentially difficult to achieve.

APEC's ability to shape international economic negotiations has already been demonstrated. The implicit threat that emanated from the 1994 APEC Summit in Seattle, of advancing trade liberalization within APEC independent of progress on the multilateral front, provided the impetus to bring the Uruguay Round of global trade negotiations to a close. By sending a message to recalcitrant European countries that freer trade within APEC represented a feasible alternative to more open global markets, the APEC leaders helped to ensure that the GATT talks would not fail (Bergsten 1994). Indeed, after the completion of the Uruguay Round, German GATT negotiator Lorenz Schomerus acknowledged: "The chief determinant of the successful conclusion of the Uruguay Round was the APEC summit in Seattle; they sent us a clear message" (quoted in Funabashi 1995, 107). Similarly, the groundwork laid at the Subic Bay APEC Economic Leaders' Summit in November of 1996 helped pave the way for an agreement to remove barriers to trade in information technology products at the WTO Ministerial Conference in Singapore the next month.[16]

There exist similar opportunities for APEC to intervene strategically in multilateral environmental efforts. In fact, some of the biggest opportunities to protect the environment are grounded in a reduction in trade barriers and protection. For example, if APEC made a commitment to reduce agricultural protectionism—eliminating export subsidies, domestic price supports, import restrictions, and unjustified sanitary and phytosanitary standards—the upcoming WTO negotiations on agriculture might be affected dramatically. Just as the intervention of the 14-member Cairns Group during the Uruguay Round arguably contributed to the significant reforms in agricultural protection (Schott 1994), APEC could spur a new round of agricultural trade liberalization.

The reduction of energy subsidies presents another opportunity both to improve allocative efficiency and to ameliorate the harmful pollution effects of excessive subsidy-induced consumption of fossil fuels (World Bank 1997). APEC action could jump-start multilateral efforts to reduce these subsidies. As with agricultural trade liberalization, such reduction would yield both economic and environmental benefits (K. Anderson 1992; Charnovitz 1996a).

---

16. The opportunities for APEC to "ratchet up" the process of trade and investment liberalization have not yet been exhausted. APEC countries have also expressed a desire to reach agreement on issues that have not yet been satisfactorily resolved at the multilateral level, such as antidumping policy, or that have not even been discussed, including competition and antitrust policy. If such agreements can be reached among APEC countries, they could be presented to WTO members for global adoption (APEC 1994b; Bergsten 1994). In the trade arena, at least, commentators have concluded that APEC fills the gap in "intra-state architecture between the global system represented by the General Agreement on Trade and Tariffs (GATT) and the network of bilateral relationships" (Clarke 1995). And Renato Ruggiero, WTO director, recently noted that APEC could increase the WTO's effectiveness through economic negotiations at the regional level (WTO, press release, 12 May 1997).

APEC might also ratchet up multilateral efforts to combat climate change. If APEC, representing a diverse group of developed and developing countries and a number of the pivotal states on this issue, could achieve consensus on an appropriate path toward reducing greenhouse gas emissions, an important foundation for advancing the issue on the worldwide level would have been laid.[17]

APEC as a Laboratory for Experimentation

An APEC environmental forum could also act as a testing ground for future multilateral environmental policy mechanisms. While the benefits of smaller-scale experimentation have been given great weight in the context of federal systems—for example, in the United States, Australia, and Canada—comparatively little attention has been paid to the potential for regional institutional structures to serve as laboratories for various international environmental strategies.[18]

APEC might also become the comprehensive testing ground for "joint implementation" (JI) projects,[19] bringing developed and developing countries together in common efforts to mitigate climate change. APEC would be a particularly useful venue to test JI since its members include many countries that favor the use of JI, including the United States, Canada, and Australia, together with those countries that are more hesitant, including China, Malaysia, and Indonesia.[20] Success with JI projects at a regional level would boost confidence in this mechanism as a cost-effective approach to addressing climate change at the global scale.

APEC could also work to reduce pressures for a "race toward the bottom" in environmental standards and address fears that developing-country access to developed-country markets will be limited by the latters'

---

17. APEC need not act as a formal environmental negotiating bloc or caucus, but rather as a forum available to test and refine possible approaches. And, of course, APEC need not intervene where multilateral efforts have been fruitful, as in the case of the Montreal Protocol. APEC's value will emerge when multilateral efforts have stalled or are inadequate.

18. The value of regional experimentation in the economic realm is well understood. Both the US-Canada and Australia-New Zealand free trade agreements, for example, helped to define the baseline for liberalized trade in services provisions that were incorporated into the Uruguay Round GATT negotiations (Schott 1994). Similarly, the NAFTA investment chapter was used as a precedent for the development of APEC's nonbinding investment code; it is also serving as a model for the OECD's Multilateral Agreement on Investment.

19. Joint implementation entails developed countries paying for emissions reductions in developing countries—where per unit emissions reductions are likely to come most cheaply—and receiving credit toward their own emissions reduction obligations.

20. JI is contentious because of the equity and sovereignty concerns it raises. From an equity perspective, JI is said to be unfair because it allows developed countries to buy their way out of taking domestic measures to mitigate climate change. The sovereignty issue arises from a fear that JI will allow developed countries to influence development patterns in less-developed nations.

strict regulations. Since these issues could become flash points at the multilateral level as well as within APEC (Runnalls 1997), APEC could test various approaches to defusing these tensions such as "harmonized" product and process standards or environmental dispute settlement procedures.

Experience for Future Global Governance

Regional environmental management can, in the short run, compensate for deficiencies in global environment management structures; in the long run, it can provide institutional experience to help ensure that future global institutions are properly structured and efficiently operated. In this regard, APEC can serve an instrumental purpose, as an intermediate institution on the path to an optimal multitiered environmental governance structure.

Some of the areas in which APEC's involvement might yield benefits include the creation of dispute settlement procedures sensitive to environmental concerns, the development of legal norms and mechanisms to govern transboundary harms, and the identification of ways to accommodate the participation of nongovernmental actors in supranational environmental management.

"Engagement" Benefits

Another virtue of APEC is that it brings together countries that are on opposite sides of the North-South environmental divide. The gulf between the developing South and the developed North has often looked unbridgeable. Progress on international environmental issues has been particularly slow in the wake of the 1992 Rio Earth Summit, at which North-South tensions produced an unfocused and unactionable document—Agenda 21—and little in the way of a concrete action plan for sustainable development (Esty 1993a). Because developing nations face pressing local and national public health and ecological problems—including threats to food security, inadequate drinking water supplies, lack of sanitation systems, and polluted airsheds—while industrialized countries give greater priority to longer-term and more diffuse harms—such as ozone layer depletion and climate change—regional environmental management in APEC provides a mechanism to accommodate the different priorities of its members and to address localized environmental harms and transboundary issues simultaneously. In fact, the progress made in the trade realm in the face of serious obstacles augers well for APEC's fashioning a common position on critical environmental issues.

In addition to the general opportunity to close the North-South environmental gap, APEC specifically offers an opportunity to engage China in constructive diplomacy (Funabashi 1995). Indeed, the environment provides an especially promising issue on which to practice cooperation.

APEC furthermore counts among its members a number of the pivotal environmental states—the United States, China, Indonesia, Mexico, and Japan—whose performance will profoundly shape the world's ecological future and whose leadership will be critical to efforts to manage the regional and global environment (Esty 1998). APEC also includes Malaysia, Thailand, and Singapore, countries whose concerns about the neocolonial "environmental imperialism" of the North have been a source of particular tension in recent international environmental dialogues.

On a broader level, a unique form of international dialogue is evolving within APEC—what Funabashi (1995) calls the "APEC way." It resembles neither the traditional Western policy process, characterized by formalism and legalism, nor the traditional Eastern way, characterized by flexibility, consensus, and personal relationships. Instead, the APEC way is an amalgam of the two modes of interaction, which may be especially valuable in providing a way forward on seemingly intractable international environmental issues.

Environmental Underpinnings for APEC Economic Integration

Apart from APEC's specific ability to optimally respond to regional-scale harms and to act as a "second-best" institutional response, thus compensating for deficiencies at the local and global scales, over time stronger coordination on environmental issues will be needed over time to provide support for deepening economic integration. Specifically, the success of efforts to keep APEC markets open (let alone open them further) cannot be guaranteed without attention to the environmental content of intra-APEC trade.

Environmental issues are important in the trade arena, not just because of their economic impacts but because trade goals are not—and cannot be—pursued in isolation from other policy aims, including environmental aspirations. The public insists that transactions and trade occur within boundaries defined by shared values (Rodrik 1997). Interest in social arrangements—including environmental rules that undergird the market—exists in all APEC countries, although wealthier publics clearly can better afford to voice their moral concerns.

Americans, in particular, have never defined themselves as purely economic beings. They find the prospect of cheaper goods through trade attractive, but not at the expense of moral principle. Thus, more than many nations, the United States has shown a willingness to forgo the benefits of international trade when the public believes that a moral issue is at stake.[21] The ongoing debates over whether to grant China most favored

---

21. In addition to concerns about environmental values, pressures for commitments to basic human rights and baseline labor standards are also likely to grow as the pace of economic integration quickens.

nation (MFN) status in the wake of human rights abuses represents one manifestation of this sentiment.

Americans are often willing to press their ethical stand even when it is unclear that doing so will improve the situation (Srinivasan 1995). While some observers suggest that this behavior is actually motivated by protectionist inclinations (Bhagwati 1993a), others recognize that the willingness to forgo trade derives, at least partially, from sincere moral beliefs. As Rodrik (1997, 33) observes in commenting on the "new" agenda for trade policy in general and the push for environmental conditions in particular: "it would be a mistake not to recognize that [these demands] reflect genuine discomfort in the importing countries with the moral or social implications of trade."[22] There is little doubt, for example, that the outrage across the United States about the dolphin deaths caused by Mexican tuna-fishing practices was *not* motivated by a desire to help competing US fishermen.[23] It reflected a genuine desire to see dolphins protected.

As trade expert Gary Hufbauer (1989, 73) notes, "Trade policy has never been pursued with single-minded attention to economic gain." And even the GATT recognizes that some foundations for trade would be unacceptable. Notably, GATT Article XX(e) permits countries to ban or restrict imports that are the product of prison or slave labor.

Every nation restricts the operation of certain markets and blocks some economic transactions as unacceptable (Walzer 1983; Rodrik 1997, 35). Some societies limit very little. Others proscribe much more. In determining the boundaries of "blocked exchanges," communities establish the baseline obligations of membership and, in so doing, define themselves. Free trade cannot be sustained in a context of serious disagreement over what is in bounds and what is out.

Jurisdictions that believe that the actions of their trade partners have dipped below community-determined minimum standards might not be able to maintain their commitments to freer trade. The dynamic that demands political integration (and the creation of ethical standards for trade) alongside economic integration can be seen at work in every deeply integrated free trade area. When the states of the American union consoli-

---

22. Alan Krueger's (1996) analysis of recent US child labor legislation, which seeks to ban the importation of goods made with child labor, supports Rodrik's claim. Indeed, Krueger found that the sponsors of the 1996 Child Labor Deterrence Act in the US Congress came disproportionately from districts with high-skill labor, not the low-skill labor most likely to benefit from legislation constructed with protectionist intent.

23. Obviously, in some cases, the motives for pushing an environmental agenda will be mixed. The US Corporate Average Fuel Economy (CAFE) requirements, for example, which set mileage standards for cars on the basis of each manufacturer's fleetwide average fuel efficiency, was adopted because it was perceived to be the policy approach to improving vehicle mileage that was least likely to hurt US car companies.

dated into a national market early in this century, powerful pressures to create minimum federal standards emerged. As President Franklin D. Roosevelt declared, in arguing for national labor standards in the United States: "Goods produced under conditions which do not meet a rudimentary standard of decency should be regarded as contraband and ought not to be allowed to pollute the channels of interstate trade" (quoted in Esty 1994a, 166). The European Union today faces similar pressures—and is responding with a comparable set of EU-wide "directives" that establish baseline standards for all members.[24]

APEC may not yet be at the point where the level of economic integration it has achieved demands greater noneconomic (including environmental) integration. But that point will come, and the fundamental disconnect between the APEC vision of ever-deepening economic integration and the reality of limited parallel noneconomic coordination will soon loom large.[25] If the APEC nations are serious about their economic goals, they must become more serious about their environmental commitments—and the need for building community around a set of common values.

Objections to APEC Environmental Management

Although the logic of managing some environmental programs at the APEC level appears strong, skeptics may still voice doubts. Wouldn't an APEC environmental regime entail a loss of national sovereignty? They might also ask why a management structure is needed at all, when issues could be dealt with on an ad hoc basis. And given that a number of functions we envisage for APEC could be performed by a reformed or reconstituted global management structure, why not direct attention to that end? Moreover, if regional environmental cooperation is desired, why is APEC the appropriate level of aggregation? Why not pursue environmental goals through subregions such as ASEAN, Australia–New Zealand Closer Economic Relations (ANZCER), and NAFTA? And there will undoubtedly be objections that an APEC environmental program will move political decision making further away from the citizenry, as well as worries about creating a large APEC bureaucracy to administer an APEC environment program.

---

24. As Sapir (1996) stresses, the harmonization of policies represents a core dimension of the compact on which the European Union rests.

25. We are not suggesting that APEC economic integration needs to be accompanied (at this time) by the development of political institutions à la European Union, but simply that parallel attention needs to be paid to noneconomic issues.

Loss of National Sovereignty

Regional environmental management need not entail a loss of national sovereignty.[26] The structures we propose as responses to transboundary harms might appear to violate the principle of territorial sovereignty, but, in fact, it is the harms themselves that spill across borders and compromise territorial sovereignty, not the creation of mechanisms to respond to them. Ecological interdependence is a fact of life on this planet. Pronouncements in defense of national sovereignty do not stop pollutants at the border.

A further dimension of the sovereignty concern arises from the prospect that an APEC environmental program might impinge on the freedom of domestic regulators, including environmental officials, to set the standards and promulgate the policies they deem appropriate.[27] To some extent this fear is well-founded. But the payback for coordinating policies at the regional level—economic welfare gains on the order of tens of billions of dollars—is considerable. In short, if countries expect to get the full spectrum of benefits from economic integration, they have to be prepared to pay a modest price in supranational collaboration.

The Sufficiency of Ad Hoc Management

The most pointed criticisms of an expanded APEC environmental program derive from the suggestion that it is not needed. Why not handle regional resource and pollution issues on an ad hoc basis as they arise, involving only those whose interests are at stake? The answer is simple: ad hoc solutions are inefficient and do not work.

Notwithstanding Coase's theorem (1960), which suggests that a small number of parties can negotiate the internalization of externalities in a manner that will lead to economically efficient outcomes, environmental experience teaches otherwise. Korea has gotten no satisfaction from China in response to its entreaties for reduced SO_2 emissions. Pacific fisheries continue to fall precipitously despite regional seas agreements. The United States and Canada have been unable to reach agreement on quotas for Pacific salmon fishing.[28] South Korea and Japan remain at loggerheads

---

26. A number of aspects of the concerns about losing sovereignty are considered in chapter 5, which examines the many tensions at the economy-environment interface.

27. Efforts to set baseline, harmonized, or tiered environmental standards, for example, place limits on domestic policy-setting freedoms. Similarly, pressure to eliminate subsidies might be viewed as an incursion into domestic power to determine redistributive policies.

28. Tensions are running so high that Canadian fisherman blockaded an American passenger ferry in the Canadian port of Prince Rupert for three days in July 1997. The Canadians are upset that American fishermen, looking to catch Alaskan pink salmon, also "accidentally" caught 320,000 Canadian sockeye salmon, thrice the usual incidental catch. For their part, American fishermen believe that they have exercised incredible restraint at a time when treaty negotiations have stalled (*Los Angeles Times*, 30 July 1997; *New York Times*, 24

over fishing treaty negotiations (*Korea Times*, 24 July 1997; *Korea Herald*, 5 August 1997). And disputes among China, Taiwan, and Vietnam have prevented the successful conclusion of such an agreement for the South China Sea. The difficulty in reaching accords, even among small numbers of parties, highlights the need to clarify property rights and establish environmental norms to deal with transboundary regional harms.

Even when Coasean solutions can be found, as exemplified by Japan's side payments to China to subsidize scrubbers on Chinese coal-burning power plants, the outcome may be morally, if not economically, suboptimal. The Japanese payments to China, for example, violate the "polluter pays" principle to which APEC countries have committed themselves. Broader resort to "victim pays" solutions might well be seen as unfair by those asked to fund responses to harms that they did not cause.

Furthermore, Coasean bargaining works only when transactions costs are low. But uncertainties about the relevant property rights, disputes over the extent of externalities, and strategic behavior to avoid liability mean that transactions costs are rarely low. Finding solutions will often be complicated, moreover, by the very nature of government-to-government negotiations, which are frequently undertaken on behalf of hundreds or thousands of enterprises whose interests must be reconciled and whose ultimate compliance with any agreement often cannot be taken for granted. Causal complexities and scientific uncertainties further raise transactions costs, meaning that such costs will never be low in the environmental realm; they are especially likely to be high in the context of transboundary harms. Indeed, the reason why regulation is needed in the environmental domain in the first place—to correct market failures—explains why ad hoc intervention does not work well.

Skeptics might conclude that weak performance is a lesser evil than having a heavy-handed APEC environmental protection agency. But the alternative to inadequate national policies need not be an intrusive regional-scale environmental bureaucracy. A carefully tailored program of regional environmental "governance" aimed at ensuring a more systematic response to transboundary harms and more efficient national policy activities offers great promise.

Regional versus Global Management

Arguably, some of the tasks we propose for APEC—capacity building and attention to regional harms—might also be taken up by global institutions. There is little reason, however, to be optimistic about the likelihood that the existing ad hoc international management structure will adequately address these tasks. A newly constituted Global Environmental

---

July 1997). Of course, the problem here arises in part because many entities and individuals are involved, not just two governments.

Organization would be well placed to strengthen capacity in developing countries and would be of a scale large enough to ensure that all of the costs and benefits of regional resource use and pollution activities were appropriately incorporated into the policymaking calculus. But, as we noted above, the creation of a GEO faces significant hurdles, which is precisely why APEC can make a contribution to global environmental initiatives—ratcheting up multilateral efforts, acting as a venue for testing ideas, and developing structures to compensate for the inefficacy of global management.

There are a number of reasons, independent of the political infeasibility of global structures, why taking regional action on some environmental issues makes more sense than leaving them to the global arena. A forum such as APEC is more or less representative of the global community but smaller and therefore easier to manage; it can thus more easily pilot important policy and institutional initiatives.

APEC also provides—from a game theory perspective—a better setting for negotiations on global issues than a plenary world forum. Having only 18 parties at the table is far more conducive to constructive discussions than the nearly 200 countries that sometimes participate in multilateral talks. It is well understood that the more players there are in a game framework, the more confusing the menu of available actions, the more unpredictable the payoffs, and the smaller the zone of agreement (Dixit and Nalebuff 1991).[29]

Finally, given that the objective of APEC members is to form an Asia Pacific "community"—albeit with a small "c"—the incentive to make progress on important environmental issues both to improve regional welfare and to undergird continuing economic integration is greater than at the global level. APEC's members share both an ecological interconnectedness and an economic interdependence, which together are more likely to catalyze progress on environmental issues than are the weaker bonds that exist at the global level.

Appropriate Level of Regional Aggregation

Situating responsibility for all environmental issues in existing regional structures—ANZCER, ASEAN, NAFTA, or other less formal subregional groups—promises suboptimal results. There are several reasons why situating some responsibility for environmental management at the APEC level makes sense. First, to the extent that certain problems, such as the

---

29. We are not making the claim that multilateral negotiations require the agreement of all participants, since success frequently hinges on the agreement of a limited number of key countries and coalitions. However, just as this applies at the global level, it also applies within APEC; arguably, the agreement of only five or six key nations is required to precipitate broader agreement within the whole of APEC.

depletion of regional fishing stocks, are truly transpacific in scope, APEC represents the best structural match. Other regional environmental problems, including acid rain and problems relating to shared coastal zones, that involve a subset of APEC countries might be dealt with on a subregional level. However, with the possible exception of the North American CEC in dealing with US-Mexico border issues, most subregional harms have been poorly addressed by existing subregional organizations,[30] a failure that creates an argument for APEC involvement.

Important benefits would be derived, moreover, by having one forum deal with the full range of regional and subregional transboundary issues. In particular, it makes sense to apply common norms and principles when seeking solutions to transboundary issues, rather than to have each issue resolved using different guidelines. A common approach holds out the prospect of an evolving framework of norms and principles that can not only be applied to future regional issues, but can serve as the foundation for the development of customary international law with respect to transboundary spillovers.

Second, the derivative environmental management functions we have proposed for APEC in this chapter—reinforcing efforts at the national and global levels—are better handled at the broader APEC scale than by subregions. It would not be optimal, for example, to leave capacity building to ASEAN, because none of ASEAN's members have environmental programs that are sufficiently advanced to offer the significant capacity improvements that Australia, Canada, Japan, or the United States can. Similarly, if efforts are to be made to ratchet up environmental efforts at the multilateral level, APEC, with its economic size and political muscle, is best positioned to do so. The nations of ASEAN, or even NAFTA, could hardly be expected, for example, to advance subsidy reform on their own.

Third, APEC—by virtue of its diverse membership—represents a microcosm of the global community in a way that other regional groupings do not. As a consequence, any results it achieves are more likely to be transferable to the multilateral level. Indeed, with its blend of Confucian, Islamic, Japanese, Western, and Latin American cultures, APEC covers at least five of Samuel Huntington's (1994) "civilizations." And as we have noted, APEC's membership cuts across the North-South fault line, with member countries that span the economic development spectrum, from per capita incomes of less than $1,000 to over $30,000.

Fourth, APEC is more flexible than other regional groupings. APEC initiatives can be pursued either with the agreement of all 18 members or by some subset of members[31] appropriate to the issue or willing to proceed at a particular point in time.

---

30. As we discussed above, ad hoc attention among the affected parties to problems of regional acid rain and of managing the South China Sea has not been successful.

31. Cases in which just a few members decide not to endorse an APEC agreement have become known as taking the "18-x" approach, with the "18" signifying full membership. The Information Technology Agreement concluded in Manila in 1996 is an example of such

Finally, APEC can provide a neutral forum, with a broad range of outside arbiters, when two or more countries find themselves in an intractable dispute. US-Canada salmon-fishing tensions, for example, have not been successfully dealt with bilaterally or within the NAFTA context. APEC might offer a venue more conducive to working through the issues, making available other countries to mediate the dispute.[32]

Moving Decision Making away from Citizenry

APEC-scale environmental management undeniably moves decision making farther away from the citizenry. Centralized policymaking, because it increases distance, always entails some loss in direct political participation.

The establishment of regional (and ultimately global) governance structures can be seen as the price that must be paid for trade and investment liberalization. Economic integration requires some environmental decision making at the scale at which trade takes place. But it is possible to minimize the public distance from political decisions through procedures to encourage NGO participation in the policy development process. Specifically, NGOs can play a very useful role in ensuring that grassroots opinions are effectively communicated to distant decision makers, such as APEC leaders. They can also transmit and explain the results of decisions made at centralized levels back to the widely dispersed citizens. NGOs can, in effect, act as the connective tissue between citizens and new forms and levels of governance.

Growing Bureaucracy

For many, the greatest fear is that of a large APEC environmental agency. But from the start, APEC's members have steered away from the EU-style bureaucracy that has developed to support the single market and the European Union's regional administrative, political, and judicial infrastructure. In its 1994 report to ministers, the APEC Eminent Persons Group

---

an agreement. Alternatively, sometimes just a few countries will decide to pursue a given proposal. The APEC "business visa" arrangement, for example, involves only Australia, the Philippines, and South Korea.

32. Just as negotiating among APEC's 18 members offers advantages over a 200-party negotiation, resolving disputes involving, say, two parties within the APEC forum offers benefits. As we noted above, small numbers of parties frequently fail to reach Coasean solutions. In these cases, dispute resolution *within* APEC offers substantial promise—pressure from peers in the forum, together with the consistent application of mutually agreed-on norms for transboundary environmental disputes, increases the likelihood that parties who could not agree on their own, or in a subregional framework, may be able to do so within APEC.

was at pains to point out that they were "not proposing creation of another . . . EU" (APEC 1994b, 53).

Environmental governance within APEC does not necessitate a big bureaucracy. NAFTA's Commission for Environmental Cooperation, with its staff of two dozen, provides a valuable model of how a lean organization can manage a quite far-reaching program of regional cooperation. Similarly, the OECD's Environment Directorate, with a comparatively small staff of 60, has helped to develop environmental norms and guidelines such as the polluter pays principle (OECD 1975) and to harmonize standards in realms such as chemicals regulation. It has also supported policy and technology exchange.

Conclusion

APEC has an indispensable role to play in abating direct harms to the environment, ensuring the integrity of the international economic system, and reducing tensions at the economy-environment interface that threaten the organization's commitment to trade and investment liberalization. By virtue of its geographic scope there will be some regional issues for which APEC represents the theoretically optimal government response level. In other cases, deficiencies at the national and global levels make APEC action the best practical alternative—better, in particular, than continued substandard efforts or inaction.

- APEC, more than any other institution, is *optimally* situated to facilitate the internalization of externalities and the management of resources at the regional level.

- APEC can make unique contributions to issues that theoretically should be dealt with at the national and global levels but that, because of practical and political constraints, have received insufficient and unsatisfactory attention. In this regard, APEC represents a valuable *second-best* response.
  - APEC can improve environmental policymaking at the *national level* by (1) helping its less-developed members overcome regulatory capacity constrains, (2) encouraging its members to collaborate on common environmental problems, and (3) sharing important environmental information among governments, NGOs, and the public.
  - APEC can address shortcomings at the *global level* by (1) improving on poor multilateral results through strategic interventions that employ its economic and political muscle, (2) acting as a testing ground for future global initiatives, and (3) taking the initiative to establish structures of its own to compensate for absent or deficient structures at the worldwide scale.

It is essential to pursue the above environmental management functions now and to strengthen environmental coordination over time. In helping to ensure that the environmental consequences of growth are being addressed locally/nationally, regionally, and globally, and by finding ways to defuse tensions between economic and environmental policies, APEC can contribute to building a true Asia Pacific community that will allow the process of economic integration to continue.

7

Toward Optimal Environmental Governance

Underlying the analysis in the previous chapter are two fundamental issues that go to the heart of environmental governance. How do we determine what is the appropriate level of government to respond to various environmental issues? This is the *jurisdictional question*. And how do we overcome regulatory failures and political constraints to optimize the performance of each level of government? This is the *policy optimization question*. In this chapter, we step back from an APEC focus to examine these questions broadly and to develop a generalized theory of optimal environmental governance.

The economics literature provides a ready answer to the jurisdictional question: to ensure optimal investment in a collective good such as environmental protection, political boundaries must be coterminous with the scope of the public good. In other words, the scope of a regulating government's authority or jurisdiction must match the scope of the externality that it seeks to address. In the case of physical pollution spillovers, the implications of this "matching principle" are quite straightforward.

Economic interdependence, however, complicates the issue of selecting and defining the optimal jurisdiction, since trade and investment linkages can lead to behavior that may have no physical spillover effects but does have real economic or psychological impacts on out-of-jurisdiction citizens. And the deeper the integration, the greater the exposure to economic and psychological spillovers—and thus the more intense the pressure to attend to these nonphysical externalities.

In particular, as trade links broaden, countries become more sensitive to the competitiveness impacts of variations in environmental standards.[1] When the goods exchanged are valued at a few million dollars, the impact will be small, and the risk of serious economic spillovers or of triggering a race toward the bottom in environmental standards is similarly minimal. When the level of trade rises to the billion-dollar level, the impact of economic spillovers will be much greater, capturing political and public attention as well as heightening the concerns of domestic industry. Thus, little notice was given in the 1980s to Chinese exports to the United States. Today, with an annual flow of goods on the order of $40 billion (IMF, *Direction of Trade Statistics 1996*), considerable attention is paid to perceived "unfair" advantages enjoyed by Chinese firms, including those obtained through China's suboptimal environmental standards.

By bringing citizens of different countries into closer contact with one another, economic integration fuels demands to transform a purely economic community into something more—a political community in which occupants are expected to adhere to certain minimum standards. In other words, the formation of an economic community, as we explain below, will necessarily be followed by the development of a wider sense of community. How deep and broad the set of behavioral baselines will be and how far they move from being minimum standards toward higher ethical aspirations will be determined by the depth and strength of the community in question, which is in turn partly a function of the breadth of the relevant economic ties.

Even if all environmental issues are appropriately allocated among the various jurisdictional levels, systemic regulatory failures and political constraints can lead to suboptimal environmental governance. We thus argue for a system of checks and balances that minimizes these welfare losses. In particular, we conceive of environmental governance as a system in which a range of actors—both governmental and nongovernmental—cooperate and compete, both vertically and horizontally, to sharpen the performance at each policymaking level.

As the discussion below shows, our two key questions—that of jurisdictional allocation and optimal governance strategies—are not distinct inquiries, to be undertaken one after the other, but are related and must be pursued in concert. Gaps at one level can be compensated for at another. Moreover, they are ongoing inquiries; evolution in capacity and

---

1. As we discuss in detail below, low environmental standards do not necessarily represent an unfair competitive advantage. In some cases, differences in circumstances—climate, geography, population density, income levels, etc.—justify less-stringent regulation, and the lower standards will be a legitimate dimension of comparative advantage. But in other circumstances, the standards chosen may not match public environmental preferences or may fail to internalize transboundary spillovers, in which case the lax requirements can be seen as inappropriate.

performance over time will make the optimal division of policymaking change across levels of government and among the actors at each level.

Jurisdictional Allocation

The issue of how to allocate responsibility for various environmental issues to jurisdictions at different geographic scales has received a great deal of attention in recent years at both the national level—especially in the United States,[2] Canada, and the Philippines—and at the supranational level, particularly within the European Union. In the United States, it has become fashionable to argue that authority over environmental regulation should be returned to the states in the name of "federalism" (Bill Clinton, State of the Union Address, 24 January 1995; Gingrich 1995, 9). In the European Union, localist opponents of environmental decision making in Brussels rally under the banner of "subsidiarity" (Kimber 1995; Lenaerts 1995). The common theme is support for decentralized environmental decision making, based on a belief that most environmental problems are local in scope and on a sense that political decisions made nearby are more likely to match citizen desires and thereby have greater legitimacy. But while such physical proximity to the citizenry is an important consideration in determining jurisdictional allocation, it cannot be the only factor. The jurisdictional allocation rule not only must respect the need for "proximity of government" (Lenaerts 1995) but also should minimize the welfare losses from environmental harms and regulatory failures (Esty 1996b).

The Dictates of Federalism and Subsidiarity

Far from supporting a simple presumption in favor of decentralization, a nuanced understanding of federalism and subsidiarity guides us to a more sophisticated jurisdictional allocation rule. Responsibility for environmental issues should be allocated on the basis of which level of governance is best equipped to address the issue in question.

As Elazar (1987, 5) observes, federalism involves the "linking of individuals, groups and polities in lasting but limited union in such a way as to provide for the energetic pursuit of common ends while maintaining the integrities of all parties." Federalism thus entails a combination of self-rule and shared rule. There are many types of "federal arrangements," reflecting a variety of ways to allocate power between the central government and state or provincial and local authorities (Elazar 1991). In Mexico,

---

2. Contributors to the environmental federalism debate in the United States include Fischel (1975), Stewart (1977), Gray (1983), Oates and Schwab (1988), Revesz (1992), Krier and Brownstein (1992), and Esty (1996b).

for example, the states hold very little power and almost all significant decisions (including the stringency of environmental standards) are made in Mexico City. But in Canada, the provinces retain considerable authority, making national initiatives difficult to execute. The United States falls somewhere between these two models. APEC itself is a federal structure, marked by especially loose ties and minimal power delegated to the center. Federalism is not—and should not be taken as—synonymous with decentralization. Instead, federal arrangements reflect the specific desires of constituent communities to share power among various levels of government.

Subsidiarity, a concept related to federalism, has been used in the European Union to settle jurisdictional questions, especially when Brussels and its members states have concurrent jurisdiction, as they do with respect to the environment (Trachtman 1992). Subsidiarity mandates that governmental action be taken at higher jurisdictional levels only if and insofar as the proposed objectives cannot be achieved by lower jurisdictional levels.[3] But subsidiarity, like federalism, should not be seen as a guarantee of proximity of government—and thus as mandating decentralization—in all situations; rather, its preference for proximity applies only in those cases in which situating power at a lower level of government does not compromise an effective policy response.

In the context of environmental policy, a general presumption in favor of decentralization is misplaced (Esty 1996b). The real implication of both federalism and the related concept of subsidiarity is that while we might have a political preference for allocating power over environmental issues to the lowest jurisdictional level, that should be understood as the lowest level that can appropriately address the mischief in question. And in some cases this means governance at higher jurisdictional levels, since the benefits of localized representation and governance will be overwhelmed by the need for effectiveness. In particular, as we saw in chapter 4, super externalities can be addressed only by intervention at an overarching level. Far from being inconsistent with either federalism or subsidiarity, the need for regional (and global) governance structures flows directly from the diversity of problems that must be addressed, some of which are supranational in scale.

The logic of regional environmental policymaking as the best way to overcome regulatory failures in some instances does not mean that public dissatisfaction with decision making at a distance should be ignored.

---

3. See, for example, Article 3b of the Treaty Establishing the European Community, as amended by the Treaty on European Union: "In areas which do not fall within its exclusive competence, the Community shall take action, in accordance with the principle of subsidiarity, only if and insofar as the objectives of the proposed action cannot be sufficiently achieved by the Member States and can therefore, by reason of the scale or effects of the proposed action, be better achieved by the Community."

On the contrary, whenever a highly centralized level of government is identified as optimal for a particular problem, there exists a special burden on officials at that level to be attentive to the need to communicate with the distant citizens in whose name they act.

Optimal Environmental Areas

For a jurisdictional response to be structurally adequate it must encompass all the cost bearers and beneficiaries of a resource use decision or environmental protection measure. When a jurisdictional response satisfies this criterion we say that it is the *optimal environmental area* (OEA). Which costs and benefits are salient can, however, be the source of considerable disagreement. In particular, do we look only at physical impacts, or are economic and psychological welfare effects also important?

Physical Super Externalities

The primary determinant of the scale of the OEA is the physical footprint of environmental harms and benefits. For example, the worldwide scale of the problem of climate change means that the globe is the appropriate OEA for dealing with it. Similarly, the depletion of fishing stocks in the Pacific is a problem of the regional commons, making the group of Asia Pacific nations the appropriate OEA to address the issue.

The need to take into account the full spectrum of physical costs and benefits to select the optimal policy jurisdiction—increasingly at higher jurisdictional levels, as our understanding of the broad reach of many environmental harms improves—is widely accepted (e.g., Farber 1996). The physicality of pollution spillovers and the tangibility of resulting harms to the environment and to public health create a strong public demand that such effects be factored into regulatory decisions. Economic theory, moreover, dictates that the scope of the governing jurisdiction match the scope of the physical costs and benefits of an environmental activity—be it resource use, pollution, or protection—to ensure allocative efficiency and optimal policy outcomes (Olson 1969; Baumol and Oates 1988).

Economic Externalities and Economic Integration

There is significant disagreement about the extent to which economic costs and benefits that flow from a jurisdiction's environmental policy choices should be factored into determining the appropriate scale of the OEA. In particular, if lower environmental standards in jurisdiction A impose economic costs on jurisdiction B (industrial migration, lost market share, lower profitability, etc.), or cause jurisdiction B to set suboptimally low environmental standards to minimize those economic costs, is suprajurisdictional cooperation warranted to ensure that the costs and benefits to both jurisdictions of their respective environmental policy choices are included in the regulatory calculus? In other words, is there an externality that should be internalized?

Of necessity, every domestic decision affecting economic policy will have international economic effects through adjustments to terms of trade (Krugman and Obstfeld 1994; Cooper 1994). But do these effects, if attributable to environmental policy differentials across countries, provide a basis for expanding the OEA to include the affected jurisdictions? The answer depends on the reason why the variations in policy exist: Do the cost differentials reflect legitimate differences in comparative advantage or are they an unfair distortion in the marketplace? As Bhagwati (1993a, 167) points out, there are "legitimate reasons for diversity in environmental regulation across countries. . . . [D]iversity of environmental regulations internationally reflects underlying diversity of endowments, technological know-how, and preferences over time and currently between income and pollution." These differences are the foundation of comparative advantage and provide the basis for gains from trade among nations (Ricardo 1973). Recall, further, that the economic gains from trade provide environmental benefits by creating increased private- and public-sector capacity to pay for environmental protection and greater public demand for it.

But where competitiveness concerns threaten to precipitate a welfare-reducing race toward the bottom, we may argue for an expanded OEA to address the attendant economic externality. Such races may be more common than the existing empirical and theoretical literature leads us to believe (see chapter 5). Although there is limited evidence that higher environmental standards affect productivity and competitiveness, leading in turn to industrial flight to pollution havens, jurisdictions nevertheless frequently engage in strategic behavior in setting environmental standards and in determining how strictly to enforce their rules.

In some cases, a "race" induced by sensitivity to competitive position will actually improve welfare by forcing governments to regulate more efficiently (Tiebout 1956; Fischel 1975; Oates and Schwab 1988; Revesz 1992). But the regulatory market in which jurisdictions compete for industrial location is far from perfect and can thus be expected to deliver inefficient, welfare-reducing outcomes in many cases. Indeed, whenever (1) the possibility of externalizing part of the cost of pollution, (2) regulatory incapacity, or (3) public choice distortions cause a jurisdiction to deviate from its own optimal environmental policy, other jurisdictions will find that their welfare-optimizing environmental standards may not be the ones they would have selected were they "island" jurisdictions (Oates and Schwab 1988; J. D. Wilson 1996; Esty 1996b).

The likelihood of a race dynamic increases as economic integration deepens. As long as jurisdiction A is a comparatively unimportant destination of jurisdiction B's exports or if jurisdiction A is an unimportant international competitor, then differential environmental standards matter very little. But as the level of interaction grows, so too does the exposure to economic externalities. The growing value of US-China trade vividly makes this point. In 1995 Chinese exports to the United States topped $24 billion and United States exports to China were $16 billion (IMF, *Direction of Trade Statistics 1996*), up from $3 billion and $7 billion, respectively, just 10 years earlier. Add to this the fact that Chinese and US companies are, and will increasingly be, competing for market share in third-country markets, and the growing interest in supposedly "unfair" differences in environmental standards is not hard to understand.

Differential standards alone do not justify intervention. But if there is evidence that physical pollution spillovers exist or that one party to a trade relationship has standards regarding localized harms that systematically deviate from its own optimum, expansion of the OEA to address the perceived or actual economic costs may be justified. The need to act in this context arises from the same logic that compels supranational cooperation and WTO disciplines to address beggar-thy-neighbor trade policies such as tariffs, import quotas, and strategic currency devaluations. Where regulatory failure is serious and widespread and economic integration is significant, there will be a strong case for some type of environmental policy discipline or harmonization.

The historical precedents for such a response are instructive. Indeed, fears of unfair competitive advantage among the states motivated federal regulation of air and water quality in the United States in the 1960s (Esty 1996b). Similar concerns have also driven the harmonization of environmental standards in the European Union (Esty and Geradin 1997). ASEAN, too, is exploring the development of regional harmonization of environmental standards (ASEAN 1992; 1995). In brief, when economic spillovers are real and threaten to result in suboptimal environmental regulation, the size of the OEA should be set so as to capture the economic externality even in the absence of physical spillovers.

Psychological Externalities, Economic Integration, and "Community"

Given the task of identifying an OEA that is structurally adequate—large enough, that is—to include all the costs and benefits of a particular environmental issue or policy response, another question must be addressed: What happens if the effect on welfare derives from moral or aesthetic preferences and is thus purely psychological? Specifically, will a suprajurisdictional response be needed to address psychological harms suffered by people as a result of behavior outside their own jurisdiction that imposes no physical or economic costs? Should American animal welfare advocates be able to have their views factored in when decisions are made about Mexican fishing practices that may kill dolphins or about Thai shrimping operations that threaten endangered sea turtles? What if Canadians feel bad about the high levels of toxic chemicals to which Chinese factory workers are exposed?[4]

The answer to these questions, we believe, is intimately connected to the idea of "community." The concept of community is important because it arises from a sense of shared values and connotes a degree of obligation by individual citizens to adhere to common norms and rules. If, therefore, those suffering psychological harms are part of the same community as those causing the harm, the victim's views are generally factored into the policy calculus. If those suffering psychological welfare losses live in another political community, they will have no right to have their views reflected in the policy process. Difficulties arise because communities exist along a continuum from very tight to very loose, with many putative supranational communities falling in the latter category. But even in the most loosely structured international communities, some psychological welfare losses—if they arise from especially egregious behavior—will be deemed cognizable.

The degree to which jurisdictions are economically integrated can, moreover, affect the depth of the political community they form and determine whether a right exists to demand certain behavior from others. In general, the stronger the economic ties, the tighter the community, and the greater the content of the baseline ethical standards to which each citizen can hold all others.[5] Close-knit communities will often demand much of their citizens, spelling out rules governing many aspects of life and providing informal norms that are even more encompassing. As the ties of community loosen, so too will the expectation of conformity to common standards.

In the case of federations such as Australia, Canada, and the United States, there is no doubt that the constituent subjurisdictions together constitute a strong community, not just founded on shared values but supported by entrenched and accepted community institutions. With minor exceptions, the residents of these communities feel that they are primarily members of the Australian, Canadian, or American polity and only secondarily citizens of their particular state or province. Being part of such a community requires a commitment to certain national behavioral

---

4. These examples are subtly different. The tuna-dolphin and shrimp-sea turtle situations involve harm that is extraterritorial to any country, while that of the toxic chemicals involves impacts *in* China. The claim to have a right to be heard on problems arising in the global commons is probably stronger.

5. In the 19th century, this "moral" underpinning for free trade emerged in the form of British discomfort with closer economic ties with the slaveholding American South (Haskell 1985). More recently, the public outcry in the United States over the subpar labor conditions in Central America under which American TV talk show hostess Kathy Lee Gifford's clothing line was produced reflected the same tension (*Boston Globe*, 20 October 1996).

standards. All these countries have a legislated set of federal minimum requirements in areas such as the environment, labor, human rights, health, and social security. When some person or subgroup breaches these minimum standards, other citizens may feel aggrieved and, by virtue of their common membership in the community, they will have a legitimate basis for demanding that those violating the established norm correct their behavior, even if there is no physical spillover from the misdeed. Such a national political identity explains, for example, why the Australian federal government took into account the demands of non-Tasmanians to save valuable old-growth tropical forests when it overrode the plans of the Tasmanian government to dam the Franklin River. Similarly, President Clinton, in declaring a large swath of Utah to be a national monument (*New York Times*, 19 September 1996), took into account the conservation preferences of non-Utah residents.

Moving down the spectrum of political communities from most integrated to less integrated, we find a number of looser, newly federalizing communities such as the European Union (EU). The EU's 40-year history of trade and investment liberalization, its ambitious "single market" economic integration program, the trend toward social and cultural integration, the establishment of political institutions—including a Brussels-based EU regulatory structure, a European Parliament, and Court of Justice—mark it as a rapidly deepening community. As intra-European economic ties have strengthened, the European Union has broadened the set of minimum standards that govern participation in the community into a variety of areas, including the environment.[6]

Still further down this spectrum lies the integration of Canada, Mexico, and the United States through NAFTA. While this is clearly a weaker political community than the European Union, expanded North American economic integration has created pressures for the development of a broader set of community norms. In fact, "side agreements" addressing environment and labor standards had to be concluded before the United States would ratify NAFTA. These demands for noneconomic integration can be attributed partly to related economic concerns (e.g., competitiveness), but they also reflect the idea that being part of a community involves having a shared set of values that guide behavior.

Given this economic-political linkage, there is a limit to the degree to which economic integration can proceed without parallel noneconomic integration. Economic integration and broader community building must advance together to ensure that noneconomic tensions do not spill over into the economic realm (Farber 1996, 1270-73). Would Malaysians in the state of Johore be willing to accept products from Sarawak if they felt

---

6. For a discussion of psychological spillovers in the EU context, see Wils (1994).

that the goods coming into their state were produced under morally unacceptable conditions? Integration on social issues—through the development of, and commitment to, standards that are acceptable to all community members—facilitates further economic integration. As economic destinies become intertwined, the need to manage the unanticipated impacts of that integration will require added attention, for important noneconomic harms (such as labor displacement and environmental degradation) may well appear to be aggravated by the liberalization process (Rodrik 1997; Greider 1997).

Understanding the social imperatives of deepening economic integration is particularly important for APEC, which represents a new federal creation, albeit a nascent one. Deeper APEC integration—through further trade and investment liberalization, harmonization of competition policy, and, ultimately, macroeconomic cooperation—will need to be accompanied by the development of minimum standards of behavior with respect to social issues, including the environment. When these standards are not met, APEC's nations should expect that citizens in other countries may be concerned and respond by demanding remedial steps. Since APEC is a relatively weak community, however, the content of the shared values and therefore the extent of the community baseline initially will probably be rather limited. Psychological externalities will rarely give rise to a right to demand adherence to communitywide standards.

As a result, although many Americans are deeply distressed by certain Asian environmental lapses—the killing of sea turtles by Thai shrimp fishermen, destruction of coral reefs in the Philippines, the construction of highly polluting power plants in China—the localized effects of these choices do not represent an affront to APEC community standards. No matter how deep their psychological harm, those who are suffering do not have a right *within the APEC context* to require better performance. As a consequence, the unilateral action of the US government, prodded by animal rights activists, to impose trade sanctions on Thailand in response to objectionable shrimping practices may not be appropriate.[7] This conclusion does not preclude those who are unhappy about the choices made elsewhere from trying to bring about better environmental practices through cajoling or through offers of training, funding, or other inducements. Moreover, since the content of the behavioral baseline will evolve with deepening integration, there may come a time when APEC coalesces into a community whose members can make a broader set of environmental demands on each other.

---

7. Of course, US citizens do have a right to choose to withdraw from further APEC integration—and further opening of their market to APEC exports—if they are uncomfortable with the behavior of their trading partners. Concomitantly, other participants in the APEC process may want to push Thailand not to act in ways that lead to a US withdrawal from APEC.

The challenges of dealing with psychological spillovers is compounded within APEC by three factors: the rapid pace of economic integration, growing public concerns in the United States and elsewhere about the implications of integration and the prospects of a globalized economy more generally, and disparate views about the importance that needs to be placed on noneconomic issues[8]—differences that both have a cultural basis and can be attributed to varying degrees of wealth and development. In sum, the commitment of APEC's members to a grand economic plan but a small "c" Asia Pacific political community cannot be squared. This disconnect may become increasingly conspicuous in the next few years.

The challenge is clear: integration on noneconomic issues, like the environment, must proceed at a pace that, on the one hand, provides comfort to developed countries that social issues are being attended to,[9] and, on the other, satisfies developing members that the values of richer countries are not being imposed upon them unjustifiably in a way that disrespects their sovereignty, their capacity to meet advanced environmental goals, or their conception of the issues to which their nation should accord the highest priority.[10] The balance will not be easy to strike.

There is no ready answer to the question of when psychological externalities will be salient in determining the appropriate scale of the OEA. What we do know, however, is that in each specific case when out-of-jurisdiction citizens demand attention to their psychological preferences, an inquiry will need to be made into the relevant community's identity and depth. Ultimately, value preferences must be respected as a matter of right where a community exists (in a strong sense) and when the behavior of some citizens does not meet communitywide expectations.

From Optimal Areas to Optimal Governance

The conclusion from the previous section is that for every environmental issue there is an OEA—based primarily on the physical scope of the harm,

---

8. The sharp difference between APEC members on the importance of noneconomic issues is brought into focus by ASEAN's decision to admit Burma as an ASEAN member despite human rights concerns. ASEAN's policy of "constructive engagement" is grounded on a " 'hands-off' policy toward the 'internal affairs' of other nations and the primacy of economic relationships over political and human rights concerns" (*New York Times*, 1 June 1997). Conversely, the American approach has traditionally sought to link economic engagement to political freedom, labor rights, and environmental policy.

9. The demand for integration along social dimensions is not just external, emanating from abroad. Citizens in countries where social standards are low often pressure their own governments to improve social performance.

10. Efforts to advance economic integration on a global scale face the same pressures and constraints that exist within APEC regarding the imperative of parallel integration on noneconomic issues such as environmental standards.

and secondarily on the reach of economic and psychological effects of environmental decisions—that should be the guide to situating governance of that problem. In other words, the size of the OEA helps to answer the jurisdictional question about where to allocate responsibility for environmental regulation.

While the OEA concept is clearly helpful, it does not provide a useful rule of application. Every environmental harm has a unique geographic footprint, defined by the reach of the relevant physical, economic, and psychological externalities. This implies an almost infinite number of OEAs and corresponding jurisdictional responses. Mundell (1961), in proposing a theory of optimum currency areas, had to contend with the very same problem, since a parallel principle suggests a separate currency for each discrete economic region in every country. In the environmental domain, as in the realm of currency, administrative inefficiency can quickly overwhelm any advantages that accrue to regulating at the optimal scale. Too many regulatory structures, each tailored to a particular environmental problem, produce chaos rather than effective results. The international community's experience with ad hoc international environmental management demonstrates this principle of diminishing returns when policy responses are individualized.[11]

Thus, the challenge is to balance the desire to respond precisely to the geographic scope of environmental harms against the need to minimize administrative and regulatory inefficiency. To do this, we need a theory of optimal environmental governance that helps us to limit the number of OEAs. Domestically, most countries have found it useful to have two (i.e., local, national) or three (i.e., local, state/provincial, national) levels of environmental policy activity. Internationally, we see similar benefits to two or three primary tiers of environmental coordination.

The argument for global structures of environmental governance is impeccable because only a world-scale response will be structurally adequate when harms are global. Arguably, a global management structure could also take responsibility for regional-scale environmental harms. There are, however, a number of reasons to establish separate regional environmental management structures. First, the separation between national programs and a global response is too big, leading to losses in policy efficacy and efficiency. Second, because countries in a region share considerable ecological connectedness, they have a greater incentive to cooperate than is likely to be found in a global setting. Third, because economic integration often proceeds regionally, it provides a basis for attention to environmen-

---

11. Considerable theoretical work (Posner 1992; Ehrlich and Posner 1974; Diver 1983) has been done on the optimal specificity of regulations. The key issue is whether the benefits of particularization outweigh the inevitable administrative costs of narrowly tailored rules.

tal issues to ensure that progress on the environmental front parallels the deepening economic integration. Finally, in the APEC context, and as we see in greater detail below, regional structures of environmental management can help to overcome systemic deficiencies at both the national and global levels, optimizing their performance.

Optimizing the Performance of Each Level of Governance

As important as where we govern—the jurisdictional question—is how we govern—an issue of regulatory competence and efficiency. How to optimize the environmental performance of each governance level once a role for that level has been identified is therefore a separate and crucial concern. Even if all environmental issues are assigned to the theoretically optimal level, there are significant practical constraints that limit how well particular jurisdictions will perform. For example, while our theory suggests that localized harms such as pollution of rivers and lakes should be handled at the national or subnational level, the regulatory agencies at the national and subnational levels in many countries are severely hampered by regulatory incapacity. Thus, even though a national government may be theoretically best suited to a particular task, many countries will perform poorly because their environmental agencies are simply not up to the job. Similarly, although our allocation rule suggests that global harms should be addressed at a worldwide scale, we know that the existing structures of international environmental management are performing poorly, and that political constraints, at least in the short run, prevent the reforms required to improve them.

The prevalence of regulatory failures and political constraints requires us to examine whether the obstacles to improved performance at the optimal governance level might be overcome by substituting another level for the ineffective one. Indeed, the prospects of one level of governance improving the performance of others provides, in large part, the basis for APEC's role in environmental management (see chapter 6).

Improving Performance

By virtue of their role in addressing and compensating for the market failures that are the source of many environmental problems, governmental actors are central to environmental management. It is important, however, not to see governmental actors as the sole agents for addressing ecological and public health harms. Nongovernmental actors—businesses and environmental groups in particular—can make valuable contributions to the policy process and to environmental protection efforts.

Businesses make many decisions that can harm the environment, as they consume resources and pollute. But they are also responsible today for most investments in environmental protection (Esty and Gentry 1997).[12] The actions that businesses take regarding industrial safety, emissions and effluent reduction, resource conservation, waste management, life cycle product analysis, and environmental risk and crisis management are also central to environmental performance (Powers and Chertow 1997; Shrivistava 1994).

Through their policy and advocacy work, monitoring, training efforts, and, in some cases, direct attention to specific issues, environmental groups make important contributions to public health and ecological protection all around the world (Shabecoff 1993; Easterbrook 1995; Harday, Mitlin, and Satterthwaite 1992). NGOs also communicate the nature and extent of environmental problems to the public and help to build the political concern on which meaningful regulatory efforts must be grounded (Haas, Keohane, and Levy 1993; Keohane and Levy 1996). More broadly, NGOs contribute, particularly in developing nations, to the building of democratic institutions in "civil society" (Heyzer, Riker, and Quizon 1995).

Cooperation and Competition

The challenge is not just to help each government to improve its own environmental performance but to optimize the performance of the environmental "system" as a whole by overcoming the regulatory and political constraints that reduce the efficacy of each level of governance. Meeting this challenge requires systematic interaction among the various environmental actors.

The interaction between nongovernmental entities and the government may take the form of either cooperation or competition. In many countries, both businesses and environmental groups work with governments to identify issues, develop policy alternatives, and implement environmental programs.[13] The literature identifies a wide range of supporting

---

12. Indeed, in the developing world, foreign investment now tops $200 billion per year. Whether these private capital flows are channeled into environmental infrastructure and whether all development projects reflect appropriate pollution controls are the main factors in determining if the growth experienced will be sustainable (Esty and Gentry 1997).

13. Given that at least some of Asia's tremendous economic success—in countries such as Japan, Korea, Malaysia, and Indonesia—can be attributed to close relationships between the public and private sector (World Bank 1993) we should be eager to further explore the possibilities of business-government cooperation in the environmental field.

roles for NGOs, including work as (1) service providers, often as government subcontractors (Bebbington and Farrington 1993); (2) watchdogs or private enforcement agents (Wapner 1995; Cameron and Ramsey 1995; Sands 1992); (3) lobbyists (Zadek and Gatward 1996; Cameron and Ramsey 1995; Covey 1995); (4) stakeholders (Shell 1996) or countervailing interests (Eikeland 1994); (5) agents of civil society enriching the public dialogue and representing interests not reflected within national governments (Spiro 1994; Susskind 1994); (6) policy analysts or expert advisers to governments (Charnovitz 1996b; Susskind 1994; Cameron and Ramsey 1995); (7) mobilizers of public opinion (Lindborg 1992; Clark 1995); (8) bridges between state and nonstate actors connecting local and global politics (Princen and Finger 1994; Gordenker and Weiss 1996); (9) change agents offering new viewpoints (Susskind 1994; Ahooja-Patel, Drabek, and Nerfin 1986; Jakobeit 1996); and (10) consultants to industry (Eikeland 1994).

While cooperation will often be valuable, there are many cases in which environmental governance will benefit from competition among actors.[14] In the environmental domain, the most constructive competition is often between governments and NGOs (Esty 1997d). By advancing alternative data, science, risk analyses, cost-benefit studies, policy options, and program evaluations, NGOs force governments to constantly reassess and justify their environmental actions. Given the high degree of uncertainty in many aspects of environmental policymaking and the fast pace of change in environmental sciences, such a process of regular review is not just valuable, it is essential.[15]

Interaction—both cooperative and competitive—can occur not only "horizontally" among actors at one level of environmental governance but also "vertically" across levels. The possibility that regional structures can reinforce national and global ones lies at the heart of our proposal for an APEC environmental program. The opportunity to establish a multitiered governance structure—which may then provide both support

---

14. Some commentators have argued that environmental governance will benefit from regulatory competition among horizontally arrayed governments (Revesz 1992). However, as we noted in chapter 5, interjurisdictional competition in environmental policymaking frequently results not in optimal environmental performance but in a welfare-reducing race toward the bottom.

15. Interaction between environmental actors should not be one way. Governments can also help to develop the capacity of NGOs and business to contribute to better environmental performance. For example, governments may facilitate development of a more vibrant NGO community by giving legal recognition and legitimacy to NGOs, and by creating or encouraging the participation of NGOs in policy forums (Heyzer, Riker, and Quizon 1995, 29-30). Governments may also facilitate greater private-sector research and development in environmental technologies—through joint technical and scientific research or by financial incentives that encourage more research and development than is being provided by the market.

and creative tension—represents one of the fundamental arguments in favor of any federal system (Braden 1995). The benefits of vertical checks and balances across the local, state/provincial, and federal governments are well known in many countries with federal structures (Kincaid 1991). Additional strength can be achieved by extending this architecture to the international domain.

Conclusion

Optimal environmental governance involves two endeavors:

- *Allocating responsibility over environmental issues to the appropriate jurisdictional level.* Authority to respond to a particular environmental issue should be allocated to the jurisdictional level that can properly address the mischief in question. Primarily, this means ensuring that the jurisdiction selected—the optimal environmental area—is geographically matched to the scope of the physical spillover effects of an activity on the environment. The OEA must also be large enough, in some cases, to cover those who are economically and psychologically affected by production or resource use decisions and by a government's environmental policy choices.

- *Optimizing the performance of each level of governance.* Systemic regulatory and political constraints prevent optimal environmental performance. Performance can, however, be improved by interaction among levels of governance and through cooperation with and competition from nongovernmental actors. In this regard, an APEC environmental program (especially one that engages NGOs and businesses) not only fills a gap in the environmental management hierarchy but also offers the promise of better performance for governing bodies at the national and global levels.

8

APEC's Existing Environmental Efforts

Almost since its inception, APEC's leaders have talked about the need to address the environmental stress and degradation that has accompanied the economic growth in their region (O'Meara 1997). At the Manila Summit in 1996 the leaders affirmed a "commitment to sustainable growth" (APEC 1996). Recently, the environment ministries in each APEC country have begun the process of transforming the concern that development be sustainable into an environmental work program. The ministers have asked each APEC working group and policy committee to integrate environmental considerations into their work programs.[1] Special attention has been focused on environmental issues related to urbanization, clean production techniques, and the marine environment. In addition, the broader issues of food, energy, environment, economic growth, and population have been identified as areas of core interest. Unfortunately, the organization's efforts to date are long on rhetoric and short on substance. Not much has been done beyond gathering and sharing information. Success in meeting the environmental challenges that APEC members face individually and collectively will require far more. Better national cooperation is one step, but real progress will require regional coordination.

APEC'S Environmental Vision

In its first report in 1993, the APEC Eminent Persons Group argued that "APEC members should ensure that they are embarked on a course of

---

1. See box 1.1 for a brief discussion of APEC's institutions and processes.

sustainable development" (APEC 1993a, 46). Picking up on the need to focus on sustainable development, the APEC leaders responded, at the Blake Island Summit in 1993, by committing APEC to "protect the quality of our air, water, and green spaces, and manage our energy resources and renewable resources to ensure sustainable growth and provide a more secure future for our people" (APEC 1993b). At the historic 1994 Bogor Summit, at which the commitment to free trade across APEC was enunciated, the leaders declared that their shared vision for the community of Asia Pacific economies was based on an "approach which . . . embrac[es] the three pillars of *sustainable growth*, equitable development and national stability" (APEC 1994a, emphasis added).

At the Osaka Summit in 1995, the leaders noted with concern that "the Asia-Pacific region's fast-expanding population and rapid economic growth are forecast to sharply increase the demand for food and energy, and the pressures on the environment." With these stresses in mind, they agreed "to put these interrelated, wide-ranging issues on the long-term agenda and consult further on ways to initiate joint actions so as to ensure that the region's economic prosperity is sustainable" (APEC 1995a). This proclamation has now evolved into the Food, Energy, Environment, Economic Growth, and Population (FEEEP) initiative. Most recently, at the Subic Bay Summit in November 1996, the leaders called on ministers to "intensify their work on sustainable growth and to report on their progress [at the Leaders' Summit] in Vancouver in 1997" (APEC 1996).

Not only have APEC's leaders collectively embraced the environmental cause, but a number of prominent heads of state have personally expressed concern over APEC environmental matters. At Subic Bay in 1996, President Jiang Zemin of China declared that "effective measures needed to be taken to strengthen Asia-Pacific cooperation in the realm of environmental protection" (*Beijing Review*, 23-29 December 1996, 7). Just a few days earlier, President Clinton, in Australia en route to Manila, similarly called for enhanced efforts to "care for our shared environment" (Reuters North American Wire, 22 November 1996). President Fidel Ramos of the Philippines has said that he places "great emphasis on the preservation of the environment because we know that, after painstaking efforts, we finally stand on the threshold of unprecedented growth and change. That threshold—unless we watch our step and look when we cross—could very well be the brink of environmental disaster" (speech, Sustainable Development Ministerial Meeting, 11 July 1996). During the Subic Bay Summit, which he hosted, Ramos actually interrupted his discussions with the leaders of other APEC countries to meet with a group of environmental NGOs. Prime Minister Jean Chrétien of Canada has further promised that the environment will be a top agenda item at the APEC summit that he hosts in Vancouver in 1997.

APEC's environmental ministers have been charged with turning the leaders' rhetoric into action. Meeting for the first time in Vancouver in

1994, at the suggestion of Chrétien, the ministers produced an "APEC Environmental Vision Statement" and a "Framework of Principles for Integrating Economy and Environment in APEC" (see appendices A and B). The vision statement declares that sustainable development and trade and investment in the region should be promoted "by integrating environmental considerations into relevant policy development and economic decisions throughout the region." This directive has translated into efforts to integrate environmental concerns into the work programs of each of APEC's working groups.

The framework of principles, drawing on the 1992 Rio Declaration, lays out nine cornerstones for APEC efforts to "reconcile the objectives of economic growth and efficiency with improved environmental outcomes." These are

- sustainable development,

- environmental cost internalization,

- science and research,

- technology transfer,

- the precautionary principle,

- trade and environmental policy integration,

- environmental education,

- innovative sustainable development financing, and

- a narrow role for APEC—putting responsibilities on APEC only when the organization can add value, and emphasizing the need to avoid duplication of the functions of other bodies.

Moving beyond the development of a vision and the laying out of principles, the environment ministers, meeting again in Manila in July 1996, agreed that APEC and its members should focus attention on three issues: sustainable cities and urban management, clean technology and clean production, and sustainability of the marine environment.

Progress to Date

The declarations of the leaders and the work of APEC's environment ministers have together laid the foundations for APEC's existing three-pronged environmental work program:

- integration of environmental and economic considerations in APEC's working groups;

- attention to sustainable cities, clean technologies, and the marine environment; and

- long-term focus on food, energy, environment, economic growth, and population.[2]

Integration of Environmental and Economic Considerations

As Zarsky and Hunter (1997, 16) note, while APEC's leaders may be the architects of its environmental agenda, the working groups and committees are the engineers. These staff-level bodies have been directed to fully integrate environmental considerations into their programs—and they have done so with varying degrees of enthusiasm and success.

The Regional Energy Cooperation Working Group, currently "shepherded" by Australia, has to date been the most active in the environmental field. It has launched a variety of information-gathering and dissemination activities including seminars, workshops, surveys, and reports, which look at energy efficiency, clean energy technologies, and the transfer of energy-related technologies and research and development. The group has also released a set of 14 "Non-Binding Energy and Environmental Policy Principles" and has recently begun to examine the prospects for harmonizing energy standards for electrical appliances across APEC.

The Marine Resources Conservation Working Group is helping to improve the capacity of APEC countries to manage red tides and algal bloom problems, and it is collecting information on coastal zone management and sensitive coastal habitats. Its work program for 1997 includes preparing inventories of ocean and marine polluting industries, assessments of the cross-boundary impacts of coastal activities, and an action plan—APEC's first in the environmental realm—for the management of red tides.

The environmental work of the Human Resources Development Working Group has focused on the need for better environmental curricula in the education of engineers, expanded environmental training for administrators and managers in the Asia Pacific region, and ways to promote academic collaboration on sustainable development. The group has also conducted research, seminars, and education and training courses to promote better utilization of international quality assurance standards.

---

2. In addition, a number of APEC's members have expressed interest, ahead of the Vancouver Leaders' Summit, in reducing barriers to trade in environmental goods and services. An APEC focus on liberalization of the environmental product market, however, is not worth priority policy focus, because tariffs are already low, and it is strongly in the importing country's interest to acquire new environmental technologies and environmentally benign goods and services.

The Tourism Working Group has published a report identifying environmentally sensitive areas in APEC and eco-tourism management techniques in use across APEC. The Industrial Science and Technology Working Group, which has held workshops on cleaner air technologies and marine environment monitoring, has also established an acid rain monitoring network. The Fisheries Working Group has done little beyond conducting a study on the environmental impacts of fishing on coral reefs and holding workshops on sustainable aquaculture and destructive fishing techniques.

In sum, the activities are basically limited to gathering and disseminating information. An internal evaluation by APEC's Economic Committee (APEC 1997a) acknowledges that activities to date, while numerous, are small-scale and do not go beyond capacity building. While we have argued that capacity building in APEC is valuable (chapter 6), the current program does not systematically address the major capacity bottlenecks visible across APEC. The overall picture is one of ad hoc attention to environmental concerns, disconnected from any overarching strategy for achieving sustainable development.

The major obstacle to success in pursuing an environmental agenda centered on APEC's working groups and committees is that pollution and resource concerns are not a primary focus of these bodies. In fact, five of APEC's ten working groups do not even mention the environment in their vision statements. It appears, furthermore, that the directive to integrate environmental concerns into work programs has produced few new efforts to address environmental issues. Instead, working groups are simply reporting on activities that were already under way or planned. These problems are exacerbated by the lack of technical expertise on public health and ecological issues within the working groups, a weakness that cannot be surprising given that the groups are designed primarily as vehicles for economic policy. The groups lack any basic, analytic foundation for their environmental efforts. They have no real sense of where the serious problems lie, what might be done to address them, and which ones APEC can begin to remedy.

The idea of making environmental considerations part of everything APEC does is not, in and of itself, a bad one. Unfortunately, the integration efforts have been poorly executed. To build meaningful environmental and economic policy bridges would require not only dedication to environmental progress within each group but also an emphasis on developing interdisciplinary approaches cutting across and among working groups and committees.

The absence of an overarching APEC structure to manage and oversee the efforts of the working groups adds to the organizational challenge. There is little coordination across the groups and no mechanism to hold the groups accountable for progress. Thus, while weaving environmental sensitivity into the fabric of APEC makes sense as an aspiration, APEC has gone about it wrong.

Sustainable Cities, Clean Technologies, and the Marine Environment

Some working groups are undertaking work in pursuit of the action program laid out at the 1996 APEC "Sustainable Development" Ministerial Meeting in Manila. At that meeting, APEC members agreed to focus on three priority areas: (1) sustainable urbanization, for which Canada has taken responsibility in the absence of a relevant working group; (2) clean production and clean technology, which is being advanced by the Industrial Science and Technology Working Group; and (3) sustainability of the marine environment, for which the Marine Resources Conservation Working Group has assumed responsibility.

In June 1997, the environment ministers met in Toronto to promote further progress on this agenda but achieved little. In fact, a number of people close to or involved in the process have said privately that the Ministerial Meeting was a disaster.[3]

At the end of their Toronto deliberations, the ministers approved a strategy for sustainable cities that calls for special emphasis on pollution prevention and control, environmentally sustainable infrastructure development, and the needs of poor urban settlements. In their proposal, they included the following specific measures:

- facilitation of city sustainability by sharing sustainable urbanization "best practices," developing guidelines for sustainable planning, and establishing an Internet website to showcase environmental solutions for sustainable cities; and

- encouragement of investment by sharing examples of innovative approaches to financing, by examining economic instruments as tools to promote sustainability, and by promoting cooperation among environment, trade, finance, and other ministries.

The strategy for clean production and clean technology, developed by Australia, Taiwan, and the United States, espouses two goals: to achieve "dramatic" progress in reducing environmental impacts through the promotion of cleaner production technologies, policies, and practices; and to achieve broader adaptation of cross-disciplinary policies and methods for cleaner production through institutional, professional, and private-sector

---

3. The failure to achieve meaningful progress in Toronto should not be viewed as fatal to APEC's environmental efforts. Instead, the weak output from the Toronto Ministerial simply reflects the poorly-thought-through current policy course and creates an opportunity for APEC to pursue a new environmental agenda, along the lines proposed in chapter 9.

partnerships. To advance this agenda, the ministers meeting in Toronto endorsed the development of tools to facilitate cleaner production, enhancement of research networks, capacity building to improve information sharing, the development of industrial environmental performance indicators, and dissemination of information electronically.

Finally, APEC's environment ministers adopted a strategy designed to ensure the sustainability of the marine environment. Its objectives are to develop integrated approaches to coastal management, reduce and control marine pollution, and manage marine resources sustainably. The measures put forward to achieve these objectives are research and exchange of information, technology, and expertise; capacity building; education and training; and public- and private-sector partnerships.

The inadequacy of each of these efforts is plainly apparent. Rhetoric, for example, about the need for "broad-based societal change in thinking throughout the APEC economies, which embraces the sustainability of cities as a fundamental concept for human prosperity and environmental health" (APEC 1997b) is not matched with any comparable commitment to action. The tools at APEC's disposal to accomplish this goal, together with the equally ambitious goals of the other two focus areas, are primarily limited to exchanging information, strengthening research networks, sharing approaches and best practices, integrating public and private actors, and constructing an array of internet websites. There exists a serious incongruity between the APEC vision and its action programs.

Food, Energy, Environment, Economic Growth, and Population (FEEEP)

Cognizant, perhaps, of the limitations of the initiatives reviewed above, APEC's members are now focusing on a new sweeping action agenda called the "FEEEP" initiative. Aiming to make FEEEP—originally proposed in Osaka in 1995—the environmental centerpiece of its efforts as host of the 1997 Leaders' Summit, Canada plans to present the leaders with a paper that identifies the key FEEEP issues. The hope is that Malaysia will follow up at the 1998 summit by addressing the policy implications and outlining a series of recommendations for action.

The issues that fall under the FEEEP umbrella are undoubtedly important. But in covering almost everything, the FEEEP initiative emphasizes nothing. Limited political capital will be spread thin, making concrete progress on sustainable development unlikely. With its long-term time horizon and vaguely defined objectives, there is a real risk that the FEEEP initiative will produce a broad and ambitious action declaration with no tangible content.[4] Indeed, the FEEEP agenda looks like a program of

4. The FEEEP initiative looks strikingly like Agenda 21, the overly broad and now plainly dysfunctional product of the Rio Earth Summit (Daniel C. Esty, *Newsday*, 25 June 1997).

general environmental needs that has been crossed with a list of issues to which nobody objects and reduced to a level of generality that commits no one to anything specific.[5] APEC can ill afford an environmental program that fails to deliver concrete results. Such an outcome leaves APEC open to further criticism that it is a "talk shop" through which little that is worthwhile can be achieved.

Crafting a sensible APEC environmental agenda demands careful consideration not of environmental needs in general but of the specific pollution control and resource management requirements that arise in the context of regional economic integration. The agenda must be further refined with an eye toward APEC's political, financial, and environmental capacity, focusing on issues where APEC can provide "value added" and do something that is not being done or that cannot be done as well in some other forum. The key is to get APEC's members moving toward sustainable development rather than just talking about it.

On its own terms, therefore, APEC's environmental program is unlikely to succeed. First, the obstacles to successful integration of economic and environmental considerations in the working groups seem daunting. Second, given the very modest action items on which agreement has been reached, there appears to be little prospect of making a significant contribution to the sustainability of cities, the use of cleaner production technologies, and the sustainability of the marine environment. Third, FEEEP seems destined to elicit little more than grandiloquent discourse that does not get translated into action.

A Broader Critique

More troublingly, if we evaluate APEC's efforts by referring to the core regional environmental management functions identified in chapter 6, the existing program looks wholly inadequate. First, its weak efforts to address the sustainability of the marine environment notwithstanding, APEC has done nothing to address the "super externalities" that drive regional-scale environmental harms. Ensuring that transboundary spillovers do not go unattended is a critical function not only as a matter of environmental policy but also to maintain the integrity of regional economic interactions. Second, despite much talk about capacity building in various working groups, APEC has not moved to establish a systematic program to support the national policy efforts of its members. Finally, APEC's existing environmental agenda does not in any way reflect a recognition of the important role APEC can play in ratcheting up multilat-

5. Early efforts to address the FEEEP issues are far from encouraging. At an APEC FEEEP symposium held in Saskatoon, Canada, 2-4 September 1997, agreement was limited to more exhortations to gather information and conduct further research.

eral environmental efforts or in providing experience for future global environmental management.

There are two other important reasons to be concerned about APEC's current environmental course. First, the potential for making environmental progress has been severely restricted by the decision to lodge APEC's sustainable development activities within the organization's economic and technical cooperation ("ecotech") program.[6] The focus on "cooperation" limits the tools available for effecting change.[7] Measurable improvements in pollution control and resource management across the Asia Pacific region will be achieved only if APEC also takes advantage of environment-related opportunities available through trade "liberalization" and "facilitation" efforts. For example, significant environmental benefits will accrue to APEC and its members if they can lead the way toward elimination of agriculture and energy subsidies (a liberalization measure) and reduce cross-country differentials in environmental standards (a facilitation measure). In short, APEC needs to make the leap from nation-to-nation cooperation to regional coordination in the environmental realm.

A second reason to be concerned about APEC's existing program arises from its failure to address any of the important issues at the economy-environment interface that threaten to derail trade liberalization and the broader process of regional economic integration. In particular, no attention has been paid to developing-country fears about environmental restrictions on market access and the use of trade measures to achieve extraterritorial environmental objectives (e.g., the shrimp-sea turtle dispute between the United States and Thailand). Similarly, little has been done to blunt developed-country worries about "unfair" competitive advantages accruing to those with lax environmental standards.

In sum, APEC's environmental program does not reflect a serious approach to sustainable development. Eileen Claussen, the US assistant secretary of state, had it right when she observed that APEC has not yet become "a credible force for environmental protection" (*Toronto Globe and Mail*, 10 June 1997).

Conclusion

If words alone could "green" the Asia Pacific, the job would already be done. Unfortunately, the leaders' exhortations about sustainable develop-

---

6. In Manila in 1996, the leaders endorsed a framework of principles for economic cooperation and development, focusing on the following themes: developing human capital; fostering safe, efficient capital markets; strengthening economic infrastructure; harnessing technologies of the future; *promoting environmentally sustainable growth*; and encouraging the growth of small and medium enterprises (APEC 1996, emphasis added).

7. As Yamazawa (1997) makes clear, APEC's current ecotech framework will never enable its members to go beyond seminars, study/research, and information gathering to achieve visible progress.

ment have not been translated into a meaningful action program. Reliance on working groups without the inclination or expertise to integrate economic and environmental goals; an ambitious focus on cities, clean technologies, and the marine environment backed by little more than promises to cooperate and share knowledge; and a misguided long-term focus on the all-encompassing issues of food, energy, environment, economic growth, and population, without any real prospects for serious short-run action to alleviate APEC's pressing environmental concerns, amount to a recipe for failure.

APEC must discard its current environmental approach. The challenge as APEC moves toward the upcoming summit meetings in Vancouver and Malaysia is to understand the roles that a regional body like APEC can fill and the environmental issues on which it can add real value—and to develop a concrete action agenda whose success can be objectively measured. Only then will APEC be positioned to move decisively from vision to action.

9

An APEC Environmental Agenda

The dramatic economic success of many of the Pacific Rim nations over the last 30 years is unparalleled in history. Unfortunately, serious environmental effects—many negative—have accompanied the region's economic growth. These adverse ecological and public health impacts have not diminished the appetite for further growth in the region, as evidenced by ongoing efforts to advance an ambitious program of trade and investment liberalization. But growth is not—and must not be—APEC's sole concern. Its members aspire to "stability, security and prosperity for [their citizens]" (APEC 1996)—in other words, the maximization of social welfare more broadly and over time. The member countries can achieve this goal only if they improve their environmental performance through a commitment to sustainable development. Environmental progress not only contributes to social welfare but also builds domestic support for continuing economic integration at a time when citizens are concerned that important social goals—environmental quality among them—are being sacrificed at the altar of free trade.

If "sustainable development" is to be anything more than an empty slogan, however, APEC must move beyond the limits of its existing unfocused environmental work program and make a fresh start. This chapter provides a menu of ideas with which to begin the process.

Criteria for an Effective Environment Program

For an APEC environment agenda to be durable and have high impact, each initiative on the agenda must have sound analytic and theoretical

Figure 9.1   Dimensions of a sound APEC environmental initiative

Does the initiative address the
underlying cause of a serious
harm or an important economy-
environment tension?

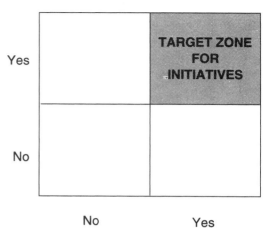

Does APEC have something significant to
contribute in addressing the harm or tension?

underpinnings. In particular, when considering any initiative for inclusion on APEC's agenda, two questions must be asked (figure 9.1).

First, does the initiative address the underlying cause of a serious pollution harm or resource management issue, or an important tension at the economy-environment interface? If the answer is "yes," we know that the initiative offers either the prospect of a measurable improvement in environmental performance, and thus social welfare, or an important opportunity to sustain the commitment of APEC's members to freer trade.

Second, does APEC have something significant to contribute in addressing the harm or tension? An affirmative response indicates that the proposal either takes advantage of APEC's unique regional scale to address regional problems or compensates for deficiencies in environmental management at the national or global levels.

Only where we can answer "yes" to both questions has an initiative made it onto our short list of proposals for APEC. Of course, it may not make sense to pursue all these initiatives—or, at least, not all of them immediately. In selecting the final roster of initiatives, the following questions must be asked: Will the proposal engage APEC's leaders? Does the proposed program have broad political appeal? And, most important, is the initiative practical and achievable?

Political Leadership and Appeal

APEC's leaders must be engaged by any proposed environmental agenda item because only they can ensure success. The current program—which has been driven "down" from APEC's environment ministers and been allowed to percolate "up" from its working groups—has manifestly failed to translate APEC's environmental rhetoric into measurable progress. Moreover, APEC's track record shows that the group's most important advances owe their success to the efforts of the leaders at their annual summits.[1]

Of course, if the leaders are to become excited about environmental action, "big ticket" initiatives that spark their interest must be identified. Leaders look for something spectacular that will deliver headlines, as did the comprehensive Bogor free trade commitment and the sectoral information technology agreement announced in Manila.[2] While the existing efforts to gather and disseminate information, support research efforts, and enhance regulatory capacity are important components of better long-term environmental policymaking, "soft" initiatives will not get high-level attention.

Beyond the need for individual environmental initiatives to attract attention, APEC's environmental program as a whole must meet two important criteria to ensure its appeal. First, the program cannot consist solely of initiatives that build on further trade liberalization. While there are important environmental projects that coincide with this core trade mission[3]—for example, the reduction of agricultural subsidies—a number of APEC's Asian members, especially Indonesia, Malaysia, and Singapore, are concerned that the focus to date on liberalized trade has crowded out attention to "facilitation" and "ecotech" activities, which they view as equally critical to the APEC goal of creating an Asia Pacific "community." Our agenda has thus been designed to include initiatives that cover all of APEC's three pillars—liberalization, facilitation, and ecotech.

Second, to succeed, the proposed environmental agenda for APEC must respect the differing, and often conflicting, priorities of APEC's developed and developing members (UNDP, *Human Development Report 1991*; Beckerman 1996). For an APEC environmental agenda to command consensus, APEC's developed members will need to be sensitive to the need to

---

1. Numerous studies have shown the central role of charismatic, committed leaders (e.g., Keohane 1996, 26).

2. As Krause (1997) has noted, however, it "may not be possible to pull a rabbit out of the hat every year."

3. While some APEC members—Canada and Japan among them (*Japan Times*, 2 July 1997)—have proposed liberalizing trade in environmental goods, such an initiative misses the mark. With barriers to trade in these goods already low, little measurable improvement in environmental performance can be expected to result.

devote some energy and resources to addressing the pressing concerns of developing nations—namely, issues relating to food security, to the provision of environmental infrastructure for water supply and sanitation, and to localized air pollution. At the same time, APEC's developing members must understand that, in return, conservation and regional and global transboundary harms, issues of importance to developed countries, must also be addressed.

Recognizing what it will take for an environmental agenda to have a chance of success—the commitment of APEC's leaders and political appeal—by no means denies the significant political obstacles to substantive environmental progress. The greatest difficulty lies in convincing APEC countries that cooperating regionally on environmental issues is in their national interest, just as they are convinced of the need to pursue trade liberalization regionally and globally.[4] Toward this end, each of the major environmental initiatives that we have developed has not just an environmental logic but an economic logic that provides compelling reasons to cooperate through APEC.[5]

Practical and Achievable

To give APEC's environmental effort momentum and to convince critics of its value, the agenda will need to be practical and achievable.[6] Primarily, the focus must be on action and on results-based performance. If actual impact is the measure of success, APEC's proposal to focus on the Food, Energy, Environment, Economic Growth, and Population (FEEEP) project

---

4. Boer, Ramsay, and Rothwell (1997) argue that the Asia Pacific countries are already beginning to see that environmental cooperation is to their mutual benefit.

5. Even when the net economic benefits of a policy reform are clear, entrenched interests that believe they will be affected adversely will resist change. The elimination of environmentally damaging agricultural subsidies in APEC countries (a measure proposed below), for example, faces an uphill battle because Japanese, South Korean, and Taiwanese farmers, as well as American sugar growers, will likely resist elimination of agricultural price supports. APEC can, however, help to keep the focus on the broad public gains to be had and can serve as a forum in which linkages across issues can be made. In the case of farm subsidies, the countries that might oppose this reform are those that have benefited the most from an open trading system. Discussions in the APEC context might serve to remind these nations of the benefits they have obtained from freer trade and thereby encourage them to make the tough domestic political decisions necessary to ensure reform. APEC can employ a variety of tools and mechanisms to facilitate the making of these hard political choices. For example, deadlines for action can be spread across time, with countries being allowed to "back-load" their efforts.

6. At the time of the 1995 Leaders' Summit in Osaka, for example, *The Economist* (11 November 1995) impatiently proclaimed that "[i]f this year's APEC summit comes out with more grand commitments, deferred into the distant future, it will be hard to take them, or APEC, seriously." In a similar vein, the *Financial Times* (25 November 1996), the day after the Manila Leaders' Summit, renamed APEC "A Perfect Excuse to Chat."

in Vancouver and Malaysia cannot help but fail, since the initiative incorporates no commitment to action. Each of our proposals, in contrast, lends itself to the development of a clear action program with identifiable performance indicators.

Advancing a practical and achievable agenda requires not only a clear program of implementation but also an understanding of the capacity constraints that many APEC members face. Since budgets are tight everywhere and APEC's industrializing nations feel considerable development pressures, the demands of economic efficiency as well as environmental improvement must be kept in mind. Our program, furthermore, responds to the regulatory incapacity that characterizes the environmental efforts of many of APEC's developing members. Finally, careful attention has been paid to questions of legal capacity, particularly the limited "fast-track" authority of the current US administration.

The need for practicality is also evident in our judgment about how to make progress in getting countries (and their citizens) to pay for the pollution harms they cause. While numerous supranational or multilateral bodies and instruments have proclaimed the polluter pays principle (OECD 1975; 1994) to be the foundation of better environmental policy,[7] the principle is honored largely in the breach (Bodansky 1995).

Talking about—and declaring support for—the polluter pays principle has not translated into real efforts to impose costs on polluters, at least as far as emissions with regional and global effects are concerned. Advancing this principle as the cornerstone for an APEC environmental program requires a sophisticated multistep approach. First, programs that *pay the polluter* should be stopped. Thus we emphasize reducing subsidies for energy consumption and agricultural production. The next step should be *partial implementation* of the polluter pays principle, phased in over time in recognition of the inability or unwillingness of many countries to make the leap to full implementation immediately. Initially, countries might be required to pay for a portion of the costs of their activities, determined by their capacity to pay, with support from a multilateral fund to soften the blow. Over more time (perhaps 20 years), countries should move to *full implementation* of the principle.[8]

Initiatives for Vancouver and Beyond

We offer below four major environmental initiatives for the 1997 APEC Summit in Vancouver or for subsequent summits in Malaysia (1998),

---

7. Forcing polluters to pay for the environmental harms they cause not only minimizes externalities but imposes costs on those responsible for incurring them, which is appealing from an equity perspective.

8. At every step, the focus must be on private-sector action and the potential to harness market forces to environmental goals.

New Zealand (1999), Brunei (2000), or China (2001). By pursuing these initiatives in parallel, APEC's members could both demonstrate a serious commitment to sustainable development and provide a firm environmental foundation for continuing economic integration.

Joint Implementation Program

Because the parties to the 1992 Climate Change Convention are meeting again in Kyoto, Japan, two weeks after the Vancouver Leaders' Summit,[9] APEC's leaders are likely to ask each other how a successful outcome at Kyoto can be assured. With the heads of so many of the world's largest and fastest growing greenhouse gas contributors sitting around the table in Vancouver, the ensuing discussion could profoundly influence the Kyoto outcome.

The Kyoto conference is attracting significant attention, for among the many transboundary environmental issues, climate change towers above the rest in its potential impact—environmentally and economically (Cline 1992)—and its political urgency. But the deep divide between developed and developing countries—over how to stem the growth of greenhouse gas emissions, who should be required to take action, and what the distribution of costs should be—has made progress in changing policy slow. APEC might help to bridge the gap with a regional initiative designed to get North and South to pull together on "joint implementation" (JI) projects to reduce emissions at the lowest possible cost.[10]

Our theory of structural sufficiency and optimal environmental governance suggests that global "super externalities," such as climate change, should be dealt with by institutions that are worldwide in scope. To date, however, multilateral efforts to stabilize "greenhouse gas (GHG) concentrations in the atmosphere at a level that would prevent dangerous (human-induced) interference with the climate system" (United Nations Framework Convention on Climate Change, Article 2) have progressed slowly (UNEP 1997; World Watch Institute 1996). With global efforts faltering, APEC could, and perhaps should, step in to fill the breach.

No matter what else is agreed on in Kyoto, it will be important to establish a mechanism by which industrialized countries are able to meet some or all of their emissions reduction obligations through projects undertaken in the developing world—where most of the high-return (maximum emissions reduction per dollar invested) opportunities exist. Since the planet does not care where the reductions come from, why should we? In this regard, it makes sense to stretch the world's inevitably

---

9. The Conference of the Parties to the United Nations Framework Convention on Climate Change will hold its third session 1-10 December 1997.

10. As we noted in chapter 6, joint implementation is designed to facilitate emissions reductions where they will be cheapest by allowing developed countries to pay for emissions reductions in developing countries and receive credit for doing so against any commitments they make to reduce their own greenhouse gas emissions.

limited budget for climate change controls as far as possible with a major commitment to joint implementation.

Toward this end, APEC should develop a JI program which could be presented for multilateral approval in Kyoto. Some developing countries have been hesitant to back JI, suggesting that it lets industrialized countries off the hook by allowing them to buy their way out of making reductions at home. But the benefits of joint implementation are too great to be obscured by political grandstanding. The chance to attract investment and to obtain efficiency-enhancing and less-polluting technologies has already made converts of a number of developing Latin American and Eastern European countries and, similarly, is likely to find support among Asian policymakers.

By securing a JI agreement in Vancouver, APEC's members could set the stage for a broader multilateral commitment to such projects. Even if the Kyoto conference fails to secure agreement on a global JI initiative, APEC should offer itself up as a laboratory for climate change policy experimentaticn and proceed with a set of JI projects on its own. Success within APEC would have a powerful demonstration effect and might well convince skeptics that joint implementation offers a critical step forward in addressing climate change.

Subsidies Reduction or Elimination

The reduction or elimination of energy and agriculture subsidies promises a win-win outcome for APEC's members. Cutting subsidies would deliver substantial economic welfare gains and would significantly reduce the environmental impact of many subsidies programs (K. Anderson 1992; World Bank 1997).[11] And given that APEC's members have already committed to free trade in the region by 2010/2020, the elimination of subsidies fits perfectly into the basic APEC strategy—it simply involves implementing the already agreed on goal of freer trade.

Agricultural Subsidies

A focus on farm subsidies not only is a logical component of the Bogor commitment to trade liberalization but also would build on the steps taken during the Uruguay Round of global trade negotiations.[12] While

---

11. It is important to note that not all subsidies have negative environmental impacts. On balance, however, the negative environmental impacts of "bad" subsidies far outweigh the positive impacts of "good" subsidies (OECD 1996).

12. The Uruguay Round agreement on agriculture commits countries to reduce farm export subsidies by 36 percent over six years, requires a 20 percent reduction in aggregate domestic support to farmers (exempting direct income payments), requires the conversion of nontariff barriers into tariff equivalents, and opens minimum access quotas for products whose trade was largely blocked by past protection (Schott 1994, 43-44).

Uruguay Round efforts "establish[ed] for the first time significant multilateral disciplines on trade-distorting farm programs" (Schott 1994, 11), much work remains to be done.[13]

The economic benefits of continued reform are significant. Agricultural production subsidies—both price and nonprice supports—in OECD countries exceeded $300 billion in 1995 (Earth Council 1997, 23). Production subsidies in some countries—the United States, Japan, South Korea, and Taiwan (and to a lesser extent Australia and New Zealand)—remain significant. One study has estimated that if these subsidies were eliminated through agricultural liberalization in APEC countries alone, income in APEC would increase by $106 billion annually (Dee, Geisler, and Watts 1996). In addition, governments would reap a windfall in reduced payouts, which now sometimes run as high as 1.5 percent of GDP.

The reduction of subsidies for agricultural inputs, particularly water, also promises large economic benefits. Subsidies for drinking water and irrigation in APEC's developing countries are high—in the vicinity of $45 billion per year in the developing world (Earth Council 1997, 15).[14] In the United States, irrigation subsidies have been estimated at between $2 billion and $2.5 billion,[15] and in Australia, water charges are largely nominal in the major agricultural region, the Murray-Darling river basin. Eliminating these subsidies would not only save governments money but would deliver economic efficiency gains by promoting wiser use of water.

The economic benefits alone of reforming agricultural subsidies provide the basis for action. When the environmental benefits of subsidy reform are also figured in, the case for reform becomes irrefutable (Charnovitz 1996a; Hammer and Shetty 1995). Removing production subsidies, for example, will reduce environmentally damaging chemical-intensive farming on marginal lands. And reducing water and irrigation subsidies will make water use significantly more efficient. In many of APEC's developing countries, as little as 30 percent of the water made available for irrigation is actually consumed (Xie, Kuffner, and LeMoigne 1993). Once irrigation subsidies have been removed, governments may be able to take actions to reverse the long-term deterioration of irrigation systems—particularly in Mexico and China—that they were previously unable to

---

13. The need to keep attention focused on the liberalization of trade in farm products was highlighted by the recent Cairns Group Ministerial Meeting in Brazil, which called for a new round of WTO agricultural negotiations prior to the year 2000.

14. In many developing countries, water users are not even charged an amount that covers the operating and maintenance costs of supplying water, let along the capital costs of constructing and upgrading water delivery facilities (Repetto 1986). In Thailand, for example, user fees amount to only 28 percent of operating and maintenance costs.

15. Irrigation subsidies in the United States take the form of "ability to pay" pricing and interest-free loans for construction of irrigation infrastructure.

afford because their limited budgets were expended on subsidies (World Bank 1997).[16]

Energy Subsidies

An "APEC Subsidies Initiative" that eliminates fossil fuel energy subsidies is the single biggest measure APEC could take to protect the environment and human health. Moreover, energy subsidies reform, like agricultural liberalization, promises substantial economic gains. Not only would governments be able to pocket their former multibillion-dollar outlays, but national incomes would grow as a result of the economywide efficiency gains that would follow the removal of price-distorting subsidies.

The economic cost of energy subsidies is enormous (*The Economist*, 14 June 1997). Worldwide fossil fuel subsidies stood at $330 billion in 1985 (Burniaux, Martin, and Oliveira-Martins 1992) and $250 billion in the early 1990s (Larsen 1994; IEA 1995a).[17] These subsidies, which equal 20 to 25 percent of the value of world fossil fuel consumption at world prices, indicate massive price distortions (Larsen and Shah 1992). Fossil fuel subsidies are of particular concern in a number of APEC countries, including Japan,[18] the Philippines, China,[19] Australia, and Canada.

Reducing energy subsidies would both take the pressure off governments fiscally and deliver significant economic benefits to consumers, households, and industry. First, reductions in energy subsidies are likely to spur significant improvements in energy efficiency. In China, for example, efficiency jumped by over 30 percent as the coal subsidy rate was reduced from 37 percent in 1984 to 29 percent in 1995 (World Bank 1997). Similar results could be achieved across APEC. Second, energy consumption falls by an estimated half a percentage point for each percentage point increase in price (K. Anderson 1995a),[20] with significant cost savings from lower energy use. Third, as the public health effects traceable to fossil fuel emissions decline, multibillion-dollar savings in health care expenditures will be generated.

---

16. While many of APEC's members have achieved significant reductions in subsidies for pesticides and fertilizers, continued reductions will limit environmental damage to agricultural lands—which ultimately affects agricultural productivity—lessen dangerous runoff in waterways, and reduce harms to human health.

17. Figures are in constant 1995 dollars.

18. In Japan, effective producer subsidies for coal amount to around $160 per ton (Michaelis 1996; IEA 1995).

19. As a result of market reforms since 1995, "preliminary findings indicate that coal prices in China are now close to international prices" (de Moor 1997; see also Earth Council 1997, 47; World Bank 1997). Of course, world prices still reflect subsidies in other nations and do not include the cost of externalities arising from coal consumption.

20. Exact estimates vary from country to country (e.g., Hope and Singh 1995; Julius 1986; Tybout and Moss 1992; Eskeland 1994).

The most disturbing feature of fossil fuel subsidies is that the more environmentally damaging the fuel, the bigger the subsidies (Earth Council 1997, 32). Coal receives the highest subsidies, followed distantly by oil and then natural gas. Because of this skewing, a reduction in subsidies will have a dramatic and positive impact on the environment. Higher prices for the most environmentally damaging fossil fuels will, by increasing energy efficiency and reducing consumption, significantly reduce particulate, NO_x, SO_2, and CO_2 emissions. Reducing coal subsidies in the OECD countries alone would cut global greenhouse emissions by between 1.5 and 5 percent (US Department of Energy 1989; Okugu and Birol 1992; K. Anderson and McKibbin 1997). Other analysis indicates that the elimination of global fossil fuel subsidies could reduce CO_2 emissions by about 10 percent in China and 12 percent in Indonesia (Larsen and Shah 1992). Reductions in emissions will deliver significant environmental benefits, including reductions in, or at least slower growth of, greenhouse gas emissions; less damage to buildings, forests, and lakes from acid rain and particulate emissions; a lower incidence of serious health problems due to the inhalation of air pollutants; and reduced habitat destruction and biodiversity loss from coal mining.

The proposal to eliminate or reduce subsidies has a strong analytic and theoretical basis. In particular, it addresses the need to minimize the effects on the environment of price-distorting policies in the agriculture and energy sectors.

Because many of the effects of subsidies—both physical and economic—spill across national boundaries, collective action on the part of APEC would be especially helpful. Since subsidies are a global problem, worldwide action by the WTO might seem to be preferable to an APEC initiative. Successful multilateral efforts, however, seem unlikely in the immediate future, which is precisely why APEC can and should act. As this study argues, APEC has an important role to play in ratcheting up multilateral efforts where they are unsatisfactory. An APEC Subsidies Initiative could pave the way for global subsidy reductions. Given that the WTO is scheduled to review agricultural protection with a view to further liberalization prior to the year 2000, the pursuit of the agricultural component of our APEC subsidies proposal in 1997, 1998, or 1999 would be particularly timely.

While substantial economic and environmental gains can be achieved by reducing or eliminating subsidies—programs that pay the polluter—doing so must be seen as just a first step toward full implementation of the polluter pays principle. Further policy reforms will be required to fully internalize the costs of agricultural production and energy consumption. Removing coal subsidies, for example, will not produce socially optimal fuel pricing, because coal would still be underpriced to the extent that market prices do not reflect the pollution that arises as a result of burning coal. Once APEC's members have eliminated subsidies they should turn their attention to ensuring that the full social costs of agriculture and energy-related activities are internalized.

Sustainable Pacific Fishing

An initiative designed to return the Pacific fisheries to sustainability and to ensure a steady and reasonably priced supply of fish would be big political news in many APEC countries and could be APEC's contribution to the 1998 Global Year of the Oceans agenda. Seafood is already an important component of the diet across the Asia Pacific region, but as incomes increase, demand for seafood as a source of protein is increasing further (Smithers and Dua 1994). APEC's nations now account for about half the world's consumption of seafood, at among the world's highest per capita rates, with several members exceeding 40 kg/per person per year. Many APEC members cannot meet domestic fish demand from local supplies. Import dependence typically ranges from 15 to 25 percent of demand and in some cases exceeds 50 percent (APEC 1995b). With nearly all the Pacific fisheries overfished or at risk of depletion, a failure to pay attention to the Pacific fisheries could threaten food security in the region.

The depletion of fisheries in the Pacific Ocean represents a classic "tragedy of the commons." The lack of private property rights leads to overexploitation of a common resource. Because there are few restrictions on fishing catches,[21] there is little incentive for a country or any single fishing boat to curb its catch when no one else does. APEC's members must engage in collective action to solve this problem. Where a problem is regional in scale, as is the case here, a cooperative regional undertaking is the optimal response.[22] The problem of overfishing can be alleviated by simulating a private property regime that creates rights in the fish. Toward this end, tradable fishing allowances for the Pacific Ocean should be created and allocated to each APEC country,[23] with the total catch allowed by these permits set at levels that would bring the Pacific fisheries

---

21. There are some minor exceptions to this. For example, both Australia and New Zealand have adopted systems of individual transferable quotas for selected species (UNESCAP 1995).

22. Of course, an APEC fishing regime would not cover some important fishing countries in the region, including Russia. But this problem can easily be rectified by inviting Russia into the regime. In fact, APEC already has in place a mechanism by which nonmembers can be invited to participate at the working group level.

23. Serious attention will need to be paid to the initial distribution of permits—not only because allocating the permits is likely to be politically sensitive, but because it will influence the magnitude of the efficiency gains that can be achieved through a tradable-permits system and the efficiency of the system as a conservation measure.

back to sustainability.[24] A starting point for such a proposal would be to allocate permits for the high seas beyond the Exclusive Economic Zone (EEZ) of each APEC country.[25] To have real impact, however, each country should also apply the permitting concept to its own EEZ, where a substantial proportion of seafood harvesting takes place.

For a tradable permit system to function efficiently, better information must be made available both to the authorities responsible for setting the level of the fishing catch and to the fishermen who will make commercial decisions about whether to buy or sell permits. Accurate projections of the supply and demand of fish will be essential to determine the overall catch ceiling for each species. APEC might also set up a "market" to facilitate the acquisition or disposition of fishing permits. Furthermore, a tradable permits scheme must be accompanied by an appropriate system for monitoring and compliance to prevent circumvention of the limitations imposed by the permit scheme.

APEC's leaders have already set the stage for a major fishing initiative by placing a priority in the 1995 Osaka Declaration on "the conservation and sustainable use of fisheries resources" (APEC 1995a). The leaders also decided that in pursuing this goal, the organization should consider applying economic instruments to address fisheries challenges. It is vital that their directive not lose force as it moves down to lower bureaucratic levels.

If APEC proves to be a useful forum for negotiation over property rights in the context of fisheries, its members may want to move on to consider other pollution and resource problems that arise from the lack of clear property rights or from the inability of those who hold rights to vindicate their positions. In particular, tradable permit schemes may prove useful in combating acid rain and climate change.

Environmental Standards and Trade Facilitation

Divergent views about the appropriate stringency of environmental standards represent a major potential flash point within APEC. As earlier chapters spelled out, APEC's developing nations see the prospect of hav-

---

24. Given the complexity of trying to bring all fishermen within the scope of such a system, it would make sense to focus initially on the comparatively smaller number of trawlers employed by large-scale fishing enterprises, rather than attempting to focus on the many small-scale subsistence fishermen.

25. The EEZ is the region of open sea extending 200 miles seaward from coastal states, in which the state maintains sovereign rights "for the purpose of exploring and exploiting, conserving and managing the natural resources, whether living or non-living, of the seabed and subsoil and the [ad]jacent waters" (UN Convention on the Law of the Sea 1982). The coastal state is therefore given freedom to determine the allowable seafood catch in its EEZ, and it is also charged with conservation of EEZ resources.

ing to meet high (developed-country) environmental standards, especially production process or method (PPM) requirements, as an obstacle to market access. More important, they view such standards as a violation of their sovereignty and a breach of their right to set their own standards consistent with their own judgments about how to trade off environmental quality against other goals.

Officials in some of APEC's industrialized nations fear that lax standards will confer an unfair competitive advantage on enterprises operating in low-standard countries, resulting in a "political drag" on their environmental policymaking process that will make it hard to maintain or elevate standards (even if it is clear that higher standards would be socially optimal) and difficult to sustain the momentum for deeper integration. Similarly, they worry that "mutual recognition" obligations related to product standards will expose their consumers to environmentally harmful goods that happen to meet developing-nation requirements.

APEC's members might limit conflicts over both PPM and product standards through an "Environmental Standards and Trade Facilitation Initiative" that carefully attends to cross-country differences in values and environmental programs. The first component of a facilitation initiative should be a renewed commitment by all APEC members—particularly APEC's developing members—to enforce their existing environmental standards and regulations. This seemingly minimal step is important because lax enforcement in APEC has widened the real differential between developing- and developed-country environmental standards.[26] With the integrity of existing environmental standards providing a baseline for economic interaction within APEC, attention might then be turned to a carefully structured program of standards "convergence" or "harmonization"[27] as a way of defusing market access and unfair competition concerns.[28]

---

26. The need to ensure the enforcement of existing environmental regulations was a central component of efforts to satisfy those critics of NAFTA who believed that lax enforcement would encourage industrial migration (P. Johnson and Beaulieu 1996).

27. Esty and Geradin (1997) explain that "harmonization" need not mean identical standards across all jurisdictions.

28. The difference between product and PPM standards is important. *Product* standards relate to the environmental performance and design attributes of goods. *PPM* standards affect how goods are made or obtained. Historically, trade rules permit countries to establish whatever product requirements they want so long as their rules do not result in arbitrary or unjustified discrimination against imports and are not a disguised restriction on trade. Thus, countries can require imported cars to have certain pollution control devices such as catalytic converters, imported fruits to be free of pesticide residues, and imported chemicals to be labeled with specified warnings. In contrast, GATT rules traditionally forbid PPM standards as an infringement of sovereignty, based on the theory that it is inappropriate for one country to tell another what production processes to employ. Thus, even nondiscriminatory PPM rules are considered illegal nontariff barriers to trade.

Product Standards

The challenge of environmental product standards is to find ways to differentiate between legitimate ecological and public health requirements and those constructed with an intent to favor domestic producers. Trade rules permit countries to determine their own preferred level of risk but forbid them from structuring their standards in ways that are not scientifically defensible.[29] A further challenge emerges from the need to balance the business advantages of harmonized standards (which permit producers to enjoy economies of scale with a single product that can enter every market) against the welfare gains of diverse standards (which allow each jurisdiction to tailor its rules to its own circumstances and citizen preferences).

APEC's current approach to this market access/regulatory sovereignty dilemma is to encourage "mutual recognition" by its members of each other's national standards (APEC 1995a; APEC 1996).[30] But in the environmental realm, a focus on negotiating "mutual recognition agreements" (MRAs) is misplaced. Mutual recognition does not work unless all participants have roughly comparable standards—so that no nation feels that its environmental precepts are violated by a commitment to allow unfettered entry to the products of others.[31] Because environmental product standards vary widely across APEC, MRAs would enable low-standard goods to be transmitted throughout the region to the distress of those whose environmental requirements are more stringent. MRAs are thus not an appropriate course to pursue here.

In many cases, formal harmonization of product standards will not be necessary. Producers learn to meet the requirements of overseas markets they wish to enter (Sykes 1995).[32] APEC might, however, facilitate this process by maintaining a database on standards in each country to assist exporters.

---

29. A WTO dispute resolution panel recently concluded, for example, that the European Union's ban on beef treated with hormones constituted a violation of GATT rules because the union permitted the sale of meat with scientifically indistinguishable naturally occurring hormones.

30. J. S. Wilson (1995) also advocates this approach to product standards.

31. Uniform standards set at high levels may cause those who would have chosen lower requirements to feel that they are being unfairly burdened. Conversely, standards set at low levels will distress those who prefer more strict environmental controls and who must let products they consider to be subpar enter their markets.

32. High product standards in large and lucrative jurisdictions such as California, for example, create an incentive for producers in other jurisdictions to meet the higher standards voluntarily to ensure market access (Vogel 1995). But this dynamic generally cannot be relied on when goods are being produced mainly for domestic consumption—thus, because most of the cars produced in China are for the domestic market there is no need for them to meet the higher, more environmentally friendly standards set by other jurisdictions.

In some circumstances, consumption of a product has transboundary—regional or global—environmental effects. For example, vehicle emissions and efficiency standards affect the amount of carbon dioxide emitted and thus efforts to combat climate change. In such cases, economic efficiency demands harmonization (Bhagwati and Hudec 1996; Nordhaus 1994)[33]—and APEC might well be able to play a role in fashioning appropriate requirements.[34]

Production Process or Method (PPM) Standards

Differences in process standards lie at the heart of complaints in developed countries that lax environmental rules in developing countries create unfair competitive advantages and downward pressure—political drag—on the environmental programs in high-standard countries. These arguments have validity. In some cases, low standards cannot be justified because of their transboundary impacts—either physical pollution spillovers or potential for triggering a race-toward-the-bottom dynamic.

But, at the same time, developing countries argue that to hold them to high standards that do not comport with their own circumstances and values is unfair and deprives them of a point of legitimate comparative advantage. In fact, because countries have different environmental endowments and preferences, absolute uniformity in PPM standards would likely be neither efficient nor advisable (K. Anderson 1996).[35] The policy goal must be to maximize the opportunity for legitimate differences to play out in welfare-enhancing divergent standards without permitting the competitive pressures thereby unleashed to cause a welfare-reducing regulatory race toward the bottom.

In striking this balance, APEC should consider adopting a multitiered system of PPM standards. Tiered standards would minimize the unconstructive competitiveness pressures that might otherwise lead to a loss of enthusiasm for trade and investment liberalization. At the same time, having standards set at a high level for developed APEC countries, at a modest level for industrializing countries, and at a baseline level for

---

33. Given differences in circumstances, and the costs involved, complete harmonization of emissions and efficiency standards might not be possible; other options, as suggested by Esty and Geradin (1997), could be pursued.

34. Skeptics might argue that harmonization negotiations would be better carried out on a worldwide scale under the auspices of the UN Environment Program or the World Trade Organization. But UNEP seems incapable of such tasks and the WTO appears unwilling to reach beyond a narrowly defined trade management role.

35. Mendelsohn (1986) demonstrates that the welfare loss from uniform standards rises as circumstances and preferences become more heterogeneous. If, in contrast, conditions and values are relatively homogeneous, the welfare loss from a harmonized standard will be relatively small—and might be worth bearing to obtain market access benefits and greater control over the race toward the bottom.

the least-developed members of APEC would ensure that the economic efficiency gains of differentiated standards would not be entirely lost.

An Environmental Standards and Trade Facilitation Initiative should appeal to those APEC members desiring an expanded commitment to trade facilitation. More important, this initiative gets to the heart of one of the central tensions in APEC—market access versus national regulatory sovereignty—that otherwise threatens the fragile trade bargain between developing and developed nations (Bergsten 1996; Tay 1996), a tension that will only increase as economic integration deepens.

Institutional Support for APEC Environmental Protection

APEC's existing institutional structure has proven to be both ineffective and, at times, too complex, creating a need for reform (Bodde 1997). When reform takes place, the emergent institutional infrastructure should include an Environment Committee, an environmental advisory body, and a dispute mediation process sensitive to environmental concerns. Without this minimal investment in institutional support, regional environmental management efforts are unlikely to succeed.

Environment Committee

APEC needs an Environment Committee to serve as the institutional home for the organization's environmental initiatives.[36] While the concept of integrating economic and environmental considerations in the program of each working group is laudable, it does not work in practice.[37] Responsibility for APEC's environmental work program and the goal of sustainable development must be lodged with a single group.

Creation of an APEC Environment Committee need not entail a large bureaucracy nor should it be the precursor to a regional environmental protection agency. Like NAFTA's Commission for Environmental Cooperation (CEC) and the OECD's Environment Directorate—both of which

---

36. APEC itself has recognized that the management of its existing environmental program is deficient and is looking at options for a coordinating mechanism. But this effort is flawed because creation of a new overarching committee or group to manage APEC's environment program is not one of the options being considered. The decision to rule out new institutional structures neglects the fact that a certain degree of institutional capacity is essential to advance APEC's environmental agenda.

37. Similarly, although national governments can stress the need for their ministries of agriculture, transportation, trade, and energy to take environmental concerns into account, no country dares go without an environment ministry to coordinate and oversee these activities.

have small staffs—an APEC Environment Committee, supported by a small secretariat in Singapore, should be established to promote collaboration among national environmental officials to achieve APEC's environmental objectives. In addition to bearing primary responsibility for coordinating and managing APEC's major environmental initiatives, the Environment Committee would manage and provide support for the calendar of meetings—of ministers, experts, and senior environment officials—required to advance the environmental program. It could also take responsibility for tracking important environmental indicators and coordinating regional capacity building.

Environmental Indicators

APEC's Environment Committee should define a set of "environmental indicators"—quantitative measures of environmental quality and public health—that each APEC country would track as a means of assessing progress in meeting environmental goals. Furthermore, to facilitate comparisons and policy refinement, each APEC country should accept responsibility for reporting on its performance, either annually or biennially. For the indicators to be successful, they should be user driven, policy relevant, and highly aggregated (Hammond et al. 1995). Scoring environmental progress numerically, in the same way that economic performance is tracked, would provide decision makers with useful information, highlight areas of concern, create pressures for countries to address issues requiring attention, and provide citizens across the APEC regions with the kind of information they need to understand environmental issues and thus articulate their concerns.

Capacity Building

A recurring theme of this study has been the need to help build environmental regulatory capacity among APEC's developing members. In performing this function, an APEC Environment Committee should focus on developing three core elements: capable people, capable institutions, and an enabling environment (Needham 1997). *Capable people* are the human resource base of managerial and technical personnel directly responsible for environmental protection. *Capable institutions* are the structures, functions, information and communication systems, resources, strategic leadership, and systems required to promote good governance. An *enabling environment* is one whose social dimensions and legal framework promote better environmental protection. Each APEC member's needs with regard to capacity building will vary. Some countries will require assistance across all three of these areas; others have weaknesses in only one or two.

Environmental Advisory Group

An APEC Environmental Advisory Group (AEAG) would strengthen APEC's environmental performance. A group of outside advisers could help to overcome several critical problems that are undermining APEC's environmental efforts.[38] At present, the lack of environmental expertise within many APEC forums means that the political commitment of the leaders to sustainable development gets lost as soon as the annual Leaders' Summit winds down. Even when innovative environmental initiatives are proposed at the working group or committee level, opposition from officials from just a few countries can scuttle them, preventing their transmission to APEC's senior officials, let alone to ministers and the leaders.

By preparing an annual report for presentation to APEC's leaders, outlining both APEC's progress in moving toward sustainable development and recommendations for further action, an outside advisory group could help to sustain the momentum for action. The group could also respond to requests from environment ministers and the Senior Officials Meeting for advice, ideas, and counsel on environmental issues, and issues at the economy-environment interface, as and when needed.

A procedure should be established by which the AEAG can elicit expert advice from both scientists and policymakers. It is also critical that there be an opportunity for NGO input into the work of the group.[39] If APEC is serious about building and fostering an Asia Pacific community, then the public needs to be engaged in and convinced of the value of the APEC process (Macaranas 1997). The need for public involvement through NGOs and civil society more broadly is especially critical in the environmental realm where uncertainties are significant, scientific knowledge evolves quickly, and public understanding of issues must be carefully cultivated. As we discussed in chapters 6 and 7, NGOs play a vital role both as intellectual competition to governments and as connective tissue, ensuring that distant international decision makers know what the thinking is at the grassroots level. This flow of information, both to and from supranational bodies such as APEC, is essential if the public's fears about the impact of regionalization—and the broader globalization process—on issues such as the environment are to be effectively addressed.

Dispute Mediation Service

In 1994, APEC's leaders noted the need for a "voluntary consultative dispute mediation service to supplement the WTO dispute settlement mecha-

---

38. D. Morgan (1996) and Hudson, Prudencio, and Forrest (1995) have similarly suggested the creation of an Environmental Eminent Persons Group. Shiroyama (1997), conversely, suggests an Environment Working Group.

39. APEC has taken promising steps to engage the business community, but no comparable effort has been made to include environmental NGOs or civil society more broadly.

nism" (APEC 1994a). This proposal builds on a desire to prevent the escalation of disputes that might negatively affect APEC liberalization efforts, the spirit of cooperation, and the process of community building.

The need to create an APEC mechanism to help mediate environmental disputes is particularly pressing because there are no established alternative forums for settling pollution or resource disputes. While the WTO actively adjudicates cases that involve environmental issues, it has proven largely unable to accommodate environmental concerns (Charnovitz 1996a). Deficiencies in the WTO dispute settlement procedure—and the GATT panel process that it replaced—can be attributed to the WTO's focus on trade objectives, the lack of transparency in its procedures, a failure to seek appropriate expert advice when environmental issues are implicated, and the prevailing GATT rules, which demand that environmental standards be the "least trade restrictive" option available, a nearly impossible hurdle to clear (Esty 1994a).[40]

An APEC dispute mediation service would be especially valuable if it were innovatively structured to address trade-environment tensions. Toward this end, rather than examining whether domestic standards being used to further health or environmental objectives are the "least trade restrictive," the service should focus on assessing whether the measure is reasonably tailored to achieving a legitimate public health or environmental goal and whether it arbitrarily or capriciously restricts trade. An inquiry of this sort would ensure that misuses of environmental policy would be unveiled, but appropriate environmental, health, and safety programs would be allowed to stand (André Dua, *The Australian*, 13 January 1997; Esty 1994b). In addition, APEC members should address the use of trade measures—multilateral and unilateral—to achieve environmental objectives. Members should agree that trade provisions in multilateral environmental agreements (MEAs) are not to be regarded as a violation of trade obligations under GATT, while the unilateral and extraterritorial use of trade sanctions should be discouraged.

Without an APEC dispute mediation mechanism that is sensitive to environmental tensions, regional economic relations and the prospects for ongoing APEC trade and investment liberalization may be undermined. It is especially important that APEC provide its member nations a means of resolving disagreements before they escalate and spill over into the economic realm. The shrimp-sea turtle dispute between the United States and Thailand and the dispute over salmon in the Pacific Northwest between the United States and Canada are good examples of controversies

---

40. The deficiencies with the WTO procedure are coming into sharper focus since an increasing number of high-profile trade disputes have environmental components, chief among them the US-Mexico tuna-dolphin case, the US-Venezuela reformulated gasoline dispute, the US-EU beef hormone case, and the soon-to-be-adjudicated shrimp-sea turtle case between Thailand and the United States.

that would benefit from an informal process that draws together the relevant actors and is guided by third-party mediators.

While such mediated outcomes would be nonbinding, they offer the potential for creativity and flexibility. Access to relevant scientific and technical experts, as well as to industry and NGOs, would enhance the process. And a focus on cooperation and coordination would improve the odds of coming up with innovative resolutions to conflicts.

Funding

One of the biggest obstacles to general acceptance of an APEC environmental program is finding ways to pay for the proposals. But environmental progress does not have to be expensive. Many steps can be taken that actually save money. And when government resources are required, the up-front costs can often be recouped through fees charged to those who benefit from improved trade flows or resource management (e.g., fishermen).

In fact, all of the initiatives proposed in this study promise net economic gains. Joint implementation, for example, offers substantial cost savings. By allowing the funds that are available for climate change mitigation to be applied wherever the cheapest emissions reduction projects can be found, JI would substantially cut the costs of meeting any emissions reduction targets agreed on in Kyoto. Not only would the proposal to eliminate subsidies save governments the hundreds of billions of dollars currently spent on subsidies, but the removal of price distortions promises allocative efficiency gains of a similar magnitude. The fisheries initiative, which would take a very modest amount of government funding to develop and administer, would yield benefits manyfold greater. The harmonization of product standards, where appropriate, and the development of a multitiered structure of PPM standards would likewise deliver large welfare gains for a minimal government investment by substantially reducing the transaction costs of trade and the capital costs of environmental investments. In brief, these initiatives would require very modest APEC administrative expenditures.

Funding would, however, be required to support the proposed Environment Committee and pay for its capacity-building and indicator-tracking efforts. Yet these expenditures, too, would be comparatively small and could be supported by voluntary contributions to an APEC Environment Fund.[41] Viewed as the overhead for economic integration, the costs of an

---

41. This proposal is along the lines of the suggestion to set up an APEC fund to support ecotech activities, made last year to President Ramos before the Manila Leaders' Summit by the "Friends of the Advisor" (made up of many members of the now-defunct Eminent Persons Group). Initial seed money might come from the $100 million that is already available through Japan's "Muruyama Fund" (Bergsten 1997).

APEC environmental program would be trivial—perhaps a few hundred million dollars to support trillions of dollars of trade and investment activity.

Importance of Private-Sector Investment

The Asian Development Bank (ADB 1997, 257) estimates that environment-related funding needs for the Asia Pacific region[42] are presently on the order of $40 billion (1990 dollars) annually and can be expected to rise to over $200 billion per year by 2020. Domestically sourced public- and private-sector funds have been able to meet only a small portion of these needs (O'Connor 1994). How can the funding gap be bridged? Certainly not through official development assistance (ODA), since only a few billion dollars are made available annually for environmental investments by the World Bank, the ADB, the Global Environment Facility (GEF), other international organizations, and bilateral foreign aid donors. Private-sector foreign direct investment (FDI) inflows to APEC's developing economies, however, now exceed $70 billion per year.[43] FDI therefore represents the only realistic large-scale source of funding for the requisite environmental investments (Esty and Gentry 1997).

FDI can be a powerful mechanism for environmental protection. It provides a source of funds for investment in environmental infrastructure such as drinking water systems, sewage treatment plants, and waste disposal facilities. And when multinational companies set up new production facilities in developing nations—either alone or in a joint venture with a local partner—they often bring with them less-polluting and more resource efficient technologies, as well as transplanting environmental management systems, transferring environmental best practices, and training local personnel.[44]

For a number of reasons, the environmental performance of multinational corporations from developed nations is often better than required by host country regulations. First, companies operating in multiple markets may adopt companywide technologies and procedures to achieve economies of scale and efficiency gains. Second, large foreign companies often take environmental stewardship seriously because they are highly visible and may present an attractive target for local enforcement officials

---

42. "Asia Pacific" in the ADB study includes East Asia, Southeast Asia, South Asia, and some of the former Soviet republics, but not North America, Australia, and New Zealand.

43. This figure compares to less than $10 billion of FDI inflows in 1985.

44. Moreover, in many places the private sector is investing in environmental improvements as a competitive strategy, especially where governments are creating incentives for innovation by carefully constructing environmental performance standards (M. Porter and van der Linde 1995a, 1995b; G. Porter 1996).

who wish to demonstrate the efficacy and stringency of their regulatory programs. In addition, the prospect of liability for environmental harms—the specter of the Bhopal disaster—often motivates better environmental performance than required by local environmental standards (Schmidheiny and Gentry 1997).

FDI-induced environmental progress is, furthermore, likely to have a leveraged effect on the host economy because the improved practices introduced by foreign firms are often adopted across the domestic industry, associated customers, suppliers, and ultimately the FDI-recipient economy as a whole (Schmidheiny and Gentry 1997).

FDI will not always result in environmental improvements. Some companies set up operations abroad with the hope that they will be able to reduce costs, including environmental compliance expenditures.[45] In other cases, FDI recipients seek to eliminate pollution control measures from projects to reduce the capital cost of their investments. In China, for instance, foreign companies eager to build power plants have fallen over each other trying to meet the demands of municipal and provincial governments to strip pollution controls out of their proposals and thereby maximize the generating capacity installed per dollar invested (Esty and Gentry 1997).

Understanding the importance of FDI as a source of possible environmental progress—and alternatively degradation—has several important policy implications. First, while APEC countries should make themselves attractive to investment, being attractive does not require lowering environmental standards (Schmidheiny and Gentry 1997). On the contrary, investors are motivated by factors such as the rule of law, security of contracts, and the capacity to repatriate profits. APEC's members can provide guarantees to foreign investors against various forms of arbitrary or discriminatory treatment by upgrading their commitment to investment liberalization through adherence to APEC's own Non-Binding Investment Code. Additionally, APEC members should support efforts to liberalize investment through the Multilateral Agreement on Investment (MAI) negotiations at the OECD in Paris.

Second, APEC's members should help to develop a mechanism that prevents strategic setting of environmental standards and blunts regulatory races toward the bottom.[46] APEC's members can accomplish this task by developing a set of environmental investment guidelines to maximize

---

45. As we noted in chapter 5, when cost variables are salient, countries may compete with each other to offer the most attractive locale by promising lax environmental standards. Such a regulatory race toward the bottom can leave all jurisdictions with suboptimal environmental results.

46. APEC's Non-Binding Investment Code already has, and the OECD's MAI contemplates, a clause calling on governments not to lower environmental standards to attract foreign investment.

the environmental benefits of FDI—and by encouraging the inclusion of such guidelines in the MAI.

As private foreign capital becomes the central engine of growth, finding ways to channel these funds into environmental infrastructure projects and to ensure that every newly constructed industrial facility has appropriate environmental controls emerges as the key to sustainable development.

Conclusion

Inattention to the environmental issues confronting APEC's members stands in the way of a better life for APEC's citizens. While economic growth has improved the quality of life, the accompanying damage done to the environment and to human health detracts from these improvements. What's more, because many environmental harms arise from externalities, problems of the commons, and price-distorting government policies, environmental problems substantially impair the allocative efficiency of the emerging regional economic system. More troubling is the possibility that tensions over market access, competitiveness, the use of trade measures to achieve environmental objectives, the environmental impacts of trade and growth, and the environmental choices selected by other nations will cause key countries to retreat from trade and investment liberalization altogether or, worse, erect new protectionist barriers.

APEC's existing response to these problems can be characterized as at best half-hearted and lacking promise. APEC must change direction to address the environmental concerns. There are a range of tasks that no other institution can perform as well as APEC. Environmental problems of a regional scale in particular need an APEC-level response. In other cases, APEC can improve on the poor or nonexistent performance of national governments and international bodies. In these areas, APEC's contribution to environmental management will be unique. In fact, from an environmental point of view, if APEC did not exist, it would need to be created.

In setting their environmental priorities, we suggest that APEC's members pursue the following agenda:

Initiatives

- Commit to an Asia Pacific "joint implementation" initiative to mitigate climate change effects.
- Eliminate or reduce agricultural and energy subsidies.
- Develop a Pacific-wide tradable fishing permits program.
- Selectively harmonize or promote convergence of environmental product and process standards.

Procedural Improvements

- Create an APEC Environment Committee to provide ongoing institutional support for APEC's environmental program.

- Establish an APEC Environmental Advisory Group of nongovernmental experts.

- Develop an environmentally sensitive APEC dispute mediation service.

APEC's members are currently at a crossroads. Should they choose the wrong path—continued pursuit of a weak and unfocused environmental program—environmental degradation will worsen, economic losses will accumulate, and countries may retreat from their commitment to open trade. But should they choose the right path—and pursue a serious environmental agenda that undergirds and reinforces economic integration—their efforts will help to build an unprecedented community of diverse cultures, geographies, and peoples.

Appendix A
APEC Environmental Vision Statement

This meeting of APEC Ministers for the Environment forged consensus on a wide range of issues, sharing the spirit of the Rio Declaration on Environment and Development. We reaffirmed the inseparable linkages between environment protection and economic growth to build an enduring foundation for sustainable development in our region.

We want to see the continued dynamic growth and growing interdependence of APEC member economies which has transformed our region. We are concerned that degradation of our environment will adversely affect our ability to sustain our economic growth. Our efforts to assure stable and sustainable development must take account of the effect of our economies and our population on the natural environment. To this end we support the outcomes of UNCED [UN Conference on Environment and Development].

We, the Asia Pacific economies are agreed that we must protect our environment and conserve natural resources. In particular, we have to improve the quality of air, water and manage energy resources to ensure sustainable development and provide a more secure future for our people. We agree to develop cooperative programs to this end.

We recognize that problems such as climate change, biodiversity loss, pollution and waste, deteriorating water quality and availability, soil erosion, population pressures, and growing energy consumption challenge all of us to cooperate more effectively in dealing with these issues. APEC should take the lead in addressing these global problems and solutions in line with the global consensus reached at UNCED.

All APEC members share a commitment to sustainable development. We support enhanced protection of our environment and greater sensitivity and concern for the environment in our economic decision-making processes by integrating environmental considerations into relevant policy development and economic decisions throughout the region. To this end, we encourage APEC working groups and policy committees to integrate environmental concerns into their work programs.

Members recognize that the market can be an efficient and flexible means of allocating resources but that market outcomes do not always take into full account relevant environmental concerns. The challenge is to achieve sustainable development while taking advantage of the dynamism that market economies provide.

We welcome the call of the Eminent Persons Group (EPG) and APEC members to embark on a course of sustainable development, without creating new forms of protectionism. We would hope the important EPG work of developing a long term vision for APEC would address equally relevant environmental and economic considerations.

We think APEC's work on the environment should add value to other environmental activities in the region through mutually beneficial work complementary to other multilateral institutions and fora.

We believe sound environment and sound economic policies are mutually supportive and that preventing environmental degradation is fundamental to sustainable development.

We will work together with our APEC Ministers to promote sustainable development, trade and investment in the region, through a vision for APEC that encourages members to integrate environmental considerations into their policymaking having regard to the attached framework of principles for integrating environmental considerations within APEC, at all levels.

APEC economies recognize the inter-relationship among poverty, unsustainable patterns of production and consumption, population growth, natural resource depletion, and environmental degradation, and the potential for regional approaches in addressing global environmental problems. We encourage an enhanced dialogue focused on opportunities for regional cooperation in priority areas such as environmental technologies, environmental education and information, policy tools, and sustainable cities, as well as earth observation and global changes research.

We urge each APEC economy to broaden consultations on sustainable development issues to provide multi-sectoral input into their policy development process. We encourage the private sector to observe their role and obligations in achieving sustainable development. We also encourage APEC senior officials (SOM) to develop ideas for multi-sectoral exchanges at the regional level, including the possible exploration of an Asia Pacific Round Table on the Environment and the Economy, and we encourage

APEC economies to develop their own mechanisms for contacts with the private sector and major groups.

We call on APEC senior officials to build on the environment work already under way in APEC working groups to develop a strategic approach, based on sustainable development principles, for environment considerations to be fully integrated into the program of each APEC working group and policy committee.

We are committed to develop policies that are sound economically and environmentally. We agree that sustainable development depends upon successful implementation of policies and programs that integrate economic, environmental, and social objectives. We believe that APEC should take the lead in achieving sustainable development.

APEC Ministers Responsible for the Environment
Vancouver, Canada
25 March 1994

Appendix B
Framework of Principles for Integrating Economy and Environment in APEC

Preamble

The challenge of sustainable development requires integration of economy and environment in all sectors and at all levels.

The experience of APEC members is that a market economy can be a very efficient and flexible means of allocating resources to meet individual preferences. Competitive market economies make for a dynamic and innovative society.

But the market will not necessarily deliver other objectives that society may have, such as meeting the basic needs of all citizens, environmental quality, and access to resources for future generations.

In seeking to reconcile the objectives of economic growth and efficiency with improved environmental outcomes, the following principles could be taken into consideration by member economies to achieve sustainable development.

Principle: Sustainable Development

Member economies should promote sustainable development and a higher quality of life for all people. All the possible measures should be seriously considered to bring about a society where "... environmental protection shall constitute an integral part of the development process and cannot be considered in isolation from it" (from Principle 4, Rio Declaration on Environment and Development).

Member economies should promote the complementary principles of reduction of poverty and improvement of the environment, consistent with Principle 5 of the Rio Declaration.

Principle: Internalization

Members should "endeavor to promote the internalization of environmental costs and the use of economic instruments, taking into account the approach that the polluter should, in principle, bear the cost of pollution, with due regard to the public interest and without distorting international trade and investment" (from Principle 16, Rio Declaration).

Principle: Science and Research

Scientific research should be fostered to increase the community's understanding of ecological system, and their interactions with the economy, employment, and human communities.

Principle: Technology Transfer

Member economies should cooperate to strengthen capacity-building for sustainable development through exchanges of scientific and technical knowledge. They should enhance the development and transfer of technologies, including new and innovative technologies, consistent with Chapter 34 of Agenda 21.

Principle: The Precautionary Approach

Member economies should, according to their capabilities, widely apply the precautionary approach in accordance with Principle 15 of the Rio Declaration: ". . . Where there are threats of serious or irreversible damage, lack of full scientific certainty shall not be used as a reason for postponing cost-effective measure to prevent environmental degradation."

Principle: Trade and the Environment

Member economies should support multilateral efforts to make trade and environment policies mutually supportive, consistent with Principle 12 and other relevant principles of the Rio Declaration.

Principle: Environmental Education and Information

Member economies, industry, consumer groups, and environmental groups should provide to all citizens information and educational opportunities that will enhance informed choices that affect the environment.

Principle: Financing for Sustainable Development

Member economies should cooperate to meet the goal of mobilizing financial resources for sustainable development, including the exploration of innovative approaches to fund raising schemes and mechanisms, taking into account conditions and priorities of APEC members.

Principle: Role of APEC

APEC members should, in promoting regional cooperation, make the best use of existing multilateral and bilateral fora, and activities of APEC to attain sustainable development. These fora and activities have contributed to the implementation of Agenda 21 in the fields of environmental priority setting, accumulation of scientific knowledge, and enhancement of capacity building. APEC members should seek appropriate ways and means by which APEC can add concrete value to these ongoing activities, avoiding duplication of functions.

Meetings of APEC ministers responsible for the environment should be held on an ad hoc basis as the necessity arises.

APEC members should consider ways to better incorporate sustainable development into the work of APEC Working Groups and Committees, where relevant, including consideration of these issues at the levels of Senior Officials Meetings and APEC Ministerial Meetings.

APEC members should achieve the integration of economy and environment considerations through conscious efforts to incorporate environmental concerns into decision making for sustainable development at all levels.

APEC Ministers Responsible for the Environment
Vancouver, Canada
25 March 1994

References

AAMA (Association of Automobile Manufacturers of America). 1997. *World Motor Vehicle Data*. Detroit: Association of Automobile Manufacturers of America.

Abbott, Frederick M. 1995. *Law and Policy of Regional Integration: The NAFTA and Western Hemispheric Integration in the World Trade Organization System*. Cambridge, MA: Kluwer International Law.

Ackerman, Bruce. 1985. Beyond Carolene Products. *Harvard Law Review* 98, no. 4 (February): 713-46.

ADB (Asian Development Bank). 1993. *Water Utilities Data Book, Asian and Pacific Region*. Manila: Asian Development Bank.

ADB. 1997. *Emerging Asia: Changes and Challenges*. Manila: Asian Development Bank.

Ahooja-Patel, Anne, Gordon Drabek, and Marc Nerfin, eds. 1986. *World Economy in Transition: Essays Presented to Surenda Patel on His Sixtieth Birthday*. New York: Pergamon Press.

Alker, Haywood R., and Peter M. Haas. 1993. The Rise of Global Ecopolitics. In *Global Accord: Environmental Challenges and International Responses*, ed. by Nazli Choucri. Cambridge, MA: MIT Press.

Anderson, Benedict. 1991. *Imagined Communities: Reflections on the Origin and Spread of Nationalism*. London: Verso.

Anderson, Kym. 1992. Effects on the Environment and Welfare of Liberalizing World Trade: The Cases of Coal and Food. In *The Greening of World Trade Issues*, ed. by Kym Anderson and Richard Blackhurst. Ann Arbor: University of Michigan Press.

Anderson, Kym. 1993. *Economic Growth, Environmental Issues, and Trade*. Centre for Economic Policy Research Discussion Paper Series 830. London: Centre for Economic Policy Research.

Anderson, Kym. 1995a. Social Policy Dimensions of Economic Integration: Environmental and Labor Standards. Paper presented at the East Asia Seminar on Regional versus Multilateral Trade Arrangements, sponsored by the NBER, Seoul (15-17 June).

Anderson, Kym. 1995b. *The Political Economy of Coal Subsidies in Europe*. Nota DiLavoro 50.95. Milan: Fondazione ENI Enrico Mattei.

Anderson, Kym. 1996. Environmental Standards and International Trade. In *Annual Bank Conference on Development Economics 1996*, ed. by M. Bruno and B. Pleskovic. Washington: World Bank.

Anderson, Kym, and Richard Blackhurst, eds. 1992. *The Greening of World Trade Issues*. Ann Arbor: University of Michigan Press.

Anderson, Kym, and Warwick J. McKibbin. 1997. *Reducing Coal Subsidies and Trade Barriers: Their Contribution to Greenhouse Gas Abatement*. Seminar Paper 97-07. University of Adelaide: Centre for International Economic Studies.

Andersson, Thomas, Carl Folke, and Stefan Nyström. 1995. *Trading with the Environment: Ecology, Economics, Institutions, and Policy*. London: Earthscan Publications.

APEC (Asia Pacific Economic Cooperation). 1993a. *A Vision for APEC: Towards an Asia-Pacific Economic Community*. First Report of the Eminent Persons Group. Singapore: APEC Secretariat.

APEC. 1993b. *APEC Leaders' Economic Vision Statement (Blake Island, USA)*. Singapore: APEC Secretariat.

APEC. 1994a. *APEC Economic Leaders' Declaration of Common Resolve (Bogor, Indonesia)*. Singapore: APEC Secretariat.

APEC. 1994b. *Achieving the APEC Vision: Free and Open Trade in the Asia Pacific*. Second Report of the Eminent Persons Group. Singapore: APEC Secretariat.

APEC. 1994c. *Environmental Vision Statement*. Singapore: APEC Secretariat.

APEC. 1995a. *APEC Leaders' Declaration of Common Resolve (Osaka, Japan)*. Singapore: APEC Secretariat.

APEC. 1995b. *Feasibility of Improving Market Information on Seafood Trade in the APEC Region*. Singapore: APEC Secretariat.

APEC. 1996. *APEC Economic Leaders' Declaration: From Vision to Action (Subic Bay, the Philippines)*. Singapore: APEC Secretariat.

APEC. 1997a. Evaluation of Economic and Technical Cooperation Program. Photocopy.

APEC. 1997b. *APEC Sustainable Cities: Agenda for Cooperation*. Singapore: APEC Secretariat.

Arden-Clarke, Charles. 1993. Green Protectionism: Differentiating Environmental Protection from Trade Protectionism. Paper presented at a conference on Striking a Green Deal: Europe's Role in the Environment and South-North Trade Relations, Brussels, sponsored by the European Parliament (7-9 November).

ASEAN (Association of Southeast Asian Nations). 1992. *Singapore Resolution on Environment and Development*. Jakarta: ASEAN Secretariat.

ASEAN. 1995. *ASEAN Workshop Report: Trade and the Environment: Issues and Opportunities*. Jakarta: ASEAN Secretariat.

Barro, Robert J. 1991. Economic Growth in a Cross Section of Countries. *Quarterly Journal of Economics* 106, no. 2 (May): 407-43.

Barro, Robert J., and Xavier Sala-i-Martin. 1992. Convergence. *Journal of Political Economy* 100, no. 2 (April): 223-51.

Barron, William, and Jill Cottrell. 1996. *Making Environmental Law in Asia More Effective*. Hong Kong: Center for Urban Planning and Environmental Management.

Bartone, Carl, et al. 1994. *Toward Environmental Strategies for Cities: Policy Considerations for Urban Environmental Management in Developing Countries*. Urban Management Programme Policy Papers 18. Washington: World Bank.

Baser, Heather. 1996. From Technical Cooperation to Capacity Development: Changing Perspectives in CIDA. *International Journal of Technical Cooperation*, no. 3 (Winter).

Baumol, William J., and Wallace E. Oates. 1988. *The Theory of Environmental Policy*. Cambridge, UK: Cambridge University Press.

Bebbington, A., and J. Farrington. 1993. Governments, NGOs, and Agricultural Development: Perspectives on Changing Inter-Organizational Relationships. *Journal of Development Studies* 29, no. 2 (January): 199-220.

Beckerman, Wilfred. 1992. Economic Growth and the Environment: Whose Growth? Whose Environment? *World Development* 20, no. 4 (April): 481-96.

Beckerman, Wilfred. 1996. *Through Green Colored Glasses: Environmentalism Reconsidered*. Washington: Cato Institute.

Bello, Walden. 1993. Trouble in Paradise: The Tension of Economic Integration in the Asia-Pacific. *World Policy Journal* 10, no. 2 (Summer): 33-40.

Bello, Walden, and Nicola Bullard. 1997. *APEC and the Environment: A Report to the Rio + 5 Conference*. Bangkok: Focus on the Global South.

Bergsten, C. Fred. 1992. The Primacy of Economics. *Foreign Policy*, no. 87 (Summer): 3-25.

Bergsten, C. Fred. 1994. APEC and World Trade: A Force for Worldwide Liberalization. *Foreign Affairs* 73, no. 3 (May/June): 20-26.

Bergsten, C. Fred. 1995. *APEC: The Bogor Declaration and the Path Ahead*. Working Paper no. 95-1. Washington: Institute for International Economics.

Bergsten, C. Fred. 1996. Globalizing Free Trade. In *The World Trading System: Challenges Ahead*, ed. by Jeffrey J. Schott. Washington: Institute for International Economics.

Bergsten, C. Fred. 1997. APEC in 1997: Prospects and Possible Strategies. In *Whither APEC? The Progress to Date and Agenda for the Future*, ed. by C. Fred Bergsten. Special Report 9. Washington: Institute for International Economics.

Bergsten, C. Fred, and Marcus Noland. 1993. *Pacific Dynamism and the International Economic System*. Washington: Institute for International Economics.

Bhagwati, Jagdish. 1993a. Trade and the Environment: The False Conflict? In *Trade and the Environment: Law, Economics, and Policy*, ed. by Durwood Zaelke. Washington: Island Press.

Bhagwati, Jagdish. 1993b. The Case for Free Trade. *Scientific American* 269, no. 5 (November): 42-57.

Bhagwati, Jagdish. 1996. Trade and Environment: Does Environmental Diversity Detract from the Case for Free Trade? In *Fair Trade and Harmonization: Prerequisites for Free Trade?*, ed. by Jagdish Bhagwati and Robert Hudec. Cambridge, MA: MIT Press.

Bhagwati, Jagdish, and Robert E. Hudec, eds. 1996. *Fair Trade and Harmonization: Prerequisites for Free Trade?* Cambridge, MA: MIT Press.

Bodansky, Daniel. 1995. Customary (and Not So Customary) International Environmental Law. *Indiana Journal of Global Legal Studies* 3: 105.

Bodde, William. 1997. Managing APEC. In *Whither APEC? The Progress to Date and Agenda for the Future*, ed. by C. Fred Bergsten. Special Report 9. Washington: Institute for International Economics.

Boer, Ben, Ross Ramsay, and Donald R. Rothwell. 1997. *International Environmental Law in the Asia Pacific*. The Hague: Kluwer Law International.

Bora, Bijit. 1995. *Trade and Investment in the APEC Region, 1980-1993*. Seminar Paper 95-16. Adelaide: Centre for International Economic Studies.

Bora, Bijit. 1996. Foreign Direct Investment. In *Regional Integration and the Asia-Pacific*, ed. by Bijit Bora and Christopher Findlay. Melbourne: Oxford University Press.

Bora, Bijit, and Christopher Findlay, eds. 1996. *Regional Integration and the Asia-Pacific*. Melbourne: Oxford University Press.

Brack, Duncan. 1996. *International Trade and the Montreal Protocol*. London: Chatham House.

Braden, John B. 1995. The Economics of Environmental Policymaking in a Multi-Layer Government Structure. In *Recent Economic and Legal Development in European Environmental Policy*, ed. by Filip Abraham. Leuven: Leuven University Press.

Brandenburg, Adam M., and Barry J. Nalebuff. 1996. *Co-opetition*. New York: Doubleday.

Brandon, Carter, and Kirsten Homman. 1995. The Cost of Inaction: Valuing the Economy-Wide Cost of Environmental Degradation in India. Paper presented at the Modelling Global Sustainability conference at the United Nations University, Tokyo (October).

Brandon, Carter, and Ramesh Ramankutty. 1993. *Toward an Environmental Strategy for Asia*. World Bank Discussion Paper 224. Washington: World Bank.

Brandts, J., and C. de Bartolome. 1988. *Social Insurance and Population Uncertainty: Demographic Bias and Implications for Social Security*. C. V. Starr Center for Economic Research Report #88-05. New York: New York University.

Brown, Lester R. 1995. *Who Will Feed China? Wake-up Call for a Small Planet*. New York: Norton.

Brown, Lester R. 1996. *Tough Choices: Facing the Challenge of Food Scarcity*. New York: Norton.

Brown Weiss, Edith. 1989. *In Fairness to Future Generations: International Law, Common Patrimony, and Intergenerational Equity*. New York: Transnational Press.

Brown Weiss, Edith. 1993. Intergenerational Equity: Toward an International Legal Framework. In *Global Accord: Environmental Challenges and International Responses*, ed. by Nazli Choucri. Cambridge, MA: MIT Press.

Buchanan, James M., and Gordon Tullock. 1962. *The Calculus of Consent: Logical Foundations of Constitutional Democracy*. Ann Arbor: University of Michigan Press.

Burniaux, J. M., J. P. Martin, and J. Oliveira-Martins. 1992. The Effect of Existing Distortions in Energy Markets on the Costs of Policies to Reduce CO_2 Emissions: Evidence from GREEN. *OECD Economic Studies*, no. 19 (Winter).

Caldwell, Lynton Keith. 1996. *International Environmental Policy*. Durham, NC: Duke University Press.

Cameron, James, and R. Ramsay. 1995. *Participation by Non-Governmental Organizations in the World Trade Organization*. Global Environment and Trade Study Working Paper no. 1. New Haven: Global Environment and Trade Study.

Carraro, Carlo, and Domenico Siniscalco. 1995. Policy Coordination for Sustainability: Commitments, Transfers, and Linked Negotiations. In *The Economics of Sustainable Development*, ed. by Ian Goldin and L. Alan Winters. Cambridge, UK: Cambridge University Press.

CEC (Commission for Environmental Cooperation). 1996. *Annual Report*. Montreal: Commission for Environmental Cooperation.

CEQ (Council on Environmental Quality). 1995. *Environmental Quality: 25th Anniversary Report*. Washington: White House Council on Environmental Quality.

Charnovitz, Steve. 1993. Achieving Environmental Goals under International Rule. *Reciel 2*, no. 1: 45-52.

Charnovitz, Steve. 1995. Regional Trade Agreements and the Environment. *Environment 37*, no. 6 (July/August): 16-27.

Charnovitz, Steve. 1996a. Improving the Trade and Environment Regimes. In *Asian Dragons and Green Trade*, ed. by Simon S. C. Tay and Daniel C. Esty. Singapore: Times Academic Press.

Charnovitz, Steve. 1996b. Participation of Non-governmental Organizations in the World Trade Organization. *University of Pennsylvania Journal of International Economic Law* 17: 331.

Charnovitz, Steve. 1997. Two Centuries of Participation: NGOs and International Governance. *Michigan Journal of International Law* 18, no. 2 (Winter): 183.

Chase, Robert, Emily Hill, and Paul Kennedy. 1996. Pivotal States and US Strategy. *Foreign Affairs* 74, no. 1 (January-February): 33.

Chertow, Marian, and Daniel C. Esty, eds. 1997. *Thinking Ecologically*. New Haven: Yale University Press.

Chia, Siow Yue, and Tsao Yuan Lee. 1993. Subregional Economic Zones: A New Motive Force in Asia-Pacific Development. In *Pacific Dynamism and the International Economic System*, ed. by C. Fred Bergsten and Marcus Noland. Washington: Institute for International Economics.

Clark, A. M. 1995. Non-Governmental Organizations and their Influence on International Society. *Journal of International Affairs* 48, no. 2 (Winter): 507-25.

Clarke, Jonathon. 1995. APEC as a Semi-Solution. *Orbis* (Winter): 81-95.

Clémençon, Raymond, ed. 1996. Economic Integration and Environment in Southeast Asia. Policy Paper no. 30. Institute on Global Conflict and Cooperation, University of California (July).

Clements, Benedict, Rejane Hugounenq, and Gerd Schwartz. 1995. *Government Subsidies: Concepts, International Trends, and Reform Options*. IMF Working Paper 95/91. Washington: International Monetary Fund.

Cline, William R. 1992. *Economics of Global Warming*. Washington: Institute for International Economics.

Coase, Ronald H. 1960. The Problem of Social Cost. *Journal of Law and Economics* 3: 1-44.

Cooper, Richard N. 1994. *Environment and Resource Policies for the World Economy*. Washington: Brookings Institution.

Cornes, Richard, and Todd Sandler. 1986. *The Theory of Externalities, Public Goods, and Club Goods*. Cambridge, UK: Cambridge University Press.

Covey, Jane. 1995. Accountability and Effectiveness in NGO Policy Alliances. In *Non-Governmental Organizations — Performance and Accountability*, ed. by Michael Edwards and David Hulme. London: Earthscan Publications.

Crowley, Peter, and Christopher Findlay. 1996. Environmental Issues. In *Regional Integration and the Asia-Pacific*, ed. by Bijit Bora and Christopher Findlay. Melbourne: Oxford University Press.

Daly, Herman E. 1993. The Perils of Free Trade. *Scientific American* 269, no. 5 (November): 50-56.

Dean, Judith M. 1992. Trade and the Environment: A Survey of the Literature. In *International Trade and the Environment*, ed. by Patrick Low. World Bank Discussion Paper 159. Washington: World Bank.

Dee, Philipa, Chris Geisler, and Greg Watts. 1996. *The Impact of APEC's Free Trade Commitment*. Staff Information Paper. Australia: Australian Industry Commission.

de Moor, André. 1997 *Perverse Incentives*. Vancouver: Earth Council.

Demsetz, Harold. 1967. Toward a Theory of Property Rights. *American Economic Review* 57, no. 2 (May): 347-59.

Demsetz, Harold. 1969. Information and Efficiency: Another Viewpoint. *Journal of Law and Economics* 12, no. 1 (April): 1-22.

Dent, F. J. 1989. Land Degradation in Asia and the Pacific. In *Environment and Agriculture*, ed. by Food and Agriculture Organization. Bangkok: Food and Agriculture Organization.

DeShazo, J. R. 1996. The Level of and Demand for Environmental Quality in Asia. Background paper for ADB 1997.

Diamond, Peter. 1977. A Framework for Social Security Analysis. *Journal of Public Economics* 8, no. 3 (December): 275-98.

Diver, Colin S. 1983. The Optimal Precision of Administrative Rules. *Yale Law Journal* 93, no. 1: 65-109.

Dixit, Avinash K., and Barry J. Nalebuff. 1991. *Thinking Strategically: The Competitive Edge in Business, Politics, and Everyday Life*. New York: Norton.

Downs, Anthony. 1957. *An Economic Theory of Democracy*. New York: Harper.

Dua, André, and Daniel C. Esty. 1997. APEC and Sustainable Development. In *Whither APEC? The Progress to Date and Agenda for the Future*, ed. by C. Fred Bergsten. Special Report 9. Washington: Institute for International Economics.

Earth Council. 1997. *Subsidizing Unsustainable Development*. Vancouver: Earth Council.

Easterbrook, Gregg. 1995. *A Moment on the Earth: The Coming Age of Environmental Optimism*. New York: Viking.

Economy, Elizabeth. 1997. *Reforms and Resources: The Implications for State Capacity in the PRC*. Washington: American Academy of Arts and Sciences.

Eder, Norman. 1996. *Poisoned Prosperity: Development, Modernization, and the Environment in South Korea*. Armonk, NY: M. E. Sharpe.

Ehrlich, Isaac, and Richard A. Posner. 1974. An Economic Analysis of Legal Rulemaking. *Journal of Legal Studies* 3: 257-86.

Eikeland, P. O. 1994. US Environmental NGOs: New Strategies for New Environmental Problems? *Journal of Social, Political, and Economic Studies* 19, no. 3 (Fall): 259-86.

Elazar, Daniel J. 1987. *Exploring Federalism*. Tuscaloosa: University of Alabama Press.

Elazar, Daniel J. 1991. *Federal Systems of the World: A Handbook of Federal, Confederated, and Autonomy Arrangements*. Essex, UK: Longman Current Affairs.

Ellickson, Robert C. 1979. Public Property Rights: A Government's Rights and Duties When Its Landowners Come into Conflict with Outsiders. *Southern California Law Review* 52, no. 6 (September): 1627-69.

Engleman, R., and P. LeRoy. 1993. *Sustaining Water: Population and the Future of Renewable Water Supplies*. Washington: Population Action International.

Eskeland, Gunnar S. 1994. *Energy Pricing and Air Pollution: Evidence from Manufacturing in Chile and Indonesia*. Policy Research Working Paper 1323. Washington: World Bank.

Eskeland, Gunnar S., and Ann E. Harrison. 1997. *Moving to Greener Pastures? Multinationals and the Pollution Haven Hypothesis*. Photocopy.

Esrey, Stephen A., et al. 1990. *Health Benefits from Improvements in Water Supply and Sanitation: Survey and Analysis of the Literature on Selected Diseases*. Technical Report 66. Arlington, VA: Water and Sanitation for Health Project.

Esty, Daniel C. 1993a. Rio Revisited: Turning the Giant's Head. *Ecodecision* (September): 90-91.

Esty, Daniel C. 1993b. Integrating Trade and Environmental Policymaking: First Steps in NAFTA. In *Trade and Environment: Law, Economics, and Policy*, ed. by Durwood Zaelke. Washington: Island Press.

Esty, Daniel C. 1994a. *Greening the GATT: Trade, Environment, and the Future*. Washington: Institute for International Economics.

Esty, Daniel C. 1994b. Making Trade and Environmental Policies Work Together: Lessons from NAFTA. *Aussenwirtschaft* 49 (January): 59-79.

Esty, Daniel C. 1994c. The Case for a Global Environmental Organization. In *Managing the World Economy: Fifty Years after Bretton Woods*, ed. by Peter Kenen. Washington: Institute for International Economics.

Esty, Daniel C. 1996a. Environment and Security: Borders and the Biosphere. In *The Convergence of US National Security and the Global Environment*, ed. by Dick Clark. Washington: Aspen Institute.

Esty, Daniel C. 1996b. Revitalizing Environmental Federalism. *Michigan Law Review* 95, no. 3 (December): 570-653.

Esty, Daniel C. 1997a. Environmental Protection during the Transition to a Market Economy. In *Economies in Transition: Comparing Asia and Europe*, ed. by Wing Thye Woo, Stephen Parker, and Jeffrey D. Sachs. Cambridge, MA: MIT Press.

Esty, Daniel C. 1997b. Environmentalists and Trade Policymaking. In *Representation of Constituent Interests in the Design and Implementation of U.S. Trade Policies*, ed. by Alan V. Deardorff and Robert M. Stern. Ann Arbor: University of Michigan Press.

Esty, Daniel C. 1997c. Stepping Up to the Global Environmental Challenge. *Fordham Environmental Law Journal* 8, no. 1 (Fall): 103-13.

Esty, Daniel C. 1997d. Why the World Trade Organization Needs Environmental NGOs. *Bridges: Public Participation in the International Trading System* 1, no. 3: 3.

Esty, Daniel C. 1998. Pivotal States and Environmental Protection. In *Pivotal States*, ed. by Paul Kennedy, Emily Hill, and Robert Chase. New York: Norton. Forthcoming.

Esty, Daniel C., and Bradford S. Gentry. 1997. Foreign Investment, Globalization, and the Environment. In *Globalization and the Environment*, ed. by Tom Jones. Paris: Organization for Economic Cooperation and Development.

Esty, Daniel C., and Damien Geradin. 1997. Market Access, Competitiveness, and Harmonization: Environmental Protection in Regional Trade Agreements. *Harvard Environmental Law Review* 21, no. 2: 265-336.

Esty, Daniel C., and Robert Mendelsohn. 1995. *Powering China*. New Haven: Yale Center for Environmental Law and Policy.

Evans, Peter. 1994. Japan's Green Aid. *China Business Review* 21, no. 4 (July): 39.

Executive Office of the President of the United States. 1997. *Study on the Operation and Effects of the North American Free Trade Agreement*. Washington: Executive Office of the President.

Fairman, David, and Michael Ross. 1996. Old Fads, New Lessons: Learning from Economic Development Assistance. In *Institutions for Environmental Aid*, ed. by Robert O. Keohane and Marc A. Levy. Cambridge, MA: MIT Press.

FAO (Food and Agriculture Organization). 1993. *Forest Resources Assessment 1990: Tropical Countries*. FAO Forestry Paper 112. Rome: Food and Agriculture Organization.

FAO. 1994a. *Selected Indicators of Food and Agriculture Development in the Asia-Pacific Region, 1983-1993*. Rome: Food and Agriculture Organization.

FAO. 1994b. *Review of the State of World Marine Fishery Resources*. FAO Technical Paper 335. Rome: Food and Agriculture Organization.

Farber, Daniel A. 1996. Stretching the Margins: The Geographic Nexus in Environmental Law. *Stanford Law Review* 48, no. 5 (May): 1247-78.

Fischel, William A. 1975. Fiscal and Environmental Considerations in the Location of Firms in Suburban Communities. In *Fiscal Zoning and Land Use Controls: The Economic Issues*, ed. by Edwin S. Mills and Wallace E. Oates. Lexington, MA: Lexington Books.

Foell, W. K., and C. W. Green. 1990. *Acid Rain in Asia: An Economic, Energy, and Emissions Overview*. Madison, WI: Resource Management Associates of Madison.

Francois, Joseph F., Bradley McDonald, and Hakan Nordstrom. 1994. *The Uruguay Round: A Global General Equilibrium Assessment*. Geneva: GATT Secretariat.

Frankel, Emil. 1997. Co-Existing with the Car. In *Thinking Ecologically: Building the Next Generation of Environmental Policy*, ed. by Marian Chertow and Daniel C. Esty. New Haven: Yale University Press.

Frankel, Jeffrey. 1997. *Regional Trading Blocs in the World Economic System*. Washington: Institute for International Economics.

Frankel, Jeffrey, David Romer, and Teresa Cyrus. 1996. *Trade and Growth in East Asian Countries: Cause and Effect?* NBER Working Paper 5732. Cambridge, MA: National Bureau of Economic Research.

French, Hilary. 1997. Learning from the Ozone Experience. In *State of the World 1997: A Worldwatch Institute Report on Progress toward a Sustainable Future*, ed. by Worldwatch Institute. New York: Norton.

Fujisaki, Shigeaki. 1995. Development and the Environment: The Experiences of Japan and Industrializing Asia. In *Development and the Environment: The Experiences of Japan and Industrializing Asia*, ed. by Reeitsu Kojima et al. Tokyo: Institute of Developing Economies.

Funabashi, Yoichi. 1995. *Asia-Pacific Fusion: Japan's Role in APEC*. Washington: Institute for International Economics.

Garnaut, Ross, Fang Cai, and Yiping Huang. 1996. A Turning Point in China's Agricultural Development. In *The Third Revolution in the Chinese Countryside*, ed. by Ross Garnaut, Guo Shutian, and Ma Gounan. New York: Cambridge University Press.

GATT (General Agreement on Tariffs and Trade). 1993. Economy-wide Effects of the Uruguay Round. GATT Background Papers. Geneva: GATT Secretariat.

GESAMP. 1993. Reports and Studies 50. London: IMO.

Gingrich, Newt. 1995. *To Renew America*. New York: HarperCollins.

Goldin, Ian, Odin Knudsen, and Dominique van der Mensbrugghe. 1993. *Trade Liberalization: Global Economic Implications*. Paris: OECD Development Centre and World Bank.

Goldstone, Jack. 1996. The Coming Chinese Collapse. *Foreign Policy*, no. 99 (Summer): 35-54.

Gordenker, L., and T. G. Weiss. 1996. Pluralizing Global Governance: Analytical Approaches and Dimensions. In *NGOs, the UN, and Global Governance*, ed. by T. G. Weiss. Boulder, CO: Lynne Rienner.

Government of Korea. 1994. Country paper presented to Regional Meeting on the State of Environment in Asia and the Pacific 1995, Myanmar (26-30 July).

Graham, John D., and Jonathan Baert Wiener. 1995. *Risk versus Risk: Tradeoffs in Protecting Health and the Environment*. Cambridge, MA: Harvard University Press.

Gray, C. Boyden. 1983. Regulation and Federalism. *Yale Journal on Regulation* 1 (Fall): 93.

Greider, William. 1997. *One World, Ready or Not: The Manic Logic of Global Capitalism*. New York: Simon and Schuster.

Grossman, Gene M. 1995. Pollution and Growth: What Do We Know? In *The Economics of Sustainable Development*, ed. by Ian Goldin and L. Alan Winters. Cambridge, UK: Cambridge University Press.

Grossman, Gene M., and Alan B. Krueger. 1993. Environmental Impacts of a North American Free Trade Agreement. In *The Mexico-US Free Trade Agreement*, ed. by Peter M. Garber. Cambridge, MA: MIT Press.

Grossman, Gene M., and Alan B. Krueger. 1995. Economic Growth and the Environment. *Quarterly Journal of Economics* 110, no. 2 (May): 353-75.

Haas, Peter M., with Jan Sundgren. 1993. Evolving International Environmental Law: Changing Practices of National Sovereignty. In *Global Accord: Environmental Challenges and Institutional Responses*, ed. by Nazli Choucri. Cambridge, MA: MIT Press.

Haas, Peter M., Robert O. Keohane, and Marc A. Levy, eds. 1993. *Institutions for the Earth: Sources of Effective International Environmental Protection*. Cambridge, MA: MIT Press.

Haggard, Stephen. 1995. *Developing Nations and the Politics of Global Integration*. Washington: Brookings Institution.

Hahn, Robert W., and Robert N. Stavins. 1992. Economic Incentives for Environmental Protection: Integrating Theory and Practice. *American Economic Review* 82, no. 2 (May): 464-69.

Hall, Colin Michael. 1992. *Wasteland to World Heritage: Preserving Australia's Wilderness*. Melbourne: Melbourne University Press.

Hammer, Jeffrey S., and Sudhir Shetty. 1995. *East Asia's Environment: Principles and Priorities for Action*. World Bank Discussion Paper 287. Washington: World Bank.

Hammond, Allen, et al. 1995. *Environmental Indicators: A Systematic Approach to Measuring and Reporting on Environmental Policy Performance in the Context of Sustainable Development*. Baltimore: World Resources Institute.

Han, Ki-Ju, and John B. Braden. 1997. Environmental Regulation and Trade: Exploring the Time Dimension. Photocopy.

Hanley, Nick, Jason F. Shogren, and Ben White. 1997. *Environmental Economics in Theory and Practice*. New York: Oxford University Press.

Hanna, Susan S., Carl Folke, and Karl-Göran Mäler. 1996. *Rights to Nature: Ecological, Economic, Cultural, and Political Principles of Institutions for the Environment*. Washington: Island Press.

Harday, Jorge E., Diana Mitlin, and David Satterthwaite. 1992. *Environmental Problems in Third World Cities*. London: Earthscan Publications.

Hardin, Garrett. 1968. The Tragedy of the Commons. *Science* 162: 1243-48.

Harrison, Ann. 1995. *Openness and Growth: A Time-Series, Cross-Country Analysis for Developing Countries*. NBER Working Paper 5221. Cambridge, MA: National Bureau of Economic Research.

Haskell, Thomas L. 1985. Capitalism and the Origins of the Humanitarian Sensibility. *American Historical Review* 90, no. 3 (June): 547-66.

Helliwell, John. 1995. Asian Economic Growth. In *Pacific Trade and Investment: Options for the '90s*, ed. by Wendy Dobson and Frank Flatters. Kingston, ON: International and Development Studies Institute.

Hempel, Lamont C. 1996. *Environmental Governance*. Washington: Island Press.

Heyzer, Noeleen, James V. Riker, and Antonio B. Quizon. 1995. *Government-NGO Relations in Asia: Prospects and Challenges for People-Centered Development*. Kuala Lumpur: Asian and Pacific Development Centre.

Hope, E., and B. Singh. 1995. *Energy Price Increases in Developing Countries: Case Studies of Columbia, Ghana, Indonesia, Malaysia, Turkey, and Zimbabwe*. Policy Research Working Paper 1442. Washington: World Bank.

Hudec, Robert E. 1996. GATT Legal Restraints on the Use of Trade Measures against Foreign Environmental Practices. In *Fair Trade and Harmonization: Prerequisites for Free Trade?*, ed. by Jagdish Bhagwati and Robert Hudec. Cambridge, MA: MIT Press.

Hudson, Stewart, Rodrigo Prudencio, and Richard Forrest. 1995. *Fixing What's Broke with APEC: First Steps toward a Sustainable Development Action Plan That Can Be Adopted at the November 1995 Osaka Ministers' Meeting*. National Wildlife Federation Trade and Environment Report. Washington: National Wildlife Federation.

Hufbauer, Gary. 1989. Beyond GATT. *Foreign Policy*, no. 77: 64-76 (Winter).

Huntington, Samuel. 1994. The Clash of Civilizations. *Foreign Affairs* 72, no. 3 (Summer): 22.

Hurrell, Andrew, and Benedict Kingsbury. 1992. *The International Politics of the Environment: Actors, Interests, and Institutions.* Oxford: Clarendon Press.

IEA (International Energy Agency). 1995a. *Energy Policies of IEA Countries, 1994 Review.* Vienna: Organization for Economic Cooperation and Development.

IEA. 1995b. *World Energy Outlook, 1995.* Paris: Organization for Economic Cooperation and Development.

IIED (International Institute for Environment and Development). 1994. *Environmental Synopsis of Indonesia.* London: International Institute for Environment and Development.

IPCC (Intergovernmental Panel on Climate Change). 1995. *Climate Change 1995: The IPCC Second Assessment Report.* New York: Cambridge University Press.

Islam, Nazrul. 1996. Income-Environment Relationship: Is Asia Different? Background paper for ADB 1997.

Jackson, John H. 1969. *World Trade and the Law of GATT.* New York: Bobbs-Merrill.

Jackson, John H. 1992. World Trade Rules and Environmental Policies: Congruence or Conflict? *Washington and Lee Law Review* 49 (Fall): 1227-49.

Jacobson, Harold K., and Edith Brown Weiss. 1997. Strengthening Compliance with International Environmental Accords. In *The Politics of Global Governance: International Organizations in an Interdependent World,* ed. by Paul F. Diehl. Boulder, CO: Lynne Rienner.

Jaffe, Adam B., Steven R. Peterson, Paul R. Portney, and Robert N. Stavins. 1995. Environmental Regulation and the Competitiveness of U.S. Manufacturing: What Does the Evidence Tell Us? *Journal of Economic Literature* 33, no. 1 (March): 132-61.

Jakobeit, Cord. 1996. Nonstate Actors Leading the Way: Debt-for-Nature Swaps. In *Institutions for Environmental Aid,* ed. by Robert O. Keohane and Marc A. Levy. Cambridge, MA: MIT Press.

Jaspersen, Frederick Z., Anthony H. Aylward, and Mariusz A. Sumlinski. 1995. *Trends in Private Investment in Developing Countries: Statistics for 1970-94.* International Finance Corporation Discussion Paper 28. Washington: World Bank.

Johnson, Pierre Marc, and André Beaulieu. 1996. *The Environment and NAFTA: Understanding and Implementing the New Continental Law.* Washington: Island Press.

Johnson, Robbin S. 1997. Food Policy in APEC. In *Whither APEC? The Progress to Date and Agenda for the Future,* ed. by C. Fred Bergsten. Special Report 7. Washington: Institute for International Economics.

Julius, D. 1986. Domestic Pricing of Petroleum Products: Efficiency and Equity Impacts in Developing Countries. *OPEC Review* (Spring).

Kalt, Joseph. 1988. The Impact of Domestic Environmental Regulatory Policies on US International Competitiveness. In *International Competitiveness,* ed. by A. Michael Spence and Heather A. Hazard. Cambridge, MA: Ballinger.

Kellert, Stephen R. 1996. *The Value of Life: Biological Diversity and Human Society.* Washington: Island Press.

Keohane, Robert O. 1996. Analyzing the Effectiveness of International Environmental Institutions. In *Institutions for Environmental Aid,* ed. by Robert O. Keohane and Marc A. Levy. Cambridge, MA: MIT Press.

Keohane, Robert O., and Marc A. Levy, eds. 1996. *Institutions for Environmental Aid.* Cambridge, MA: MIT Press.

Khor, Martin. 1992. *The Uruguay Round and North-South Sovereignty.* Penang: Third World Network.

Kim, Jong-Il, and Lawrence J. Lau. 1994. The Sources of Economic Growth of the East Asian Newly Industrialized Countries. *Journal of the Japanese and International Economies* 8, no. 3: 235-71.

Kimber, Cliona J. M. 1995. A Comparison of Environmental Federalism in the United States and the European Union. *Maryland Law Review* 54 (Summer): 1658.

Kincaid, John. 1991. The Competitive Challenge to Cooperative Federalism: A Theory of Federal Democracy. In *Competition among States and Local Governments,* ed. by Daphne A. Kenyon and John Kincaid. Washington: Urban Institute Press.

Kojima, Reeitsu, Yoshihiro Nomura, Shigeaki Fujisaki, and Naoyuki Sakumoto, eds. 1995. *Development and the Environment: The Experiences of Japan and Industrializing Asia.* Tokyo: Institute of Developing Economies.

Krause, Lawrence. 1997. Progress to Date and the Agenda for the Future: Summary. In *Whither APEC? The Progress to Date and Agenda for the Future,* ed. by C. Fred Bergsten. Special Report 9. Washington: Institute for International Economics.

Krier, James E., and Mark Brownstein. 1992. On Integrated Pollution Control. *Environmental Law* 22 (Fall): 119.

Krueger, Alan. 1996. Observations on International Labor Standards and Trade. Princeton University. Photocopy.

Krugman, Paul. 1994. The Myth of Asia's Miracle. *Foreign Affairs* 73, no. 6 (November-December): 62-78.

Krugman, Paul R., and Maurice Obstfeld. 1994. *International Economics: Theory and Policy,* 3d ed. New York: HarperCollins College Publishers.

Kuznets, S. 1955. Economic Growth and Income Inequality. *American Economic Review* 45, no. 1 (March): 1-28.

Larsen, B. 1994. *World Fossil Fuel Subsidies and Global Carbon Dioxide Emissions in a Model with Interfuel Substitution.* Policy Research Working Paper 1256. Washington: World Bank.

Larsen, B., and A. Shah. 1992. *World Energy Subsidies and Global Carbon Dioxide Emissions.* WDR 1992 Background Paper 25. Washington: World Bank.

Lawrence, Robert Z. 1996. *Regionalism, Multilateralism, and Deeper Integration.* Washington: Brookings Institution.

Lawrence, Robert Z., Albert Bressand, and Takatoshi Ito. 1996. *A Vision for the World Economy: Openness, Diversity, and Cohesion.* Washington: Brookings Institution.

Lenaerts, Koen. 1995. The Principle of Subsidiary and the Environment in the European Union: Keeping the Balance of Federalism. In *Recent Economic and Legal Developments in European Environmental Policy,* ed. by Filip Abraham, Kurt Deketelaere, and Jules Styyck. Leuven: Leuven University Press.

Lewis, Jeffrey D., Sherman Robinson, and Zhi Wang. 1995. Beyond the Uruguay Round: The Implications of an Asian Free Trade Area. World Bank. Photocopy (February).

Lindborg, N. 1992. Nongovernmental Organizations: Their Past, Present, and Future Role in International Environmental Negotiations. In *International Environmental Treaty Making,* ed. by Lawrence E. Susskind. Cambridge, MA: Program on Negotiation at Harvard Law School.

Low, Patrick, and Alexander Yeats. 1992. Do Dirty Industries Migrate? In *International Trade and the Environment,* ed. by Patrick Low. World Bank Discussion Paper 159. Washington: World Bank.

Low, Patrick, and R. Safadi. 1992. Trade Policy and Pollution. In *International Trade and the Environment,* ed. by Patrick Low. World Bank Discussion Paper 159. Washington: World Bank.

Lynch, Owen J., and Krik Talbott. 1995. *Balancing Acts: Community-Based Forest Management and National Law in Asia and the Pacific.* Washington: World Resources Institute.

Macaranas, Federico M. 1997. The Foundations for Economic Cooperation and Civil Society Participation in APEC. Speech delivered at a conference on Canada and the Challenge of APEC: The Road to Vancouver, sponsored by the Centre for International Studies, University of Toronto (27 May).

Martin, Will, Peter A. Petri, and Koji Yanagashima. 1994. Charting the Pacific: An Empirical Assessment on Integration Initiatives. *Journal of International Trade.*

McNeeley, Jeffrey A., et al. 1990. *Conserving the World's Biological Diversity.* Washington: WRI, World Conservation Union, World Bank, WWF-US, and Conservation International.

Meadows, Donella H. 1972. *The Limits to Growth.* New York: Universe Books.

Mendelsohn, Robert. 1986. Regulating Heterogeneous Emissions. *Journal of Environmental Economics and Management* 13: 301.

Menell, Peter. 1992. Institutional Fantasylands: From Scientific Management to Free Market Environmentalism. *Harvard Journal of Law and Public Policy* 15, no. 2 (Spring): 489-510.

Michaelis, Laurie. 1996. The Environmental Implications of Energy and Transport Subsidies. In *Subsidies and Environment: Exploring the Linkages*, ed. by Organization for Economic Cooperation and Development. Paris: Organization for Economic Cooperation and Development.

Ministry of Environment, Republic of Korea. 1993. *Environmental Protection in Korea.* Seoul: Government of South Korea.

Morgan, David G. 1996. *Building APEC's Institutional Architecture: Crosscutting and Participatory Mechanisms for Sustainable Development.* Paper presented at a conference on APEC and the Environment: Innovative Approaches to Trade and Environment in Asia-Pacific, San Francisco, sponsored by the Nautilus Institute for Security and Sustainable Development, the National Wildlife Federation, and the Berkeley Roundtable on the International Economy (18 October).

Morgan, Peter, and Ann Qualman. 1996. Institutional and Capacity Development, Results-Based Management and Organizational Performance. Paper prepared for Canadian International Development Agency.

Munasinghe, M., and W. Cruz. 1995. *Economywide Policies and the Environment: Lessons from Experience.* World Bank Environment Paper 10. Washington: World Bank.

Mundell, Robert A. 1961. A Theory of Optimum Currency Areas. *American Economic Review* 51, no. 4 (September): 657-65.

Myers, Norman. 1988. Threatened Biotas: "Hot Spots" in Tropical Forests. *The Environmentalist* 8, no. 3: 187-208.

Myers, Norman. 1990. The Biodiversity Challenge: Expanded Hot Spot Analysis. *The Environmentalist* 10, no. 4: 243-56.

Nader, Ralph. 1993. Free Trade and the Decline of Democracy. In *The Case against "Free Trade,"* by Ralph Nader et al. San Francisco: Earth Island.

NASA (National Aeronautics and Space Administration). 1996. 1996 Atlantic Ozone Hole Below Average Size. Press Release 96-217 (25 October).

Needham, Kristin. 1997. Capacity Development for Global Environmental Protection. Paper prepared for the Global Environment Facility.

Nguyen, Trien T., Carlo Perroni, and Randall M. Wigle. 1993. *An Evaluation of the Draft Final Act of the Uruguay Round.* Wilfrid Laurier University Working Paper. Waterloo, ON: Wilfrid Laurier University.

Noland, Marcus. 1996. Economic Cooperation in the Asia-Pacific: Openings for the US? In *Great Decisions 1996.* New York: Foreign Policy Association.

Noll, Roger G. 1989. Economic Perspectives on the Politics of Regulation. In *Handbook of Industrial Organization*, ed. by Richard Schmalensee and Robert D. Willig. New York: Elsevier Science.

Nordhaus, William D. 1994. *Managing the Global Commons.* Cambridge, MA: MIT Press.

Oates, Wallace E., and Robert M. Schwab. 1988. Economic Competition among Jurisdictions: Efficiency Enhancing or Distortion Inducing? *Journal of Public Economics* 35, no. 3 (April): 333-54.

O'Connor, David. 1994. *Managing the Environment with Rapid Industrialization: Lessons from the East Asia Experience.* Paris: Organization for Economic Cooperation and Development.

OECD (Organization for Economic Cooperation and Development). 1975. *The Polluter Pays Principle: Definition, Analysis, Implementation.* Paris: Organization for Economic Cooperation and Development.

OECD. 1993. *Assessing the Effects of the Uruguay Round.* Paris: Organization for Economic Cooperation and Development.

OECD. 1994. *The Environmental Effects of Trade.* Paris: Organization for Economic Cooperation and Development.

OECD. 1996. *Reconciling Trade, Environment, and Development Policies: The Role of Development Co-operation.* Paris: Organization for Economic Cooperation and Development.

OECD. 1997. *Economic Globalization and the Environment.* Paris: Organization for Economic Cooperation and Development.

Ohmae, Kenichi. 1995. *The End of the Nation State: The Rise of Regional Economies.* New York: Simon and Schuster.

Okugu, B. E., and F. Birol. 1992. Curbing Carbon Dioxide Emission by Axing EC Coal Subsidies. *OPEC Bulletin* 23, no. 10 (November/December).

Oldeman, L. R., R. T. A. Hakkeling, and W. G. Sombrock. 1990. *World Map of the Status of Human-Induced Soil Degradation.* Wageningen: ISRIC/UNEP.

Olson, Mancur. 1965. *The Logic of Collective Action: Public Goods and the Theory of Groups.* Cambridge, MA: Harvard University Press.

Olson, Mancur. 1969. The Principle of "Fiscal Equivalence": The Division of Responsibilities among the Different Levels of Government. *American Economic Review* 59, no. 2 (May): 479-87.

O'Meara, Molly. 1997. Riding the Dragon. *World Watch* March/April: 8-18.

Ostro, B. 1994. *Estimating the Health Effect of Air Pollution: A Method with an Application to Jakarta.* World Bank Policy Research Paper WPS 1301. Washington: World Bank.

Oxley, A. 1993. The Looming Issue of Trade and the Environment. Report prepared for the Council on International Business Affairs. Melbourne.

Oye, Kenneth A., and James H. Maxwell. 1994. Self-Interest and Environmental Management. *Journal of Theoretical Politics* 6, no. 4.

Pacific Economic Cooperation Council, Philippine Institute for Development Studies, The Asia Foundation. 1996. *Perspectives on the Manila Action Plan for APEC.* Manila: PECC, PIDS, Asia Foundation.

Pack, Howard, and John Page. 1994 *Accumulation, Exports, and Growth in the High-Performing Asian Economies.* Carnegie-Rochester Series on Public Policy 40. Amsterdam: Carnegie-Rochester Conference: 199.

Page, John. 1994. The East Asian Miracle: Four Lessons for Development Policy. In *NBER Macroeconomics Annual.* Cambridge, MA: MIT Press.

Pallemaerts, Marc. 1994. International Environmental Law from Stockholm to Rio: Back to the Future? In *Greening International Law,* ed. by Philippe Sands. New York: New Press.

Palmeter, D. 1993. Environment and Trade: Much Ado about Little? *Journal of World Trade* 27, no. 3 (June): 55-70.

Panayotou, T. 1993. *Green Markets: The Economics of Sustainable Development.* ICEG Sector Studies Series 7. San Francisco: ICS Press.

Parnwell, Michael J. G., and Raymond L. Bryant. 1996. *Environmental Change in South-East Asia: People, Politics, and Sustainable Development.* London: Routledge.

Pearson, Charles. 1987. *Multinational Corporations, Environment, and the Third World.* Durham, NC: Duke University Press.

Perot, Ross. 1993. *Save Your Job, Save Our Country: Why NAFTA Must be Stopped — Now!* New York: Hyperion.

Petri, Peter A. 1997. Foreign Direct Investment in a Computable General Equilibrium Framework. Paper presented at a conference on Making APEC Work: Economic Challenges and Policy Alternatives, Tokyo (13-14 March).

Pigou, Arthur Cecil. 1920. *The Economics of Welfare.* London: Macmillan.

Pomfret, Richard. 1996. Sub-regional Economic Zones. In *Regional Integration and the Asia-Pacific,* ed. by Bijit Bora and Christopher Findlay. Melbourne: Oxford University Press.

Porter, Gareth. 1996. Natural Resource Subsidies, Trade and Environment: The Cases of Forests and Fisheries. Paper presented at a conference on APEC and the Environment: Innovative Approaches to Trade and Environment in Asia-Pacific, San Francisco, sponsored by the Nautilus Institute for Security and Sustainable Development, the National

Wildlife Federation, and the Berkeley Roundtable on the International Economy (18 October).

Porter, Michael E., and Claas van der Linde. 1995a. Green and Competitive: Ending the Stalemate. *Harvard Business Review* 73, no. 5 (September/October): 120-55.

Porter, Michael E., and Claas van der Linde. 1995b. Toward a New Conception of the Environment-Competitiveness Relationship. *Journal of Economic Perspectives* 9, no. 4 (Fall): 97-118.

Posner, Richard A. 1992. *An Economic Analysis of Law.* Boston: Little & Brown.

Powers, Charles, and Marian Chertow. 1997. Industrial Ecology—Overcoming Policy Fragmentation. In *Thinking Ecologically: Building the Next Generation of Environmental Policy,* ed. by Marian Chertow and Daniel C. Esty. New Haven: Yale University Press.

Princen, Thomas, and Matthias Finger. 1994. *Environmental NGOs in World Politics: Linking the Local and the Global.* London: Routledge Press.

Radetzki, M. 1992. Economic Growth and Environment. In *International Trade and the Environment,* ed. by Patrick Low. World Bank Discussion Paper 159. Washington: World Bank.

Ramstetter, Eric D. 1991. *Direct Foreign Investment in Asia's Developing Economies and Structural Change in the Asia Pacific Region.* Boulder, CO: Westview Press.

Repetto, Robert. 1986. *Skimming the Water: Rent-Seeking and the Performance of Public Irrigation Systems.* Washington: World Resources Institute.

Repetto, Robert. 1995. *Jobs, Competitiveness, and Environmental Regulation: What Are the Real Issues?* Washington: World Resources Institute.

Revesz, Richard L. 1992. Rehabilitating Interstate Competition: Rethinking the "Race-to-the-Bottom" Rationale for Federal Environmental Regulation. *New York University Law Review* 67 (December): 1210-54.

Ricardo, David. 1973. *The Principles of Political Economy and Taxation.* New York: Everyman's Library.

Richardson, J. David. 1993. *Sizing Up US Export Disincentives.* Washington: Institute for International Economics.

Richardson, Sarah. 1992. Overview on Trade, Environment, and Competitiveness. In *Trade, Environment, and Competitiveness,* ed. by John Kirton and Sarah Richardson. Ottawa: National Roundtable on the Environment and the Economy.

Rodrik, Dani. 1994. *Getting Interventions Right: How South Korea and Taiwan Grew Rich.* NBER Working Paper 4964. Cambridge, MA: National Bureau of Economic Research.

Rodrik, Dani. 1997. *Has Globalization Gone Too Far?* Washington: Institute for International Economics.

Roht-Arriaza, Naomi. 1996. ISO 14001 in the APEC Context: Uses, Limitations, and Policy Alternatives. Paper presented at a conference on APEC and the Environment: Innovative Approaches to Trade and Environment in Asia-Pacific, San Francisco, sponsored by the Nautilus Institute for Security and Sustainable Development, the National Wildlife Federation, and the Berkeley Roundtable on the International Economy (18 October).

Romer, Paul M. 1986. Increasing Returns and Long-Run Growth. *Journal of Political Economy* 99, no. 3 (October): 500-21.

Roodman, David Malin. 1997. Reforming Subsidies. In *State of the World 1997: A Worldwatch Institute Report on Progress toward a Sustainable Future,* ed. by Worldwatch Institute. New York: Norton.

Rose, Carol M. 1994. *Property and Persuasion: Essay on the History, Theory, and Rhetoric of Ownership.* Boulder, CO: Westview Press.

Rowher, Jim. 1995. *Asia Rising: Why America Will Prosper as Asia's Economies Boom.* New York: Touchstone.

Runnalls, David. 1997. What the North Must Do. In *Asian Dragons and Green Trade,* ed. by Simon S. C. Tay and Daniel C. Esty. Singapore: Times Academic Press.

Ryan, Chris. 1997. The View from Australia. *Journal of Industrial Ecology,* 1, no. 1: 7-9.

Samuelson, Paul. 1954. The Pure Theory of Public Expenditure. *Review of Economics and Statistics* 36, no. 4 (November): 387-89.

Sands, Philippe. 1992. The Role of Environmental NGOs in International Environmental Law. *Development Journal of the Society for International Development* 2: 28-32.

Sands, Philippe. 1994a. International Environmental Law: An Introductory Overview. In *Greening International Law*, ed. by Philippe Sands. New York: New Press.

Sands, Philippe, ed. 1994b. *Greening International Law*. New York: New Press.

Sapir, Andre. 1996. Trade Liberalization and the Harmonization of Social Policies: Lessons from European Integration. In *Fair Trade and Harmonization: Prerequisites for Free Trade?*, ed. by Jagdish Bhagwati and Robert Hudec. Cambridge, MA: MIT Press.

Sax, Joseph. 1970. The Public Trust Doctrine in Natural Resource Law: Effective Judicial Intervention. *Michigan Law Review* 68: 471.

Sax, Joseph. 1980. Liberating the Public Trust Doctrine from Its Historical Shackles. *University of California at Davis Law Review* 14: 185.

Schmidheiny, Stephan, and Bradford Gentry. 1997. Privately-Financed Sustainable Development. In *Thinking Ecologically: Building the Next Generation of Environmental Policy*, ed. by Marian Chertow and Daniel C. Esty. New Haven: Yale University Press.

Schott, Jeffrey J. 1994. *The Uruguay Round: An Assessment*. Washington: Institute for International Economics.

Seager, Joni. 1995. *The New State of the Earth Atlas*. New York: Touchstone.

Selden, Thomas M., and Daqing Song. 1994. Environmental Quality and Development: Is There a Kuznets Curve for Air Pollution Emissions? *Journal of Environmental Economics and Management* 27, no. 2 (September): 147-52.

Shabecoff, Phil. 1993. *A Fierce Green Fire: The American Environmental Movement*. New York: Hill and Wang.

Shafik, Nemat, and Sushenjit Bandyopadhyay. 1992. Economic Growth and Environmental Quality: Time Series and Cross-Country Evidence. Background paper prepared for World Bank, *World Development Report 1992: Development and the Environment*. New York: Oxford University Press.

Shell, G. R. 1996. The Trade Stakeholders Model and Participation by Nonstate Parties in the World Trade Organization. *University of Pennsylvania Journal of International Economic Law* 17 (Spring): 359.

Shiroyama, Hideaki. 1997. Environmental Policy at APEC. Paper presented at Collaboration on Trade and the Environment, sponsored by GETS/GISPRI, New York (27 June).

Shrivivasta, Paul. 1994. Greening Business Education: Toward an Ecocentric Pedagogy. *Journal of Management Inquiry* 3, no. 3: 235.

Siwabut, P. 1992. Thailand Country Report: Planning and Management of Environmental Technology. Prepared for the UN Economic and Social Commission for Asia and the Pacific, Bangkok (January).

Smil, Vaclav. 1996. *Environmental Problems in China: Estimates of Economic Cost*. East-West Center Special Report 5. Honolulu: East-West Center.

Smithers, Geoffrey, and André Dua. 1994. *Food into Asia: The Next Steps*. Canberra: Australian Government Printing Service.

Snape, Richard H. 1994. *Trade and Multilateral Trade Agreements: Effects on the Global Environment*. Monash University Department of Economics Seminar Papers 8/94. Melbourne: Monash University.

Spiro, P. J. 1994. New Global Communities: Non-governmental Organizations in International Decisionmaking Institutions. *Washington Quarterly* 18, no. 1 (Winter): 45-57.

Srinivasan, T. N. 1995. International Trade and Labor Standards. Yale University. Photocopy.

Stewart, Richard B. 1977. Pyramids of Sacrifice? Problems of Federalism in Mandating State Implementation of National Environmental Policy. *Yale Law Journal* 86: 1196-72.

Stewart, Richard B. 1992. International Trade and Environment: Lessons from the Federal Experience. *Washington and Lee Law Review* 49: 1315-401.

Stiglitz, Joseph E. 1988. *Economics of the Public Sector*. New York: Norton.

Stone, Christopher D. 1993. *The Gnat Is Older Than Man: Global Environment and Human Agenda.* Princeton: Princeton University Press.

Stone, Christopher D. 1997. The Maladies in Global Fisheries: Are Trade Laws Part of the Treatment? Paper presented at Collaboration on Trade and the Environment, sponsored by GETS-GISPRI, New York (27 June).

Streets, David G. 1997. *Energy and Acid Rain Projections for Northeast Asia.* ESENA Occasional Paper. San Francisco: Nautilus Institute.

Susskind, L. E. 1994. *Environmental Diplomacy: Negotiating More Effective Global Agreements.* New York: Oxford University Press.

Swee, Goh Keng, and Linda Low. 1996. Beyond "Miracles" and Total Factor Productivity: The Singapore Experience. *ASEAN Economic Bulletin* 13, no. 1 (July): 1-13.

Sykes, Alan O. 1995. *Product Standards for Internationally Integrated Goods Markets.* Washington: Brookings Institution.

Tay, Simon S. C. 1996. The Way Ahead in Asia. In *Asian Dragons and Green Trade: Environment, Economics, and International Law,* ed. by Simon S. C. Tay and Daniel C. Esty. Singapore: Times Academic Press.

Tay, Simon S. C., and Daniel C. Esty, eds. 1996. *Asian Dragons and Green Trade: Environment, Economics, and International Law.* Singapore: Times Academic Press.

Tiebout, Charles M. 1956. A Pure Theory of Local Expenditures. *Journal of Political Economy* 64, no. 5 (October): 416-24.

Topping, J. C., Jr., A. Quershi, and A. Samuel. 1990. *Implication of Climate Change for the Asian and Pacific Region.* Nagoya: Environment Agency of Japan.

Trachtman, Joel P. 1992. L'État, C'est Nous: Sovereignty, Economic Integration, and Subsidiarity. *Harvard International Law Journal* 33, no. 2 (Spring): 459-73.

Tybout, J. R., and D. Moss. 1992. The Scope for Fuel Substitution in Manufacturing Industries: A Case Study of Chile and Colombia. *World Bank Economic Review* 8, no. 1 (January): 49-74.

UBS. 1996. The Asian Economic Miracle. *UBS International Finance,* no. 29 (Autumn).

UN (United Nations). 1994. *World Population Prospectus: The 1994 Revision.* New York: United Nations.

UNEP (United Nations Environment Program). 1997. *Global Environment Outlook.* New York: Oxford University Press.

UNEP/GEMS (United Nations Environment Program and Global Environment Monitoring Service). 1992. *The Impact of Ozone Layer Depletion.* Nairobi: United Nations Environment Program.

UNEP/GEMS. 1993. *Global Biodiversity.* UNEP/GEMS Environment Library 11. Nairobi: United Nations Environment Program.

UNEP/WMO (United Nations Environment Program and World Meteorological Organization). 1994. *Scientific Assessment of Ozone Depletion.* Nairobi: United Nations Environment Program.

UNESCAP (United Nations Economic and Social Commission for Asia and the Pacific). 1995. *State of the Environment in Asia and the Pacific.* Bangkok: United Nations Economic and Social Commission for Asia and the Pacific.

US Department of Energy. 1989. *The Impact of Eliminating Coal Subsidies in Western Europe.* Office of Coal, Nuclear, Electric, and Alternative Fuels. Washington: US Department of Energy.

US Department of Energy. 1995. *International Energy Outlook, 1995.* Washington: US Government Printing Office.

van Beers, C., and J. C. J. M. van den Bergh. 1997. An Empirical Multi-country Analysis of the Impact of Environmental Regulations on Foreign Trade Flows. *Kyklos* 50, no. 1: 29-46.

Van Grasstek, C. 1992. The Political Economy of Trade and the Environment in the United States. In *International Trade and the Environment,* ed. by Patrick Low. World Bank Discussion Paper 159. Washington: World Bank.

van Kamenade, Willem. 1997. *China, Hong Kong, and Taiwan, Inc.* New York: Knopf.

Victor, David G., Kal Raustiala, and Eugene B. Skolnikoff. 1997. *The Implementation and Effectiveness of International Environmental Commitments.* Cambridge, MA: MIT Press.

Viscusi, W. Kip. 1995. Equivalent Frames of Reference for Judging Risk Regulation Policies. *New York University Environmental Law Journal* 431: 437.

Vogel, David. 1995. *Trading Up: Consumer and Environmental Regulation in a Global Economy.* Cambridge, MA: Harvard University Press.

Vogler, John. 1995. *The Global Commons: A Regime Analysis.* Chichester: Wiley.

Walzer, Michael. 1983. *Spheres of Justice: A Defense of Pluralism and Equality.* New York: Basic Books.

Wapner, P. 1995. Politics beyond the State: Environmental Activism and Civic World Politics. *World Politics* 47, no. 3 (April): 311-41.

Watabe, Akihiro, and Kaoru Yamaguchi. 1996. Asian Structural Interdependency and the Environment. In *Energy, Environment, and the Economy: Asian Perspectives,* ed. by Paul R. Kleindorfer, Howard C. Kunreuther, and David S. Hong. Cheltenham: Edward Elgar.

WCMC (World Conservation Monitoring Center). 1992. *Global Biodiversity: Status of the Earth's Living Resources.* Cambridge, MA: World Conservation Monitoring Center.

Weber, P. C. 1993. *Abandoned Seas.* Worldwatch Paper 166. Washington: The Worldwatch Institute.

WEC (World Energy Council). 1993. *Energy for Tomorrow's World: The Realities, the Real Options, and the Agenda for Achievement.* New York: St. Martin's Press.

WEC. 1995. *Global Energy Perspectives to 2050 and Beyond.* London: World Energy Council.

WHO and UNEP (World Health Organization and United Nations Environment Program). 1992. *Urban Air Pollution in Megacities of the World.* Cambridge, MA: Blackwell.

Wils, Wouter P. J. 1994. Subsidiarity and EC Environmental Policy: Taking People's Concerns Seriously. *Journal of Environmental Law* 6, no. 1: 85.

Wilson, Edward O. 1992. *The Diversity of Life.* Cambridge, MA: Harvard University Press.

Wilson, John D. 1996. Capital Mobility and Environmental Standards: Is There a Theoretical Basis for a Race to the Bottom? In *Fair Trade and Harmonization: Prerequisites for Free Trade?,* ed. by Jagdish Bhagwati and Robert Hudec. Cambridge, MA: MIT Press.

Wilson, John S. 1995. *Standards and APEC: An Action Agenda.* POLICY ANALYSES IN INTERNATIONAL ECONOMICS 42. Washington: Institute for International Economics.

WMO (World Meteorological Organization). 1994. *Scientific Assessment of Ozone Depletion: 1994.* Global Ozone Research and Monitoring Project Report 37. Geneva: World Meteorological Organization.

Woo, Wing Thye, Stephen Parker, and Jeffrey D. Sachs, eds. 1997. *Economies in Transition: Comparing Asia and Europe.* Cambridge, MA: MIT Press.

World Bank. 1993. *The East Asian Miracle: Economic Growth and Public Policy.* New York: Oxford University Press.

World Bank. 1996a. *Social Indicators of Development.* Washington: World Bank.

World Bank. 1996b. *Partnership for Global Warming in Africa.* Office of the Vice President, Africa Region. Washington: World Bank.

World Bank. 1997. *Expanding the Measure of Wealth: Indicators of Environmentally Sustainable Development.* Washington: World Bank.

World Commission on Environment and Development. 1987. *Our Common Future.* Oxford: Oxford University Press.

Worldwatch Institute, ed. 1996. *State of the World 1997: A Worldwatch Institute Report on Progress toward a Sustainable Future.* New York: Norton.

WRI (World Resources Institute). 1996. *World Resources, 1996-97.* New York: Oxford University Press.

Xie, M., U. Kuffner, and G. LeMoigne. 1993. *Using Water Efficiently: Technological Options.* Technical Paper 205. Washington: World Bank.

Yamazawa, Ippei. 1997. APEC's Economic and Technical Cooperation: Evolution and Tasks Ahead. In *Whither APEC? The Progress to Date and Agenda for the Future,* ed. by C. Fred Bergsten. Special Report 9. Washington: Institute for International Economics.

Yang, Y. 1994. Trade Liberalization with Externalities: A General Equilibrium Assessment of the Uruguay Round. Paper presented at a conference on Challenges and Opportunities for East Asian Trade, Australian National University, Canberra (13-14 July).

Young, Alwyn. 1994. Lessons from the East Asian NICs: A Contrarian View. *European Economic Review* 38, no. 3-4 (April): 964-99.

Young, Alwyn. 1995. The Tyranny of Numbers: Confronting the Statistical Reality of the East Asian Growth Experience. *Quarterly Journal of Economics* 110, no. 3 (August): 641-80.

Young, Oran R., and George J. Demko. 1996. Improving the Effectiveness of International Environmental Governance Systems. In *Global Environmental Change and International Governance,* ed. by Oran R. Young, George J. Demko, and Kilaparti Ramakrishna. Hanover, NH: Dartmouth College, University Press of New England.

Zadek, S., and M. Gatward. 1996. Transforming the Transnational NGOs: Social Auditing or Bust? In *Beyond the Magic Bullet: NGO Performance and Accountability in the Post Cold War World,* ed. by Michael E. Edwards and David Hulme. West Hartford, CT: Kumarian Press.

Zaelke, Durwood, Paul Orbuch, and Robert F. Housman. 1993. *Trade and the Environment: Law, Economics, and Policy.* Washington: Island Press.

Zarsky, Lyuba. 1995. APEC, Citizen Groups, and the Environment: Common Interests, Broad Agenda. Paper presented to Citizens Forum on Trade and Environment, People's Forum 2001, Tokyo (11-12 November).

Zarsky, Lyuba, and Jason Hunter. 1997. Environmental Cooperation at APEC: The First Five Years. *Journal of Environment and Development* 6, no. 3 (September): 222-52.

Index

water management in, 38*f*, 152
Australia-New Zealand Closer Economic
    Relations, 110, 113

Basel Convention (1989), 42
Beef, EU ban on, 158*n*, 163*n*
Bergsten, C. Fred, 13, 15, 21, 29*n*, 84, 160
Bhopal disaster, 166
Biodiversity, benefits of, 51*n*, 52-53
Biodiversity loss, 51, 52*t*, 54*n*, 154
    caused by deforestation, 37, 51-52
Bioprospecting, 52
Blake Island Summit (1993), 136
Blocked exchanges, 109
Bogor Summit (1994), 10, 136, 147, 151
Border Environmental Plan (US-Mexico),
    97
Brundtland Commission, 4*n*
Brunei, 52*t*, 149
Bureaucracy, growth of, 115-16
Burma, 129*n*
Business, cooperation between
    government and, 6, 132, 132*n*, 134,
    162*n*
Business Advisory Council (APEC), 27,
    27*n*
Business Advisory Group (APEC), 3*n*
Business visa arrangements, 115*n*

CAFE. *See* Corporate Average Fuel
    Economy
Cairns Group, 105, 152*n*
Canada
    acid rain disputes with US, 44, 53, 72-
        73, 97
    biodiversity loss, 52*t*
    federalism in, 120, 126-27
    greenhouse gas emissions, 49*f*
    joint implementation projects, 106
    and jurisdictional allocation, 121
    land degradation in, 34
    market access issues, 86
    reforestation efforts in, 37
    salmon disputes, 86, 111, 111*n*, 115,
        163
    share of APEC exports, 24*f*
    subsidies in, 68-69, 153
    sustainable urbanization initiative, 140
    water and sanitation services in, 38*f*
Canadian International Development
    Agency, 99
Capacity building, 99-100, 114, 116, 139,
    142, 161

Capital formation, gross fixed, foreign
    direct investment as proportion of,
    25, 25*f*
Carbon dioxide. *See* Greenhouse gases
Carbon sinks, 48, 54, 59
Carbon tax, 89*n*
Cars, number of, increase in, 39-40, 39*n*-
    40*n*, 69
CEC. *See* North American Commission
    for Environmental Cooperation
CFCs. *See* Chlorofluorocarbons
Child Labor Deterrence Act (1996), 109*n*
Chile
    biodiversity loss, 51, 52*t*
    foreign direct investment inflows, 25,
        25*f*
    greenhouse gas emissions, 49*f*
    water and sanitation services in, 38*f*
China
    acid rain problems, 45, 53, 73, 97*n*, 97-
        98, 111-12
    air pollution in, 38*f*
    APEC investment in, 26-27
    biodiversity loss, 51-52, 52*t*
    cars in, number of, 39-40*n*
    commons problems in, 64
    deforestation in, 36-37
    environmental harms in, economic
        costs of, 33
    fisheries depletion in, 42
    foreign direct investment inflows, 23-
        26, 24*f*-25*f*
    GDP, 13*n*
    greenhouse gas emissions, 49*f*, 50-51,
        154
    hazardous waste disposal problems, 41
    joint implementation projects, 106-7
    land degradation in, 35, 35*t*
    life expectancy and infant mortality
        rates, 18*t*
    market access issues, 88
    most favored nation status, 108-9, 120,
        125
    per capita income, 15, 15*t*, 16, 16*n*, 29
    population, 78
    power generation in, 70, 128, 166
    public choice problems in, 71, 102
    share of APEC exports, 24*f*
    subsidies in, 68, 153*n*, 153-54
    transition to market economy,
        uncertainty regarding, 28
    water management in, 38*f*, 67, 152
Chinese Academy of Social Science, 33

economic growth in, 11, 12*n*, 29
Eastern Europe, development pattern, 69*n*
Eco-dumping, 85
Eco-imperialism, 91, 108
Eco-labeling, 85*n*, 88
Economic Committee (APEC), 139
Economic externalities. *See* Economic spillovers
Economic growth
  of APEC, 6, 11-31
    versus European Union, 13, 14*f*
    prognosis for, 28-31
  environmental effects of, 90-92
Economic integration
  within APEC, 12-13, 26-27
  and community building, 5, 85, 92, 108-10, 113, 125-29, 147
  economic externalities and, 123-25. *See also* Economic spillovers
  environmental underpinnings for, 108-10, 138-42
  increase in, 12-13, 26-27
  market forces and, 26-27
  political integration alongside, 109-10, 120, 126-27, 134
  political support for, 84
  psychological externalities and, 125-29
Economic magnifiers, 77-80
Economic spillovers, 60-61, 119-20, 123-25
Economic trends, 11-31
Economic zones, natural, 26-27, 26*n*
Economy-environment interface, tensions at, 8, 83-93, 143, 163
Ecotech programs, 143, 143*n*, 147
Eco-tourism management, 139
Education, public, 71, 71*n*, 101-2, 138, 175
EEZ. *See* Exclusive Economic Zone
Electrical appliances, energy standards for, harmonization of, 138
Eminent Persons Group (APEC), 3*n*, 115, 135, 162, 170
Endangered species, 51-52, 52*t*, 87*n*, 88. *See also* Biodiversity loss; *specific species*
Energy standards, for electrical appliances, harmonization of, 138
Energy subsidies, 68, 81, 105, 143, 149
  reduction of, elimination of, 9-10, 151, 153-55, 167
Environmental action agenda, development of, 9, 145-68
Environmental Advisory Group (APEC), 10, 162, 168

Environmental agreements, multilateral, 87-88, 163
Environmental degradation
  demographic and economic magnifiers of, 77-80
  as offset against quality-of-life gains, 7
  reasons for, 7
  severity of, 33*n*
Environmental expertise, lack of, 162
Environmental goals, trade measures used to achieve, 87-88
Environmental goods, trade liberalization in, 147*n*
Environmental governance
  on ad hoc basis, 110-12, 114*n*, 130
  benefits of competition for, 133
  global, future, experience for, 107
  multitiered structure of, 5, 9, 133-34
  need for, 95-117
  optimal, 8-9, 96*n*, 119-34
    from optimal areas to, 129-31
    and performance issues, 131-34
Environmental groups, 6, 92, 125-26, 128, 132. *See also* Nongovernmental organizations
Environmental harms. *See also specific harm*
  abatement of, relationship between income and, 73-77, 74*f*
  confronting APEC members, 33-55
    underlying causes of, 57-81
  economic costs of, 33-34
  geographic scope of, 53-54, 54*n*, 98-99, 130
  global, 53*n*, 53-54, 62
  improving information about, 63, 101-2
  liability for, 166
  local or national, 53
  regional, 53*n*, 53-54
    optimal responses to, 97-99
  time delay for, 62-63, 72, 72*n*
  transboundary. *See* Super externalities; Transboundary harms
Environmental imperialism, 91, 108
Environmental indicators, 102, 102*n*, 161
Environmental information, lack of, 63, 71, 101-2
Environmental investments
  cost of, 6
  private-sector, 6, 132, 132*n*, 149*n*, 165-67, 170
Environmental issues
  APEC as best institutional response to, 5, 8, 77, 81, 104-7, 116

importance of, 1-5, 83
Environmental legitimacy test, 86*n*
Environmental management certification systems, 85*n*
Environmental management program (APEC)
  effective, criteria for, 145-49, 146*f*
  existing, 135-44
  funding for, 164-67, 175
  institutional support for, 160-64
  need for, 95-117, 135
  objections to, 110-16
Environmental performance, of multinational corporations, 165-66
Environmental policymaking, 7
  and competitiveness concerns, 89-90
  decentralized, support for, 121-22
  failures in, 66-70
  and loss of political participation, 101-2, 115-16, 121-23
  multiple levels of, 130
  national, regional contribution to, 96, 99-102
  regulatory complexity of, 67, 80, 101
  regulatory incapacity for, 67, 80, 116, 124, 149
  spillovers from, 67-69
Environmental protection, responsibility for, 67, 76-77
Environmental standards
  convergence of, harmonization of, 10, 12, 119*n*, 125-128, 157-159, 164
  enforcement of, 157
  and market issues. *See* Regulatory competition
  and trade facilitation, 156-60
Environmental Standards and Trade Facilitation Initiative, 157, 160
Environmental standards initiative, 9-10, 143
Environmental value-added, of APEC, 8, 96-108
Environmental values, community-determined, 92
Environmental vision, APEC, 135-37
Environmental Vision Statement (APEC), 137, 169-71
Environment Committee (APEC), 10, 160-61, 164-65, 168
Environment Fund (APEC), 10
EPG. *See* Eminent Persons Group (APEC)
European Union (EU)
  ban on beef, 158*n*, 163*n*

bureaucracy issues, 115
carbon tax, 89*n*
community sense in, 127
dialogue with APEC, 15, 15*n*, 105
economic performance of, versus APEC, 13, 14*f*
environmental standards in, 125
establishment of, 122*n*
labor standards, 110
policy harmonization, 110*n*
share of global exports, 22, 22*f*
share of global income, 13, 14*f*
Exchange rates, 13
Exclusive Economic Zone, 156, 156*n*
Export markets
  APEC, distribution of, 23, 23*f*
  expansion of, 21
  global, APEC share of, 22*f*, 22-23
  and protectionism, 84, 87
Externalities, 58-61, 80
  definition of, 58
  economic/competitiveness, 61, 119-20, 123-25
  negative, 58-59
  policy, sectoral, 67-69, 81
  positive, 58-59
  psychological, 60-61, 61*n*, 119-20, 125-29
  regular, 59-60
  super. *See* Super externalities
  uninternalized, 60

Factor mobility, increased, 22
Fair trade, 85, 89, 89*n*, 157
FAO. *See* Food and Agriculture Organization (UN)
FDI. *See* Foreign direct investment
Federal arrangements
  APEC, 122, 128
  types of, 121-20
Federalism, 121-23, 126-27
  definition of, 121
FEEEP (food, energy, environment, economic growth, and population) initiative, 9, 136, 141-42, 142*n*, 144, 148
Fisheries
  depletion of, 42-44, 43*f*, 98-99, 123, 139
  and commons problems, 62, 111-12, 114, 155
  responses to, 9-10, 155-56, 164
  subsidies for, 68-69
Fisheries Working Group, 138

unrepresentative, 70-71, 101-2
Government failures, 66-77, 80-81
  in policymaking, 66-70, 80
  and public choice problems, 70-72, 81
  and regulatory competition, 61n
  structural, 72-77, 81
Great Lakes, 98
Greenhouse gases, 47-51, 53, 106
  climate change effects of, 50-51
  emissions of
    APEC share of, 48-49, 49f
    and commons problems, 62, 76-77
    and energy subsidies, 69, 154
    global, 50, 50f
    and standards harmonization, 159,
      159n
  mitigation of, 9, 150-51, 164
Gross domestic product
  global
    APEC share of, 13-15, 14f, 29
    increase in, 30
  per capita annual growth in, 15t, 15-16
Growth theory, 12n

Habitat destruction, 42-44, 51, 154
Halons, 47, 47n, 48f
Harmonization. *See under* environmental
  standards
Hazardous waste, 41-42, 42n
HCFCs. *See* Hydrochlorofluorocarbons
Health and environmental standards,
  and market access issues, 85-86
Health problems, caused by fossil fuel
  emissions, 40, 47, 153-54
Hong Kong, 11
  biodiversity loss, 52t
  economic prospects for, 28-29
  life expectancy and infant mortality
    rates, 17t
  per capita income, 15t, 16
  share of APEC exports, 23f
Human Resources Development
  Working Group, 138
Human rights abuses, 109, 129n
Huntington, Samuel, 114
Hydrochlorofluorocarbons, 47n

IAEA. *See* International Atomic Energy
  Agency
IEA. *See* International Energy Agency
IMF. *See* International Monetary Fund
Import bans, 87, 87n
Income
  effect of economic growth on, 91

equalization of, 17
global distribution of, 13, 14f, 29
relationship between abatement of
  harms and, 73-77, 74f
rise in, 12, 16t, 16-17, 30
India, 33, 88
Indonesia, 11
  biodiversity loss, 51-52, 52t
  commons problems in, 65
  deforestation in, 36, 36t, 53n
  economic prospects for, 30
  environmental harms in, economic
    costs of, 33-34
  foreign direct investment inflows, 25-
    26, 25f-26f
  GDP, 13n
  greenhouse gas emissions, 49f, 154
  industrialization in, 16, 18f, 79-80
  joint implementation projects, 106
  land degradation in, 35t
  life expectancy and infant mortality
    rates, 18t
  market access issues, 86
  per capita income, 15, 15t, 17
  population, 78
  public choice problems, 71
  and right to development issues, 91
  subsidies in, 68, 154
  water and sanitation services in, 37,
    38f
Industrial composition, changes in, 12,
  16-21
Industrialization. *See also* Development
  early stages of, and environmental
    protection issues, 75, 79-80
  levels of, 78-80
Industrial pollution, 67, 140-41
Industrial Science and Technology
  Working Group, 139-40
Infant mortality rates, 17, 18t
Information, environmental, lack of, 63,
  71, 101-2
Information exchange, need for, 96, 175
Information technology products, trade
  barriers to, 105, 114n-115n, 147
Interest group manipulation, 71
Intergovernmental Panel on Climate
  Change (IPCC), 48, 103
International Atomic Energy Agency,
  102n
International Energy Agency, 50
International environmental bodies
  lack of coordination between, 103

intertemporal, 62-63, 72, 72n
Market forces, and economic integration, 27-28
Matching principle, 119
MEAs. *See* Multilateral environmental agreements
Megacities, 78
Megadiversity countries, 51
Mekong Basin, 98
Methane. *See* Greenhouse gases
Mexico
  air pollution in, 38f, 39
  APEC investment in, 27
  biodiversity loss, 52t
  environmental harms in, economic costs of, 33
  federalism in, 121-20
  foreign direct investment inflows, 25, 25f
  greenhouse gas emissions, 49f
  population, 78
  tuna dispute with US, 87, 87n, 109, 125, 126n, 163n
  US border disputes, 42n, 97, 114
  water management in, 38f, 152
Ministerial Meetings (APEC), 3b, 140n, 140-41, 175. *See also specific meeting*
Montreal Protocol on Substances that Deplete the Ozone Layer (1987), 45, 47n, 88, 103, 106n
Moral hazard, 61n
Moral issues, in trade arena, 92, 108-9, 120, 126. *See also* Public choice issues
Most favored nation (MFN) status, for China, 108-9, 120, 125
MRAs. *See* Mutual recognition agreements
Multilateral Agreement on Investment, 166, 166n
Multilateral efforts, 102-3, 103n
  ratcheting up, 104-6, 113-14, 116, 142-43, 154
Multilateral environmental agreements, 87-88, 163
Multilateral trade liberalization, 29-30, 30n, 100
Multinational corporations, environmental performance of, 165-66
Muruyama Fund, 164n
Mutual recognition agreements, 158

NAFTA. *See* North American Free Trade Agreement

National sovereignty
  and environmental standards harmonization, 158
  and joint implementation projects, 106n
  loss of, and environmental management program creation, 110-11
  and regulatory competence issues, 73
  and trade liberalization, 83, 89, 92
Newly industrializing economies, 11, 22, 26
New Zealand
  biodiversity loss, 52t
  effects of ozone layer depletion on, 47
  fisheries depletion in, 42, 155n
  greenhouse gas emissions, 49f
  marine protection in, 98
  subsidies in, 152
  water and sanitation services in, 38f
NGOs. *See* Nongovernmental organizations
NIEs. *See* Newly industrializing economies
Nitrogen oxides. *See* Acid rain
Nitrous oxide. *See* Greenhouse gases
Non-Binding Energy and Environmental Policy Principles, 138
Non-Binding Investment Code (APEC), 166, 166n
Nongovernmental organizations, 6, 8
  capacity building efforts, 99, 116, 131-32, 162
  cooperation between government and, 9, 96, 115-16, 132n, 132-34, 162
  as link between public and government, 71, 81, 115-16, 132, 132n, 162
  and market access issues, 88
  and sustainable development issues, 92
North America. *See also specific country*
  economic performance, 11
North American Commission for Environmental Cooperation, 98, 114, 116, 160
North American Free Trade Agreement, 4, 90, 98, 110, 113-15, 127, 157
  Commission for Environmental Cooperation, 98, 114, 116, 160
  Environmental Side Agreement, 90n, 98, 127
  investment chapter, 106n
Northeast Asia. *See also specific country*
  definition of, 45n

sulfur dioxide emissions in, 45
North-South divide, amelioration of, 97,
    107-8, 114, 147-48, 150

OECD. *See* Organization for Economic
    Cooperation and Development
Official development assistance (ODA),
    6, 165
Open regionalism, 2b
Optimal environmental areas (OEAs),
    123-29, 134
  definition of, 123
  from optimal governance to, 129-31
Optimum currency areas, theory of, 130
Organization for Economic Cooperation
    and Development (OECD), 17n, 103,
    152, 154, 166, 166n
  Environment Directorate, 116, 160
  Multilateral Agreement on Investment,
    106n
Osaka Summit (1995), 136, 141, 148n, 156
Ozone hole, 45, 47
Ozone layer depletion, 45, 47, 48f, 53, 102

Pacific Basin Economic Council, 27n
Pacific Business Forum, 3n, 27n
Pacific Century, 12, 12n
Pacific fisheries. *See* Fisheries
Papua New Guinea
  biodiversity loss, 52t
  deforestation in, 36t
  greenhouse gas emissions, 49f
  marine protection in, 98
  water and sanitation services in, 38f
Pay-the-polluter programs, 69, 149, 154.
  See also Subsidies
PBEC. *See* Pacific Basin Economic
  Council
People's Summits, 5, 5n, 91n
Pesticide residues, in food, 101, 153n
Philippines
  acid rain problems, 45
  aquaculture in, 42
  biodiversity loss, 51-52, 52t
  commons problems in, 65
  currency crisis, 29
  deforestation in, 36, 36t
  Department of Environment and
    Natural Resources, 33n
  economic prospects for, 30
  fisheries depletion in, 42
  foreign direct investment inflows, 25,
    25f
  greenhouse gas emissions, 49f

and jurisdictional allocation, 121
land degradation in, 35t
life expectancy and infant mortality
    rates, 17t
marine pollution in, 44, 44n, 128
per capita income, 16
population, 78
subsidies in, 153
water and sanitation services in, 38f
Pivotal states, 53n, 108
Policy choices, of trading partners,
    discomfort with, 92. *See also*
    Regulatory competition
Policy failures, 66-70, 80, 131
  demographic and economic magnifiers
    of, 77-80
Policymaking
  environmental. *See* Environmental
    policymaking
  in nonenvironmental areas,
    environmental repercussion of, 57,
    66-67, 80
Policy optimization question, 119
Policy spillovers, 67-69, 81
Political appeal, of environmental
    agenda, 146-48
Political clout
  of environmental groups, 92
  of polluters, 71
Political decisions, public distance from,
    101-2, 115-16, 121-23
Political drag, 89, 89n, 157, 159
Political integration, alongside economic
    integration, 109-10, 120, 126-27, 134
Political support
  for economic integration, 84
  for environmental agenda, 146-48
Politicians, discount rates of, 72
Polluter pays principle, 116, 149, 149n,
    174
Polluters, political clout of, 71
Pollution
  air, 39-41, 40f, 67, 75
  caused by trade-led growth, 90-92
  industrial, 67, 140-41
  lack of information about, 63
  marine/coastal, 44, 98, 114, 128, 138,
    140-41
  urban, 38f, 39-41, 67
  water, 37, 38f, 40-41, 51, 67, 75, 98
Pollution havens, 89
Pollution spillover, 59-60. *See also* Super
    externalities; Transboundary harms

Russia, 155*n*

Salmon, disputes over, 86, 111, 111*n*, 115, 163
Sanitation, access to, 37, 38*f*, 40
Schomerus, Lorenz, 105
Seafood, APEC consumption of, 155
Seattle Summit (1994), 105
Sea turtles, dispute over, 61, 87, 87*n*, 92, 125-26, 126*n*, 128, 143, 163
Senior Officials Meeting (APEC), 162, 170, 175
Shrimping practices, dispute over, 61, 87, 87*n*, 92, 125-26, 126*n*, 128, 143, 163
Side agreements, 127. *See also specific agreement*
Singapore, 11
    air pollution problems, 53*n*
    biodiversity loss, 52*t*
    economic prospects for, 29-30
    greenhouse gas emissions, 49*f*
    life expectancy and infant mortality rates, 18*t*
    per capita income, 15, 15*t*, 16, 29
    and public choice problems, 71*n*, 101-2
    and right to development issues, 91
    share of APEC exports, 23*f*
    water management problems in, 40
Skin cancer rates, and ozone layer depletion, 47
Slave labor, 109
Social dumping, 85
Social integration, parallel to economic integration, 85, 92, 108, 125-29, 129*n*
Social welfare
    and environmental standards harmonization, 158
    maximization of, 4-5, 145
Social welfare losses, and environmental problems, 33, 120-21, 145, 159*n*
Soil degradation, 34-35
Solid waste, 41-42
SOM. *See* Senior Officials Meeting (APEC)
South China Sea, disputes over, 112, 114*n*
Southeast Asia. *See also specific country*
    acid rain problems in, 44, 45, 97-98
    climate change effects in, 51
    deforestation in, 36, 36*t*
    economic growth in, 30
    marine pollution in, 44, 98
    per capita GDP growth in, 30
South Korea, 11

    acid rain problems, 45, 53, 111
    biodiversity loss, 52*t*
    development issues in, 69*n*
    economic prospects for, 28-29
    environmental standards, and market access issues, 86*n*
    greenhouse gas emissions, 49*f*
    hazardous waste disposal problems in, 41
    industrial structure, 17, 17*n*, 19*f*
    life expectancy and infant mortality rates, 18*t*
    marine pollution in, 44
    per capita income, 16, 16*t*, 30
    share of APEC exports, 24*f*
    subsidies in, 152
    water and sanitation services in, 37, 38*f*
South Pacific Islands, marine protection in, 98
Spillovers. *See* Externalities; Super externalities; Transboundary harms; phsychological externalities
Stockholm Declaration, 91
Structural failures, 72-77, 81, 113, 116, 139-40
    in international environmental bodies, 102-3
Subic Bay Summit (1996), 105, 136
Subregional economic zones (SREZs), 25-27, 26*n*
Subsidiarity, 121-23
    definition of, 120
Subsidies, 68-69, 81. *See also specific type of subsidy*
    definition of, 68*n*
    reduction or elimination of, 9-10, 69, 105, 143, 147, 148*n*, 149, 151-55, 164, 167
Subsidies Initiative (APEC), 153-54
Sulfur dioxide emissions. *See also* Acid rain
    in Asia, 44, 45, 53
    tradable permits for, 45
Super externalities, 7-8, 59-60, 142, 150-51. *See also* Transboundary harms
    APEC ability to respond to, 96-97
    and federalism issues, 122
    physical, 123
    and property rights vindication, 65
    and structural failures, 72-77
Sustainable development, 91, 136-38, 143-44

APEC commitment to, 9, 145, 170-71, 173-74
  definition of, 4
  foreign direct investment in, 6, 23*n*

Taiwan, 11
  acid rain problems, 45
  biodiversity loss, 52*t*
  clean technology/production initiative, 140-41
  development issues in, 69*n*
  economic prospects for, 28-29
  Environmental Protection Agency, 33*n*
  per capita income, 15, 15*t*, 16, 29
  subsidies in, 152
  US trade disputes with, 87*n*, 88
Tasmania, Franklin River dispute, 60-61, 61*n*, 127
Technologies
  clean, 140-41
  effect of economic growth on, 91
Territorial sovereignty. *See also* National sovereignty
  effect on regulatory competence, 73
  and transboundary harms, 111
Thailand, 11
  acid rain problems, 45
  aquaculture in, 42
  biodiversity loss, 52*t*
  cars in, number of, 40*n*
  currency crisis, 29
  deforestation in, 36, 36*t*
  economic prospects for, 29
  environmental harms in, economic costs of, 34
  greenhouse gas emissions, 49*f*
  industrialization in, 79-80
  land degradation in, 35, 35*t*
  life expectancy and infant mortality rates, 18*t*
  per capita income, 15, 15*t*, 16
  regulatory incapacity in, 67
  shrimping practices dispute with US, 61, 87, 87*n*, 92, 125-26, 126*n*, 128, 143, 163
  waste disposal problems in, 41
  water management in, 37, 38*f*, 98, 152*n*
Tiger bones, 87*n*, 88
Time delay, for environmental harms, 62-63, 72, 72*n*
Toronto Ministerial Meeting (1997), 140*n*, 140-41
Total factor productivity, 11-12
Tourism Working Group, 139

Trade
  and environmental performance issues, 84, 108
  fair, 85, 89, 89*n*, 157
  and global welfare issues, 72, 72*n*
  growth led by, pollution caused by, 90-92
  intraregional flow of, 27
  moral content of, 92, 108-9, 120, 126.
    See also Public choice issues
  openness of, 21, 27, 83-86, 109-10, 136
  and elimination of subsidies, 151
  expected benefits of, 30-31
  volume of, 12, 21-23, 29
Trade bargain, between developed and developing countries, 83-88, 92, 97, 107-8, 143
Trade barriers, 83-85, 87, 87*n*, 105, 109, 138*n*
Trade facilitation, environmental standards and, 156-60
Trade liberalization
  challenges to, 83, 89, 92
  expected benefits of, 27, 29-30, 143, 147, 147*n*
  multilateral, 29-30, 30*n*, 100
Trade measures, used to achieve environmental goals, 87-88, 143, 163
Trading partners, policy choices of, discomfort with, 92. *See also* Regulatory competition
Transboundary harms, 7-8, 53*n*, 53-54.
  See also Super externalities
  and commons problems, 57, 62, 64-65, 76-77
  in international environmental policy context, 60, 142, 150-51
  and international litigation, 65*n*-66*n*, 114
  and national sovereignty issues, 111
  and product standard harmonization, 159
  and structural failures, 72-77, 114
Transportation subsidies, 69, 81
Tuna, disputes over, 42*n*, 87, 87*n*, 109, 125, 126*t*, 163*n*

Ultraviolet radiation, 47
Uncertainty problems, 63
United Nations (UN)
  Conference on Environment and Development (UNCED), 169
  Conference on Trade and Development (UNCTAD), 103

Other Publications from the
Institute for International Economics

POLICY ANALYSES IN INTERNATIONAL ECONOMICS Series

1 **The Lending Policies of the International Monetary Fund**
John Williamson/*August 1982*
ISBN paper 0-88132-000-5
72 pp.

2 **"Reciprocity": A New Approach to World Trade Policy?**
William R. Cline/*September 1982*
ISBN paper 0-88132-001-3
41 pp.

3 **Trade Policy in the 1980s**
C. Fred Bergsten and William R. Cline/*November 1982*
(out of print)   ISBN paper 0-88132-002-1
Partially reproduced in the book *Trade Policy in the 1980s.*
84 pp.

4 **International Debt and the Stability of the World Economy**
William R. Cline/*September 1983*
ISBN paper 0-88132-010-2
134 pp.

5 **The Exchange Rate System,** Second Edition
John Williamson/*September 1983, rev. June 1985*
(out of print)   ISBN paper 0-88132-034-X
61 pp.

6 **Economic Sanctions in Support of Foreign Policy Goals**
Gary Clyde Hufbauer and Jeffrey J. Schott/*October 1983*
ISBN paper 0-88132-014-5
109 pp.

7 **A New SDR Allocation?**
John Williamson/*March 1984*
ISBN paper 0-88132-028-5
61 pp.

8 **An International Standard for Monetary Stabilization**
Ronald I. McKinnon/*March 1984*
(out of print)   ISBN paper 0-88132-018-8
108 pp.

9 **The Yen/Dollar Agreement: Liberalizing Japanese Capital Markets**
Jeffrey A. Frankel/*December 1984*
ISBN paper 0-88132-035-8
86 pp.

10 **Bank Lending to Developing Countries: The Policy Alternatives**
C. Fred Bergsten, William R. Cline, and John Williamson/*April 1985*
ISBN paper 0-88132-032-3
221 pp.

11 **Trading for Growth: The Next Round of Trade Negotiations**
Gary Clyde Hufbauer and Jeffrey J. Schott/*September 1985*
(out of print)   ISBN paper 0-88132-033-1
109 pp.

12 **Financial Intermediation Beyond the Debt Crisis**
Donald R. Lessard and John Williamson/*September 1985*
(out of print)   ISBN paper 0-88132-021-8
130 pp.

13 **The United States-Japan Economic Problem**
C. Fred Bergsten and William R. Cline/*October 1985, 2d ed. January 1987*
(out of print)   ISBN paper 0-88132-060-9
180 pp.

14 **Deficits and the Dollar: The World Economy at Risk**
Stephen Marris/*December 1985, 2d ed. November 1987*
(out of print)   ISBN paper 0-88132-067-6
415 pp.

15 **Trade Policy for Troubled Industries**
Gary Clyde Hufbauer and Howard F. Rosen/*March 1986*
ISBN paper 0-88132-020-X
111 pp.

16 **The United States and Canada: The Quest for Free Trade**
Paul Wonnacott, with an Appendix by John Williamson/*March 1987*
ISBN paper 0-88132-056-0
188 pp.

International Debt: Systemic Risk and Policy Response
William R. Cline/*1984*   ISBN cloth 0-88132-015-3   336 pp.

Trade Protection in the United States: 31 Case Studies
Gary Clyde Hufbauer, Diane E. Berliner, and Kimberly Ann Elliott/*1986*
(out of print)   ISBN paper 0-88132-040-4   371 pp.

Toward Renewed Economic Growth in Latin America
Bela Balassa, Gerardo M. Bueno, Pedro-Pablo Kuczynski,
and Mario Henrique Simonsen/*1986*
(out of stock)   ISBN paper 0-88132-045-5   205 pp.

Capital Flight and Third World Debt
Donald R. Lessard and John Williamson, editors/*1987*
(out of print)   ISBN paper 0-88132-053-6   270 pp.

The Canada-United States Free Trade Agreement: The Global Impact
Jeffrey J. Schott and Murray G. Smith, editors/*1988*
          ISBN paper 0-88132-073-0   211 pp.

World Agricultural Trade: Building a Consensus
William M. Miner and Dale E. Hathaway, editors/*1988*
          ISBN paper 0-88132-071-3   226 pp.

Japan in the World Economy
Bela Balassa and Marcus Noland/*1988*
          ISBN paper 0-88132-041-2   306 pp.

America in the World Economy: A Strategy for the 1990s
C. Fred Bergsten/*1988*   ISBN cloth 0-88132-089-7   235 pp.
          ISBN paper 0-88132-082-X   235 pp.

Managing the Dollar: From the Plaza to the Louvre
Yoichi Funabashi/*1988, 2d ed. 1989*
          ISBN paper 0-88132-097-8   307 pp.

United States External Adjustment and the World Economy
William R. Cline/*May 1989*   ISBN paper 0-88132-048-X   392 pp.

Free Trade Areas and U.S. Trade Policy
Jeffrey J. Schott, editor/*May 1989*
          ISBN paper 0-88132-094-3   400 pp.

Dollar Politics: Exchange Rate Policymaking in the United States
I. M. Destler and C. Randall Henning/*September 1989*
(out of print)   ISBN paper 0-88132-079-X   192 pp.

Latin American Adjustment: How Much Has Happened?
John Williamson, editor/*April 1990*
          ISBN paper 0-88132-125-7   480 pp.

The Future of World Trade in Textiles and Apparel
William R. Cline/*1987, 2d ed. June 1990*
          ISBN paper 0-88132-110-9   344 pp.

**Completing the Uruguay Round: A Results-Oriented Approach
to the GATT Trade Negotiations**
Jeffrey J. Schott, editor/*September 1990*
          ISBN paper 0-88132-130-3   256 pp.

Economic Sanctions Reconsidered (in two volumes)
Economic Sanctions Reconsidered: Supplemental Case Histories
Gary Clyde Hufbauer, Jeffrey J. Schott, and Kimberly Ann Elliott/*1985, 2d ed. December 1990*
          ISBN cloth 0-88132-115-X   928 pp.
          ISBN paper 0-88132-105-2   928 pp.

Economic Sanctions Reconsidered: History and Current Policy
Gary Clyde Hufbauer, Jeffrey J. Schott, and Kimberly Ann Elliott/*December 1990*
          ISBN cloth 0-88132-136-2   288 pp.
          ISBN paper 0-88132-140-0   288 pp.

Pacific Basin Developing Countries: Prospects for the Future
Marcus Noland/*January 1991*   ISBN cloth 0-88132-141-9   250 pp.
(out of print)   ISBN paper 0-88132-081-1   250 pp.

9   Whither APEC? The Progress to Date and Agenda for the Future
    C. Fred Bergsten, editor/*October 1997*
                    ISBN paper 0-88132-248-2   272 pp.

WORKS IN PROGRESS

The US - Japan Economic Relationship
C. Fred Bergsten, Marcus Noland, and Takatoshi Ito

Trade and Income Distribution
William R. Cline

China's Entry to the World Economy
Richard N. Cooper

Liberalizing Financial Services
Wendy Dobson and Pierre Jacquet

Economic Sanctions After the Cold War
Kimberly Ann Elliott, Gary C. Hufbauer and Jeffrey J. Schott

Trade and Labor Standards
Kimberly Ann Elliott and Richard Freeman

Forecasting Financial Crises: Early Warning Signs for Emerging Markets
Morris Goldstein and Carmen Reinhart

Global Competition Policy
Edward M. Graham and J. David Richardson

Prospects for Western Hemisphere Free Trade
Gary Clyde Hufbauer and Jeffrey J. Schott

Trade Practices Laid Bare
Donald Keesing

The Future of U.S. Foreign Aid
Carol Lancaster

The Economics of Korean Unification
Marcus Noland

Foreign Direct Investment in Developing Countries
Theodore Moran

Globalization, the NAIRU, and Monetary Policy
Adam Posen

The Case for Trade: A Modern Reconsideration
J. David Richardson

Measuring the Cost of Protection in China
Zhang Shuguang, Zhang Yansheng, and Wan Zhongxin

Real Exchange Rates for the Year 2000
Simon Wren-Lewis and Rebecca Driver

Canadian customers   RENOUF BOOKSTORE
can order from   5369 Canotek Road, Unit 1, Ottawa, Ontario K1J 9J3, Canada
the Institute or from: Telephone: (613) 745-2665   Fax: (613) 745-7660

Visit our website at: http://www.iie.com   E-mail address: orders@iie.com